^{THE} SACRED

 PLACE

THE SACRED PLACE

Witnessing the

Holy in the

Physical World

EDITED BY

W. Scott Olsen
Scott Cairns

UNIVERSITY OF UTAH PRESS
Salt Lake City

© 1996 by the University of Utah Press

LIBRARY OF CONGRESS CATALOGING-IN-PUBLICATION DATA

The sacred place : witnessing the holy in the physical world / edited
by W. Scott Olsen, Scott Cairns.
    p.   cm.
   ISBN 0-87480-523-6 (cloth : alk. paper). — ISBN 0-87480-524-4
(pbk. : alk. paper)
   1. Nature—Religious aspects—Literary collections. 2. Holy, The
—Literary collections. 3. American literature—20th century.
I. Olsen, W. Scott, 1958–   . II. Cairns, Scott.
PS509.N3S23 1996
810.8'0382—dc20   96-26677

CONTENTS

ix   *Introduction:* Regarding the Body
      SCOTT CAIRNS

Part One: The Mystery
      Poetry
3   The Beautiful Changes
      RICHARD WILBUR
4   Clearness
      RICHARD WILBUR
5   Looking Outside the Cabin Window, I Remember a Line
        by Li Po
      CHARLES WRIGHT
6   Natural Theology
      KELLY CHERRY
7   Lt. Col. Valentina Vladimirovna Tereshkova
      KELLY CHERRY
9   Vertigo
      JORIE GRAHAM
11   The Visible World
      JORIE GRAHAM
14   Pastoral
      ANNIE DILLARD
15   Mornings Like This
      ANNIE DILLARD
16   The Naturalist At Large On the Delaware River Marshes
      ANNIE DILLARD
19   Allatoona Evening
      DAVID BOTTOMS

20 Under the Vulture-Tree
DAVID BOTTOMS

21 A Vision
PETER COOLEY

22 Dandelions
PETER COOLEY

23 Rosh Hashanah
RICHARD CHESS

24 Yellow Lilies and Cypress Swamp
DAVID BAKER

26 In the Limbo of Lost Words
ANN TOWNSEND

27 Evening Burning
ANN TOWNSEND

29 Nightfall After a Storm
EDWARD BYRNE

31 Aurora Borealis
NAOMI SHIHAB NYE

33 Praise
HELEN FROST

34 Deer in Dry Creek, Dusk
DAWN MARANO

37 False Cape Landing, The Horses
JANET SYLVESTER

38 Blessed Among Birds
INGRID WENDT

Prose

41 The Meekness of Angels
PAUL GRUCHOW

49 Buffalo Winter
LINDA HASSELSTROM

61 Buckeye
SCOTT RUSSELL SANDERS

68 Where He Is Now
ALVIN GREENBERG

84 The Bluest Water or Getting to the Bottom of Things
WILLIAM KITTREDGE

89 From "A Mountain"
   JOHN MCPHEE
122 Tide Pools
   DOUGLAS CARLSON
130 Widows and Dead Men
   BETH SIMON
135 Home as Eden's Picture Book: The Fiction of Sacred Space
   LYNDA SEXSON
153 Getting to Hope
   KATHLEEN NORRIS

165 *Interlude:* The Literature of Nature and the Quest
      for the Sacred
   DOUGLAS BURTON-CHRISTIE

Part Two: The Gnawing
   Poetry
181 Alfred Jacob Miller
   DIANE GLANCY
182 Asylum in the Grasslands
   DIANE GLANCY
184 The Clearing
   CHARLES O. HARTMAN
190 Midway
   SYDNEY LEA
193 Over Brogno
   SYDNEY LEA
197 God Attack
   CATHRYN HANKLA
198 Dancers at the Edge
   CATHRYN HANKLA
199 Modifies
   MICHAEL MOTT
200 Mondrian's Forest
   WENDY BATTIN
203 Seven
   WENDY BATTIN
204 It Should Be Visible
   DENISE LEVERTOV

205 What One Receives from Living Close to a Lake
DENISE LEVERTOV

206 In the Woods
DENISE LEVERTOV

207 Poem for the Last Decade
KATHARINE COLES

213 The Golden Years of the Fourth Dimension
KATHARINE COLES

218 Spiritual Fallout
DAVID BENGTSON

220 The Soul May Be Compared to a Figure Walking
DAVID HOPES

Prose

223 Pearyland
BARRY LOPEZ

231 Presences
SYDNEY LEA

241 Eve
DAVID HOPES

245 The Real Surreal: Horseshoe Canyon
REG SANER

257 Out on the Wild Fringe
RICK BASS

266 War Story
BRET LOTT

285 In the Maternity Wing, Madison, Minnesota
CAROL BLY

299 All That Is Hidden
TERRY TEMPEST WILLIAMS

306 Piety
KATHERINE MCNAMARA

331 *Afterword:* An Advent Nature
W. SCOTT OLSEN

341 *Contributors*
349 *Acknowledgments*

SCOTT CAIRNS

Regarding the Body

IT WOULD BE DIFFICULT to pinpoint the beginnings of this book. Still, there must have been a day when some early human came back to his dwelling and tried to explain to others there that he had discovered something curious, something uncanny about the next valley. It wasn't merely a greater abundance of food or the promise of better shelter. It wasn't just better water or more fertile earth. Somehow, that other place seemed larger than its physical definition. Somehow, that place evoked a feeling of reverence. One might say that then—in the desire to join an intimation of the sacred with a description of the apparent world—this book was begun.

And we're supposing that the resulting, troubled terrain of these texts will seem familiar to most readers, for most have stood near the hilltop, the stream bank, the village park, and witnessed a startling moment when some tilt of the head, or sudden turn of the mind occasioned a deeper seeing; some portal opened and we glimpsed more than is commonly observed.

And then another thing happened, every bit as curious: We turned to our friends and tried to tell them about the experience, as if in returning to the experience in language we might in some way witness it again.

This more or less *Romantic* occupation with the physical world—an occupation which engages the visible as a means of suspecting the invisible—arguably has been the central project of English literature since Milton. That is, however, until a banal taste for certainty took hold of the cultural imagination and we submitted perhaps a little too fully to empiricism and related fictions. Still, some have discovered that a religion of the empirical is not quite as satisfying as we'd like, and some have suspected that the world is larger than what might be accounted for in theories tied to what is observable upon demand, larger than what is promoted in theologies of a literal bent.

A short while ago it dawned on us that many writers were in fact trying to give voice to what we have come to call *the sacred place*. Once again, and with renewed urgency, serious writers are undertaking an unabashedly metaphysical discourse. In doing so, some have had cause to invoke what might be seen as religious typologies, either Eastern or Western or indigenous; some have resisted these typologies and have sought to construct more anthrocentric if nonetheless spiritual readings of the troubled landscape.

If I may be forgiven my "getting personal," I'd like to say, as well, that the poems, stories, and essays collected here are teaching me something about the body, the body itself, the body as intrinsic value, perhaps even the body as spiritual presence, paradoxical as that may sound. Over the months that we've been collecting works for *The Sacred Place*, I've had a periodic suspicion that I'm beginning to glimpse something I hadn't seen before.

Pierre Teilhard de Chardin commences one section of his *Hymn of the Universe* with the following, a retelling of the story of Elias, or Elijah, as some may know him:

> The man was walking in the desert, followed by his companion, when the Thing swooped down on him.

I *love* that—in naming the vehicle that would subsequently remove Elijah from Elisha's presence, Teilhard has chosen to foreground its *Thingness*. Granted, in the more familiar narrative of the King James Version, the prophet is assaulted by an array of *things*—a fiery chariot, winged horses, a whirlwind—but our habit has been to receive *these* sorts of things as mere literary substitutions for purely spiritual (as in *non-bodily*) agency. I am delighted that in Teilhard's narrative some*thing* of material substance (albeit appalling substance) is said to swoop down, utterly translate the prophet, and carry him away.

Later in his text, Teilhard names that agency somewhat differently, if more abstractly; it is *the moving heart of an immeasurable pervasive subtlety.* The two depictions work together to avail a powerful construction—a locally perceived thing with immeasurable attributes.

In part, what we witness when we observe texts such as those selected for *The Sacred Place* are the results of an ongoing love affair with matter, with the humble *stuff* of creation. Westerners in general are pretty much doomed to keep showing up for the tryst, so powerfully are we drawn to the landscapes we inhabit—the wild landscapes as well as the less wild. We slog through them, examine them, call them by many names, periodically poke at them for some clues about ourselves. *What we see* when we stand mutely before the landscape's expanse is necessarily a troubled image: is there a *there* there, or are we projecting aspects of ourselves yet again? Is some powerful agency at work in what we see, or are we just wishing (or fearing) that there were? Who can say? Who would dare?

What's most intriguing to me about the texts here is that they *do* dare. What's most attractive about them is that for the most part they resist answering that dare with reductions. They appear generally to prefer the swoon of multiple possibilities over the relative comfort of conclusions.

That preference requires that I qualify my use of *Westerners* above: I would say that these contemporary texts seem less, say, *Greek*, in their assumptions than they seem *Hebraic*—by which I mean that the phenomena they celebrate appear less *referential* than they do *inhabited*, as if the sacred scene were sacred for what it is, holds, what it embodies, not merely for what it may or may not point toward. Susan Handelman's observation in her book *The Slayers of Moses* might prove useful: "Indeed, the Greek term for word, *onoma*, is synonymous with name. By contrast, its Hebrew counterpart—*davar*— means not only *word* but also *thing*." And, I would add—bearing in mind the Hebrew Bible's creation story—such things as *words* are also *powers*. So, while a more Greek disposition might be inclined to receive material phenomena as sorry substitutions in an ontology of diminishing returns, the Hebrew disposition would more readily witness in matter and language an empowered and empowering spiritual presence.

I'm guessing that it is an unfortunate contemporary habit—maybe the result of an underdeveloped historical sense, but more likely a general disinterest in traditional theological discourse—to suppose that *belief* among predecessors was a matter of unquestioned assumptions, a matter of blithe certainty. Of course, the more time one spends with actual theological texts, the less likely one is to accuse their authors of mistaking appearances for something like reality, or metaphorical relationships for something like equations. The fact is, the more time one spends with those authors, the more one is likely to witness a well developed taste for confronting one's own *failure* to know; reading these authors helps us see that all our metaphors for the *sacred* are admittedly and necessarily provisional.

The works here seem in large part to be the result of a species of doubt that leads many writers to suspect a richness in their experience that works counter to their culture's more habitual materialisms. Call it a contemporary version of the *via negativa*, if you will. It is nonetheless a way of moving along, if a way that depends upon a series of anticipated failures, observed points at which all, or most, so far received wisdom demonstrates its provisional status, its inability to sufficiently account for and comprehend all that is suspected. This *sensation of the incommensurate* may finally be the only clue one has that any progress at all has been made—the recognition that what was *known* just moments before is once again up for grabs.

Various as they are, the works collected in *The Sacred Place* share a common reverence for the *world itself*, and—perhaps best of all— they share a common understanding that no one of them comprehends fully what that means. And while many share conventions and traditions with more transcendental dispositions, I suspect that these authors are not after transcendence at all; they seem to desire instead a sense that the humble stuff surrounding us affords a likely enough habitation for the sacred, even now. This is a significant recovery, for, as Teilhard writes:

> You thought you could do without [matter] because the power of thought has been kindled in you? You hoped that the more thoroughly you rejected the tangible, the closer you would be to spirit; that you would be more divine if you lived in the world of pure thought, or at least more angelic if you fled the corporeal? Well, you were like to have perished of hunger.

On the contrary, I suspect that the Body lies before us, and we partake of it. The Body draws us to itself, and we are sustained. The Body includes us among its members, and we are lifted up. In that expansive confusion, we proceed.

The collection which follows, therefore, should be received as an early survey of responses to the *apparent*—of pristine wilderness, the commonplace of the city, aboard ship, or within the walled garden. They are diverse responses, granted, but responses unified in having taken into account an uncanny sensation of the sacred which has attended the scene. We have made a single division among these works, arranging them in two sections, "The Mystery" and "The Gnawing." Such division cannot be made without a nagging sense of arbitrary placement, but those in the former section might be seen to provoke the sacred in relatively familiar Western terms, while those in the latter include recourse to other traditions as well. For the most part, these authors have benefited from both modern and postmodern discourses; one detects in most of these pieces a canny and careful disposition, which, on the one hand, will not deny the sensation of the sacred, but will not presume it's simple objectivity. Appropriately, the tone here leaves open the question of whether one bears witness to *something seen* or to *something by which one sees*.

What is the relation between what we call the sacred and what we witness as the apparent world? Not everyone agrees on the answers. But in fiction, poetry, and essays, the new writing is a provocative assertion that this is the turn American literature in the twenty-first century will take, a post-post-modern turn toward the natural world, the wilderness, as an empowering scene of encounter with what Coleridge would have called the *pre-phenomenal*, what we will entertain here as the *sacred*.

PART I

THE MYSTERY

Behold, I show you a mystery: We shall not all sleep, but we shall all be changed

I Corinthians 15:51 (KJV)

RICHARD WILBUR

The Beautiful Changes

One wading a Fall meadow finds on all sides
The Queen Anne's Lace lying like lilies
On water; it glides
So from the walker, it turns
Dry grass to a lake, as the slightest shade of you
Valleys my mind in fabulous blue Lucernes.

The beautiful changes as a forest is changed
By a chameleon's tuning his skin to it;
As a mantis, arranged
On a green leaf, grows
Into it, makes the leaf leafier, and proves
Any greenness is deeper than anyone knows.

Your hands hold roses always in a way that says
They are not only yours; the beautiful changes
In such kind ways.
Wishing ever to sunder
Things and things' selves for a second finding, to lose
For a moment all that it touches back to wonder.

Clearness

There is a poignancy in all things clear,
In the stare of the deer, in the ring of a hammer in the morning.
Seeing a bucket of perfectly lucid water
We fall to imagining prodigious honesties.

And feel so when the snow for all its softness
Tumbles in adamant forms, turning and turning
Its perfect faces, littering on our sight
The heirs and types of timeless dynasties.

In pine-woods once that huge precision of leaves
Amazed my eyes and closed them down a dream.
I lost to mind the usual southern river,
Mud, mist, the plushy sound of the oar,

And pondering north through lifted veils of gulls,
Through sharpening calls, and blue clearings of steam,
I came and anchored by a fabulous town
Immaculate, high, and never found before.

This was the town of my mind's exacted vision
Where truths fell from the bells like a jackpot of dimes,
And the people's voices, carrying over the water,
Sang in the ear as clear and sweet as birds.

But this was Thulë of the mind's worst vanity;
Nor could I tell the burden of those clear chimes;
And the fog fell, and the stainless voices faded;
I had not understood their lovely words.

Looking Outside the Cabin Window, I Remember a Line by Li Po

The river winds through the wilderness,
Li Po said
              of another place and another time.
It does so here as well, sliding its cargo of dragon scales
To gutter under the snuff
                        of marsh willow and tamarack.

Mid-morning, Montana high country,
Jack snipe poised on the scarred fence post,
Pond water stilled and smoothed out,
Swallows dog-fighting under the fast-moving storm clouds.

Expectantly empty, green as a pocket, the meadow waits
For the wind to rise and fill it,
                        first with a dark hand
Then with the rain's loose silver
A second time and a third
                        as the day doles out its hours.

Sunlight reloads and ricochets off the window glass.
Behind the cloud scuts,
                  inside the blue aorta of the sky,
The River of Heaven flows
With its barge of stars,
              waiting for darkness and a place to shine.

We who would see beyong seeing
              see only language, that burning field.

Natural Theology

You read it in the blue wind,
the blue water, the rock spill,
the blue hill

rising like a phoenix from ash. Some mind
makes itself known through the markings of light
on air; where earth rolls, right

comes after, our planet's bright spoor. . . . If you look, you'll find
truth etched on the tree trunk,
the shark's tooth, a shell, a hunk

of root and soil. Study from beginning to end.
Alpha and omega—these are the cirrus alphabet,
the Gnostics' cloudy "so—and yet."

If a tree falls in a forest, a sacred hind
leaps, hearing branches break;
you crawl under the log and shake

honey out of a hollow, eggs from a nest, ants from the end
of a stick; resting, you read God's name on the back of a bass
in a blue pool; God grows everywhere, like grass.

Lt. Col. Valentina Vladimirovna Tereshkova

first woman to orbit the earth,
June 16–June 19, 1963

It looked like an apple
or a Christmas orange:
I wanted to eat it.
I could taste the juice
trickling down my throat,
my tongue smarted,
my teeth were chilled.
How sweet those mountains seemed,
how cool and tangy, the Daugava!

What scrawl of history
had sent me so far from home? . . .

When I was a girl in school, comrades,
seemingly lazy as a lizard
sprawled on a rock in Tashkent,
I dreamed of conquest.
My hands tugged at my arms,
I caught flies on my tongue.

Now my soul's as hushed as the Steppes on a winter night;
snow drifts in my brain, something
shifts, sinks, subsides inside,

and some undying pulse hoists my body
like a flag, and sends me up,

like Nureyev.
From my samovar I fill my cup with air,
and it overflows.
Who knows who scatters the bright cloud?

Two days and almost twenty-three hours
I looked at light,
scanning its lines like a book.

My conclusions:

At last I saw the way
time turns,
like a key in a lock,
and night becomes day,
and sun burns away the primeval mist,
and day is, and is not.

Listen, earthmen,
comrades of the soil,
I saw the Black Sea shrink to a drop
of dew and disappear;
I could blot out Mother Russia with my thumb in thin air;
the whole world was nearly not there.

It looked like an apple
or a Christmas orange:
I wanted to eat it.
I thought, It is pleasant to the eyes,
good for food,
and eating it would make men and women wise.

I could taste the juice
trickling down my throat,
my tongue smarted,
my teeth were chilled.
How sweet those mountains seemed,
how cool and tangy, the Daugava!

Vertigo

Then they came to the very edge of the cliff and looked down.
Below a real world flowed in its parts, green, green.
The two elements touched—rock, air.
She thought of where the mind opened out
into the sheer drop of its intelligence,
the updrafting pastures of the vertical in which a bird now rose,
blue body the blue wind was knifing upward
faster than it could naturally rise,
up into the downdraft until it was frozen until she could see them
                                                    at last

the stages of flight, broken down, broken free,
each wingflap folding, each splay of the feather-sets flattening
for entry. . . . *Parts* she thought, *free* parts, watching the laws
at work, *through which desire must course*
seeking an ending, seeking a shape. Until the laws of flight and fall
                                                    increased.

Until they made, all of an instant, a bird, a blue
enchantment of properties no longer
knowable. What is it to understand, she let fly,
leaning outward from the edge now that the others had gone down.
How close can the two worlds get, the movement from one to the
    other
being death? She tried to remember from the other life
the passage of the rising notes off the violin
into the air, thin air, chopping their way in,
wanting to live forever—marrying, marrying—yet still free of the
                                                    orchestral swelling
which would at any moment pick them up, in-
corporate. How is it one soul wants to be owned

by a single other
in its entirety?—
What is it sucks one down, offering itself, only itself, for
ever? She saw the cattle below
moving in a shape which was exactly their hunger.
She saw—could they be men?—the plot. She leaned. How does one
     enter
a story? Where the cliff and air pressed the end of each other,
everything else in the world—woods, fields, stream, start of another
                                             darker
woods—appeared as kinds of
falling. She listened for the wind again. What was it in there
                               she could hear
that has nothing to do with *telling the truth?*
What was it that was *not her listening?*
She leaned out. What is it pulls at one, she wondered,
what? That it has no shape but point of view?
That it cannot move to hold us?
Oh it has vibrancy, she thought, this emptiness, this intake just
                               prior to
the start of a story, the mind trying to fasten
and fasten, the mind feeling it like a sickness this wanting
to snag, catch hold, begin, the mind crawling out to the edge of the
     cliff
and feeling the body as if for the first time—how it cannot
follow, cannot love.

The Visible World

I dig my hands into the absolute. The surface
                              breaks
into shingled, grassed clusters; lifts.
If I press, pick-in with fingers, pluck,
I can unfold the loam. It is tender. It is a tender
maneuver, hands making and unmaking promises.
Diggers, forgetters. . . . A series of successive single instances . . .
Frames of reference moving . . .
The speed of light, down here, upthrown, in my hands:
bacteria, milky roots, pilgrimages of spores, deranged
                              and rippling
mosses. What heat is this in me
that would *thaw time*, making bits of instance
                              overlap
shovel by shovelful—my present a wind blowing through
                              this culture
slogged and clutched-firm with decisions, over-ridings,
                              opportunities
taken? . . . If I look carefully, there in my hand, if I
                  break it apart without
crumbling: husks, mossy beginnings and endings, ruffled
                              airy loambits,
and the greasy silks of clay crushing the pinerot
                              in . . .
Erasure. Tell me something and then take it back.
Bring this pellucid moment—here on this page now
                  as on this patch
of soil, my property—bring it up to the top and out
                              of

sequence. Make it dumb again—won't you?—what
                                        would it
take? Leach the humidities out, the things that will
                                        insist on
making meaning. Parch it. It isn't hard: just take this
                                        shovelful
and spread it out, deranged, a vertigo of single
                                        clots
in full sun and you can, easy, decivilize it, un-
                                        hinge it
from its plot. Upthrown like this, I think you can
                                        eventually
abstract it. Do you wish to?
Disentangled, it grows very very clear.
Even the mud, the sticky lemon-colored clay
hardens and then yields, crumbs.
I can't say what it is then, but the golden-headed
                                        hallucination,
mating, forgetting, speckling, inter-
                                        locking,
will begin to be gone from it and then its glamorous
                                        veil of
echoes and muddy nostalgias will
be gone. If I touch the slender new rootings they show me
                                        how large I
am, look at these fingers—what a pilot—I touch, I press
                                        their slowest
electricity. . . . What speed is it at?
What speed am I at here, on my knees, as the sun traverses now
                                        and just begins
to touch my back. What speed where my fingers, under the
                                        dark oaks,
and suddenly touched, lit up—so white as they move, the ray for
                                        a moment
on them alone in the small wood.
White hands in the black-green glade,
opening the muddy cartoon of the present, taking the tiny roots
                                        of the moss

apart, hired hands, curiosity's small army, so white
in these greens—
make your revolution in the invisible temple,
make your temple in the invisible
revolution—I can't see the errands you run, hands gleaming
for this instant longer
like tinfoil at the bottom here of the tall
whispering oaks . . .
Listen, Boccioni the futurist says a galloping horse
has not four
legs (it has twenty)—and "at C there is no sequence
because there is no time"—and since
at lightspeed, etc. (everything is simultaneous): my hands
serrated with desires, shoved into these excavated
fates
—mauve, maroons, gutters of flecking golds—
my hands are living in myriad manifestations
of light. . . .
"All forms of imitation are to be despised."
"All subjects previously used must be discarded."
"At last we shall rush rapidly past objectiveness" . . .
Oh enslavement will you take these hands
and hold them in
for a time longer? Tops of the oaks, do you see my tiny
golden hands
pushed, up to the wrists,
into the present? Star I can't see in daylight, young, light
and airy star—
I put the seed in. The beam moves on.

Pastoral

—Max Picard, *The World of Silence*, 1948.
Trans. Stanley Godman, 1952.

Sometimes when a peasant moves with the plough and the oxen
Over the broad surface of the field,
It is as if the vault of the sky might take

Up into itself the peasant, the plough, and the oxen.
It is as though time had been sown into silence.
The eye of the gods falls on the figures, and they

Increase. A bird flies slowly into the sky.
Its movements are trails that keep the silence enclosed.
Animals lead silence through the world of man

And always put silence down in front of man.
The cattle: the broad surface of their backs . . .
It is as if they were carrying silence.

Two cows in a field moving with a man beside them:
It is as if the man were pouring down silence
From the backs of the animals on to the fields.

Mornings Like This

—David Grayson, *The Countryman's Year*, 1936

Sunday. What still sunny days
We have now. And I alone in them.
So brief—our best!

So much is wrong, but not my hills.
I have been thinking of writing
A letter to the President of China.

Mornings like this: I look
About the earth and the heavens:
There is not *enough* to believe—

Mornings like this. How heady
The morning air! How sharp
And sweet and clear the morning air!

Authentic winter! The odor of campfires!
Beans eighteen inches long!
A billion chances—and I am here!

And here I lie in the quiet room
And read and read and read.
So easy—so easy—so easy.

Pools in old woods, full of leaves.
Give me time enough in this place
And I will surely make a beautiful thing.

The Naturalist at Large on the Delaware River Marshes

Charles C. Abbott, M.D., *Waste-land Wanderings*, 1887

CONFESSIONS

I once witnessed a riot in wrendom.
I have insisted that the cardinal-redbird
is not a mocker. I take it all back.

I am free to confess that woodpeckers
have failed to interest me.
I know of two fine boulders in the meadows,

but I use them only for stepping-stones—
never as texts. My last public talk
about them was disastrous.

I saw a purple grackle's nest.
I resolved to climb the tree.
The birds looked on approvingly.

It now remained for me to descend.
Through some strange miscalculation
I failed to secure a footing, and fell.

The scars on my back made an excellent
map of the Micronesian archipelago.
It most vividly recalled

the apparently instant appearance
of every woman in the village
when my horse ran away and landed me
in the duck-pond on the common.

ANOTHER CONFESSION

In numerous little sink-holes,
I find the skeletons of small fishes.
I pick them from the mud.

The imprint of their shriveled
forms is left—fossil
impressions for the naturalist

of ten thousand years to come.
This is possible, of course, so
I wrote on the smooth surface

from which I lifted a minnow,
Fundulus multifasciatus.
Will it not startle the paleontologist

of the indefinite future to chisel
from rock an already labelled fossil?
I trust that he will not go mad.

LATE WANDERINGS

Now that nesting is over, many
find next to nothing to sing about.

When a blast from the north blows
the brown rushes, above the roar
can be heard a tone of sadness,

a cry, "We weep! we weep!"

"Keep up, keep up, keep!"

"Chesapeake, O Chesapeake!"

Was there not yet something
that I could watch even
by the gloaming's uncertain and waning light?

Allatoona Evening

Half a mile through a briar scrub thickening to woods,
I've lugged it like a sack of stones
and come to these shadows opening the cove.
A jon boat waits among the water lilies,
restless as wind, a paddle
in the bow, as though night were a current
to be muscled through.

On the horizon
a red glaze still treads water,
and in my silence, crickets choir the treeline.
Wave after wave, they call me to lay down
my anger. And the tree frogs
with them, barking out of the needles,
the copperhead skirting rushes,
sidling into the shallows—
lay it down, they say, on the green stones
beside this water.

A whippoorwill, an echo,
and above the drooping shoulders of the willows
delicate bats tumbling for flies—
lay it down, they say, your ambition,
which is only anger,
which sated could bring you to no better place.
Nothing is more beautiful than your emptiness,
and over the lake
these three stars soaking up twilight.

Under the Vulture-Tree

We have all seen them circling pastures,
have looked up from the mouth of a barn, a pine clearing,
the fences of our own backyards, and have stood
amazed by the one slow wing beat, the endless dihedral drift.
But I had never seen so many so close, hundreds,
every limb of the dead oak feathered black,

and I cut the engine, let the river grab the jon boat
and pull it toward the tree.
The black leaves shined, the pink fruit blossomed
red, ugly as a human heart.
Then, as I passed under their dream, I saw for the first time
its soft countenance, the raw fleshy jowls
wrinkled and generous, like the faces of the very old
who have grown to empathize with everything.

And I drifted away from them, slow, on the pull of the river,
reluctant, looking back at their roost,
calling them what I'd never called them, what they are,
those dwarfed transfiguring angels,
who flock to the side of the poisoned fox, the mud turtle
crushed on the shoulder of the road,
who pray over the leaf-graves of the anonymous lost,
with mercy enough to consume us all and give us wings.

A Vision

I look out at the flowers in the yard.
As if by lightning they have been delivered from their bodies,
crushed and black from last night's frost.
My summer garden: such labor, such tenderness,
fell to the preparation of the soil, the seeds,
rising or not, then the sprouts, lush on the warming air,
before the gashes of color when they were blossoming.
My delphiniums, no, my red-tongued salvia,
I suppose I will miss you most among the worshipped
until some of you appear next year. Now the burden of autumn.
Since I awoke, the flowers have been babbling
unceasingly in their new tongues, being dead,
recognizing in me the soul of a brother
in whom death has planted such darkness, such hunger,
he is greedy for their words, even consuming them, glutted.

Dandelions

Once I knew what dying was
in a field run wild with thousands
going to seed. I stood there, dumb,
at the edge of town, myself,
where May was what the earth gave up
to clouds, cloudless, & summer kept the wind
that hadn't risen yet. I waited,

twelve years old. I stand here even now,
stripping off my clothes, going down
naked on my knees, shaking, shaking
their lives away, their heads
fireworks of skulls in the last fire
turning finally to snow, turning to air.
This is how the blessed will rise I think

years later, but this day nothing
human or in images can touch me,
pushing their heads against the sun,
multiplying the field, the road
to town, until I find just one in bloom
& then before I dress & turn back home
rub all my body gold, losing the world.

Rosh Hashanah

On this day a slow but wise King
At the palace window surveys his kingdom.
Our souls fly to meet their father.
Abandoned, our bodies converse with pigeons
And rivers, ticks and stones: their souls
Have also flown to appear before their father.
As pure today as they were ten thousand years ago,
The souls float on a river of divine light
And do not interest him. He desires
Our bodies—scarred, bent, wired, pierced, singed . . .
He examines the surfaces on which we walk,
Measures the walls against which we're thrown,
Weighs the air we breathe, samples the water
In which we bathe.

                The rest of the year he pities
Those souls. Today he rubs the bodies, fills the eyes
With beauty, tickles the ears with truth, he touches the toes
Of a man who has smoked for a hundred years
And the belly of a baby who glows with milk,
Forgetting not the crab or rat or beetle or moth,
Not the oak or phlox flickering on the side of the road.

Yellow Lilies and Cypress Swamp

1.

So green against the standing water they're
nearly black, the sudden, wild lily stalks
cup their flames like candlesticks beyond which,
as though it bears no end, the cypress swamp
continues into steam and smoke. How the
lilies grow here is anybody's guess—
an errant seed buried in some bird's wing.
Or they caught a hard spring blow, floating down.
They bloom amber in landscape hazed dull green,
darkly cool, yet dangerous enough we
must watch our step or fall upon the strange,
hard cypress knees bunched around each trunk.

And how the cypresses reach through shallow
pools for sturdiness, thickened at the base,
stretched like softened sinew. They span upwards
of seventy feet, delicate, high, arched
canopy of leaves, gauze-white in the light.
Above water their short knees go rough, dry.
Below they're veined, yellow-red, like agates
broken open or the small, torn tissues
of a body turned stone by cold neglect.
They shine in a black, clean foot of water—
mosses cling to them. Wild lilies burning
in a cypress swamp. We wish to hold them.

2.

High, lighted altar. Pews of fine-planed board.
And mourners filing past the burnished, closed

casket to kiss his photograph, to touch
the bright brass fittings, say their goodbyes now
that it's too late. When the preacher stands to
lead us all in song we recall beauty
is most likely in these solemn places.
Not the song, too pious and commanding,
not the stained glass lighting or white candles
thawing onto hand-rubbed ebony, not
the few friends torn apart, here to heal, but
like a sudden slash of blood in wind one
redwing blackbird flashing past a clear pane
under which spreads a fist of lilies in a vase—
like landscape cupped, held, kept. One gorgeous flame.

In the Limbo of Lost Words

After our love, I lie in the shadow of your shoulder
and drift to the sound of the seventeen-year locusts outside,

their lonely tenor buzz that rises and falls together
and as suddenly stops, and flares out again.

Their background rhythm sweeps against the sides of the house,
rustles like late leaves, a soft desperate rasping,

the *ave, ave, ave* syllables of air, skin against skin.
When we came upon her yesterday, inside the chapel shadows,

the young girl soloist abandoned herself to the words she read,
her translation like an absence of language. Her music

cast itself away and away, pulsing on, until the silence
of an empty room took its place, where the heat of day

is only lamplight through the stained windows.
It filters across the dusty floor. It lights

upon a pale blue wall, indiscriminate in what it touches.
And the mocking, mating voices of the locusts return again

in their regular pilgrimage out of the earth,
out of the dark, into the shadows.

Evening Burning

  Vapor trails unfurl in the north sky,
dissolving as they slide,

  but the rain approaches—
cool, a sueded glove brushing,

  finger by finger,
across his forehead. The old leaf-smell hovers,

  broken-down wet rot
cupped in the curves

  of hillsides. Behind the house
the perpetual fire burns

  and he pushes leaves and twigs
into the dugout pit,

  its comforting red mouth.
Smoke divides around him—

  burning leaves leap up,
bright sparks, a cloud of fireflies.

  The church bells toll in town,
calling the wind

  to evening mass.
If he works slowly,

it will burn all night
while the rake-flattened grass slowly

unbends, and the starlings
step in formation

to mine the ground for grubs.
In the grove of trees,

the raised rough skin of the trunks
pebbles and shines

as the last light
catches hold of the bark, its grooves

and indentations, the pockmarks
of woodpeckers, the natural

abrasions. He leans a hand there,
in support, and the living skin

is so cold, so slick with moss,
it's wet before the rain comes down.

EDWARD BYRNE

Nightfall After a Storm

Sunset and evening star
And one clear call for me!
—Alfred, Lord Tennyson

I.

Each wedge of sunlight edges
    through this sky now crowded
        with clouds suddenly
incandescent, spreading
    lavish color, conferring
        blessing upon all.

II.

The skeletal limbs of winter
    trees stir a cold
        north wind, offering
clear evidence of the storm's
    end, removing nightfall's
        final obstacles.

III.

Stars surface, rearranging
    everything. The entire
        horizon is altered as we
glimpse far past the fast slide
    of dusk, a welcoming
        we might almost return.

IV.

As more distant constellations
lift through that tidal
shift, joy drifts
in this quick tip of night sky.
How ardent the stars
are when gone so long.

Aurora Borealis

It was speaking to me
putting out its long
single finger
and pointing
maybe it could hear me shout
shimmering parenthesis
put me in my place
my place was
low down
turning up
and over
Alaska Gas
Sam's Sourdough Cafe
I was not cold
standing in snow
for hours
leaping under
green swoop
one finger swelled
rippled fringe
staggering swish
I was running outside
by myself
not by myself
it came so close
I almost felt
more than I had been
waiting for
what word

what possible telling
everying different
here on out
you saw nothing
knew nothing
till now
now what
do you know

Praise

after a line by Hannah Wilson
and rocks found by Laurie Hughes

I wake one morning and all that I love is alive.
Light across frost-glazed field, pale green
where yesterday it was brown, and the day before
dusted with snow. Clear indrawn breath is what wakes me.

Light across frost-glazed field, pale green—
cows, wolf, moccasins, mud of a sycamore forest, mastodon
dusted with snow. Clear indrawn breath is what wakes me.
Grey weight of these fossiliferous rocks has shown me

cows, wolf, moccasins, mud of a sycamore forest, mastodon,
sea fans waving in aqua light—an epiric sea.
Grey weight of these fossiliferous rocks has shown me
all who have swum or walked here and loved

sea fans waving in aqua light—an epiric sea
shallow across the whole wide land.
All who have swum or walked here and loved—
I see you this morning and sing, clear green

shallow and wide, across the whole land
where yesterday it was brown and the day before.
I see you this morning and sing, clear green.
I wake one morning and all that I love is alive.

Deer in Dry Creek, Dusk

I.

Desperation brings them
      down the mountain
to this oak- and sage-choked alley,
      hoof-drag through the mesh of scrub,
still shadows dark and lean as grief
      etched against the spent wild rye.
Fifteen head all nodding now
      by Larkin's buckled water heater
and the sprung mattress a solemn Tidwell
      heaved up and over the cliff
one year, evicting bad tenants.
      From a cloudless spring like last
the thaw tumbles too fast, too soon
      routing gullies here in ragged rows:
come summer deer wear a thin trail
      to this near-ruined place for no more
than a taste of parched bitterbrush.
      In late July they stop traffic
and idle conversation and linger among us
      welcomed like family turned up
unexpected at suppertime.
      October, seems every garage in town
has one strung up from the rafters;
      see the men and their boys at work
in flame orange, straddling the cool, limp bucks,
      wading rivers of opened veins.

II.
Up the slough I see Sam, or maybe Sam,
he says, it could be a nickname
his father gave him once.
But he knows his age well enough:
Five, he says, and wants to know
who am I, climbed all this way
to find him, crouched in oak
and sage, lost with a lap of bones.
Deer, he says, and shows me then
how pleased his mother will be.

Questions. I have those, these
thirty-four years beyond him.
Too many, Sam says, like his sister,
Sarah, with the loud voice, like
how and where and what now?
Sam knows everything
he will ever need: this dwindling day,
a long walk to nowhere for no reason,
the alpenglow on the foothills here
and the stripped bones he carries.

III.
It's nothing but hard scrabble, up and down,
but coming down is easy, compared.
The choices are clearer. Always.
And this is when I find them, on a different fork,
the bones of winterkill: the vertebrae still locked;
the pelvic basin, unfolded in the cheat grass
like hands, having delivered a prayer. The femora.
The jaw. The hoof. The locusts. The hot August sun.
I collect what I can carry, wish a blessing
over my sacrilege, and I bring the bones home.
What will you do with them, he asks when I am back,
and this is how I know
how far apart two people can stand in one room.

In my hands, the bones are nearly weightless,
luminous; cool now as if spirited already
through the chill of atmospheres several times thinner.

False Cape Landing, The Horses

I have never seen them sidle
across the meadow's grassy space
to stop in shade or teeming rain
under the wax myrtle tree.

The signs, though, that they cede to me
when I pass by, remain—a few
tough hairs unsubtly scratched against
the tree's gray trunk, above a wheel

of earth churned into mud, congealed
as if in it blind horses turned
some heavy work. I circumscribe
the zone they've marked, one latitude,

where light is bread, and time is good
as flesh that, hungering,
takes all this in. Above the bay,
its edging reeds the depth of tone

a sunset scatters when it's done,
locusts stroke blue air into
flames that flash against the side
a leaping fish twists into light.

The self without itself's not quite
scribbled across the water's skin.
As usual, the mystery
chooses somewhere broken to begin.

Blessed Among Birds

for Ralph

Blessed among birds, is how my husband
likes to put it, and maybe it's true: that flock of
six or eight kinglets too young for their ruby red crowns or even

those characteristic white eye rings, flicking through our backyard
apple-tree leaves around my head so close I could have reached out and
touched each one as it clung upside down to a leaf, picking the

undersides clean, or perched on a twig—tip of beak to
tip of tail the length of my own little finger—fearlessly
sizing up my mountainous form frozen, like lava,

mid-motion, but
shining (surely the feeling
was shining) like gold,

the true Midas touch of their chip
chip-chipping
pitched so high the human ear almost

can't take it in. I know
my husband hasn't
Saint Francis in mind, although

when he says what he says about blessings, suddenly
here I am, as Giotto never painted me, high on the east
cathedral wall in Assisi, the upper

cathedral, built on top of that other, more somber
nave and transepts we studied so long (craning our necks to find
Biblical scenes preserved in all their brilliance by almost-

darkness) we almost
didn't have time for the brightness above: blue and gold
and light streaming through space so

unexpected our souls
were flying, the birds
hovering over the head of Saint Francis,

perched on his shoulder,
hadn't a thing
over us. No,

what he's remembering, when I mention the kinglets, is how
two weeks ago over in Eastern Oregon,
walking together near Benson Pond at dusk, I was

whacked on the head by a great horned owl.
I know
this could sound funny, and that

was my reaction, too: I laughed
although the whole top of my scalp throbbed
from the force of the blow. It was hard.

It felt like someone had taken a board flat
to the top of me, someone had sneaked
up from behind in that mystical field of knee-high grass

we waded through in half
light, finding the path to the cottonwoods faint
but true, and all of that empty sky ours.

But no one had told us this was a hard-hat area, who
would have imagined *Danger*, lured by the hoot, hoot, soft
lullaby deep in the trees? *Athena*,

my husband said later, hoping to comfort
me. *Athena has tapped you, marked you with wisdom.*
But wisdom was not what I felt, hunched into my collar, my eyes

following giant wings to their perch in the branches ahead.
And blessings were not right then first in my mind (although
later I saw again those claws that were blessedly not

extended), gaining my
balance,
discovering just

off to our right in the crook of a tree the owlet
so fluffy grey and rounded we thought at first it must
be a raccoon without a mask.

All of us caught
off guard. Unmoving,
all of us stunned into place.

PAUL GRUCHOW

The Meekness of Angels

ONE NIGHT MY friend John and I, on a trek across the Bob Marshall Wilderness of northern Montana, camped in a peaceful grove of pines nestled against the Chinese Wall, a spectacular, thousand-foot-high, thirteen-mile-long escarpment at the heart of the wilderness. This is grizzly bear country, and we had been seeing signs of the animal.

At dusk a strong wind arose, howling over the continental divide and whistling in the tops of the trees. The walls of our tent, when we retired for the night, fluttered and flapped. It would have blown away had we not weighed it down. Although it was the middle of the summer, the high-pitched whine of the wind carried the sound of winter and of death—bleak, desolate, mournful. Then the wind grew calmer, murmuring in the trees like water tumbling over rocks. We might have been, from the sound of it, camped beside the gentle falls of a river.

I awoke in the night, chilled, perhaps by the suggestive voice of the wind, for the air itself was mild. I had the strong sense that we were in the presence of another creature. John felt it and awoke, too. I reached for my glasses and rose on my elbows, but it was utterly dark, impossible to make out anything. We listened intently, but nothing could be heard above the wind. For a long time I listened. Then the sensation passed. We seemed alone again. I fell asleep. In the morning, the air was tranquil and the sun sparkled on a heavy dew. We looked for tracks in the vicinity of our tent, but it was a grassy place and tracks would not easily have been seen even had they been there. Whether we had been awakened by imagination, or prescience, or premonition we would never know.

The next night at dusk, as we set up a tent along a fork of the Sun River, the strong feeling of foreboding returned. I was securing the last tent pole in its grommet when John, who had turned toward the river, touched my shoulder and said quietly, "They're here, Paul."

By the time I could set the tent down and turn around, a sow grizzly bear had reached the place where our packs were hanging. She was enormous and blonde. The silver tips of her venerable hair glistened in the long angle of the sunlight filtering through the trees. She did not make a sound as she moved with athletic grace toward her purpose, her massive shoulders as fluid as water. She was like a waterfall on legs. The hump of her back was so prominent and her size so great, that in another setting I might temporarily have mistaken her for a bison cow. She did not waste a motion or hesitate for a microsecond. She was completely, assuredly in charge. Behind her trailed two darker cubs, themselves the size of black bears. We realized that she had been there all along, lurking in the willows while we ate and bathed and sallied at the edge of the river, biding her time, watching us, awaiting her opportunity.

Adrenaline flooded into my bloodstream. I was high on it before I knew it. When I opened my mouth to speak, I had difficulty catching my breath and the words quavered. "She is very beautiful, isn't she?" I said softly. She was, in the old and religious sense, awesome, mesmerizing in her grace and power, perfectly formed in every way.

We moved a few feet into the screen of some tall shrubs, a gesture that reassured us while doing nothing to secure our safety. Grizzly bears have notoriously bad eyes but keen ears and incomparable noses. The old adage is that if a pine needle falls in the forest, the eagle sees it, the deer hears it, and the bear smells it. We had been hiking for nine days without benefit of thorough baths. We stank even to ourselves. She could certainly, in the right wind, have smelled us a mile away (an odor Andy Russell, who knows grizzlies as intimately as anybody, describes as offensive, from a bear's point of view, to the point of nausea), and we were scarcely a hundred feet from her, a distance she could have covered before the charge had registered in our brains. Even so, we continued to whisper to each other as we watched. We were, suddenly, delirious.

The bear used the same foothold I had used to get up one of the anchor trees, stretched her massive right front paw—its long claws glinting—up ten feet, seized the rope, and thwacked it up and down until John's pack slid toward her. Then she clamped one of its straps in her teeth, pulled it toward her, and snapped the aluminum frame in half in her powerful forearms, as if it were a twig. She let the pieces fall to the ground, grabbed the slackened rope between her teeth, and cut it. My pack crashed down. We laughed.

"Well, there's the end of our hike," John said cheerfully.

"I suppose it's a little like watching your house burn," I said. That seemed hilarious to us, too.

I was thinking of the spectacle of fire. There was the hypnotic energy of fire in the bear's movements: the rigorous efficiency with which she undid our best precautions against her, the intelligence so belying our arrogant presumption against animal thought. We were captive not only to her power but to her wit, which had proved superior to ours.

While the darker cubs, looking too big for it, gamboled in the shadows, the adult grizzly set methodically about her work. She ripped apart the packs and searched the scattered contents, item by item, for edibles. We had intended to go out the next day to resupply; the pickings were slim, but she overlooked nothing. I knew how resourceful grizzlies can be in their diets, in ways that sometimes seem incongruous, given their size—of their fondness for ants, for ladybugs, and for the dainty strawberries that grow so profusely on the Montana Front Range.

This bear had an indiscriminate palate and a forgiving stomach. She snapped up freeze-dried foods in their foil-lined packages, gorp, candies, tea bags and pipe tobacco, toothpaste. She helped herself to bottles of sunscreen, vitamin pills, aspirins, antihistamine and Kaopectate tablets, paper and plastic, shards of cloth. She sampled bottles of insect repellent and canisters of white gas. She punctured water bottles, which popped like balloons. She latched her massive jaws around the nest of cooking pots and chomped down, puncturing them with what looked, when we inspected them later, like rifle bullet holes. Perhaps she had a bad tooth; at any rate, after the sound of lacerating metal came a particularly robust roar, one of half a dozen she sent echoing through the sparkling air of the narrow valley.

Douglas Peacock, another man intimately familiar with grizzlies, describes that roar as capable of chilling your piss. Perhaps it is, in other circumstances. Peacock, after all, claims to have survived more than forty bear charges. This was only the third time I had seen one in the wild. But those roars—directed at what, we could not tell—sounded to me magnificent, not chilling, even though a shiver ran down my spine. The bear's voice was as enormous and commanding as its physique—grander, less guttural, and more eloquent than the roars of the one lion I have heard.

"I felt," John wrote me later, "like I was approaching the throne of the 'most high.' While the grizzly was dismantling our property, and clearly ignoring us, I was thinking about what I've always been taught—everything we have in life, including life itself, is a gift. I understand that intellectually, but watching and listening to her and knowing she could wipe us out any time she wanted to, I understood emotionally about gifts."

The bear used her long, razor-sharp claws as adroitly as fingers. There was a single hard candy in the right pocket of my denim hiking shorts. She extracted and ate it, leaving only a slight tear in the shorts. She cut a quarter moon in a leather binoculars case without scratching the binoculars themselves. She shredded the stuff sack holding my sleeping bag but left the bag itself uncut. She ripped a sack holding a down vest, leaving the vest intact.

We watched her at close range for some time, spellbound and joyful. In our helplessness we had lost our fear. It felt liberating to be, for once, in charge of absolutely nothing.

Then it dawned on us that we might be safer at a greater distance. We backed cautiously away from the bear. She did not so much as glance in our direction. If she was aware of us, she ignored us with grand disdain. I have often felt such disregard in the presence of wild animals. Although I have sometimes been dismayed, I have come to cherish that lack of interest as a useful corrective, a reminder that only in our own inflated imaginations do human beings star in the center ring of creation.

By stages, we made our way out of the forest and up a steep grassy ridge. About halfway up we found a comfortable place to sit, a couple of hundred yards from the bear. We could still, indistinctly in the fading light, make out her movements. Mainly we heard her, a steady staccato of rips, shreds, and pops, accentuated now and then by a roar, perhaps of pain or frustration, or as a warning against interference, or simply for the hell of it.

We counted our blessings. How fortunate that the bear had arrived while it was still light; that she had not surprised us in our tent; that she had permitted us to get out of the way before moving in; that we were so close to the edge of the wilderness, hours rather than days from food and shelter; that we had been granted this rare, close encounter with one of the earth's legendary creatures. We congratulated each other on our luck.

"Let's face it," John said, "this is the moment you've been searching for." I had in fact once said, recklessly, that I would welcome any encounter with a grizzly bear, even one that did me injury, so long as I might be permitted to survive. In the motel room in Great Falls the night before we had gone up to Marias Pass to begin our walk, we had read of an early morning attack on a hiker in Yellowstone National Park. The woman, alone, had come around a bend in the trail, surprising a mother grizzly with cubs at close range. She had been grievously, but not fatally, wounded. From her hospital bed, silenced by a tracheotomy, she had penned a plea for the bear. It had only been doing its maternal duty, she said; she held no ill toward it.

I had often noticed that reaction in stories I had read about encounters with bears. It cheered me. Such willingness to submit to the authority of a prior claim by another species, even in the advent of harm, is rare in our culture, almost as rare as the grizzlies themselves. These encounters sometimes show us what it still means to live with humility in the world. The grizzly bear is almost uniquely capable of commanding such respect; for that reason alone its survival among us is vital. The point is not, as it is so often put, that we fear it, and that it is good for us to know fear, although that is also true, but that the grizzly demands of us some fealty to its own nature.

There was, at last, a long silence. We began to think that the bear had left. Then there was the sound again of rending fabric. Later, we would see that she had left the campground and sought out our tent, which we had erected but not staked, shredding its sides and flattening it, mangling its aluminum poles. This one act seemed gratuitous. It peeved me. The tent was nine days old, empty, and had never been near food or been slept in in clothing that had come into contact with food.

After that, we followed her progress eastward through the forest toward Benchmark, audible in the series of cracks of sticks and small timber, like firecrackers exploding. The bursts grew fainter and finally faded away altogether. We sat for some minutes after they had dissipated, listening breathlessly to be sure that she was gone. When we were certain of it, we exhaled pent-up air and rose to our feet. We were surprised to notice that it was already night, that the air was chilly, and that the nearly full moon had come up over the ridge. Never had a night seemed so tranquil.

We went down in the moonlight as far as the tent, reflecting the blue glow like a pool of water, and looked for our sleeping bags. Improbably, they had survived. The stillness of the forest was eerie, so encased, so riddled with menacing shadows. Everything seemed alive in the place now, nothing necessarily stationary or benign: the trees, the thin layer of soil, the rocks, the blue beams of the moonlight glimmering up out of the leaves. We made quickly for the freedom of the grassy ridge. Near its peak, below a stand of limber pines, we found a place where we could lie under the wide, open sky. The hillside embraced us with a welcoming grace. We wriggled into our sleeping bags, zipped them up, and prepared to receive whatever the night might bring.

We had been sleeping in forests beside clammering streams or in the high country where the wind always blows at night. So I found this night's sounds a revelation. A bat squeaked by. Somewhere a nighthawk collected a late harvest of insects, its wings buzzing, a sound familiar on the deserted evening streets of every prairie village. Upriver an owl called, and downriver another answered it.

Overhead a star plummeted in a blinding flash, the brightest either of us had ever seen. Satellites ambled this way and that. The moon hung over a sensuous line of barren hills, and the big dipper tilted toward the river, as if to resupply it. I thought of boyhood nights wandering the countryside of Rosewood Township, listening to the night breeze in the corn and to the distant barking of dogs, and dumbstruck by the shimmering, vaulting vastness of space. I felt small and young again, insignificant and secure in my insignificance, kept and attended, all of life's mystery still stretching out ahead of me, undiscovered.

Suddenly there was a loud, deep twang, like the sound of a bass fiddle string being plucked. We started.

John sat up in his sleeping bag. "What was that?" he asked.

"A wood frog," I said, gathering my wits. "A lovelorn wood frog."

Just when we had forgotten it, the frog called again in its oddly mechanical and impossibly loud way, the sorriest love song in all of nature. One more twang, and it fell silent.

"Not very persistent, either, poor thing," I said.

We were determined to keep a wakeful vigil until the dawn came, out of some sense of circumspection, I suppose. Something about the encounter with the bear—the animal itself, or the violence of the meeting, or the sense of having been spared—required it of us. We had entertained briefly the prospect of early death and had been granted stays of execution. Our lives seemed now acutely fresh and full of promise. It was not a moment one ought to shrug away. So I was chagrined to notice, when I opened the eyes I had been resting only for a moment, that the moon had gone down. Above me arched the Milky Way, so dense with stars that they looked, to my dim eyes, continuous, unfathomable, a great radiance at the heart of the universe. For the second time that night I felt tiny and secure, untouched by any prospect except to savor the one before me.

And then the hour before dawn arrived, crisp and clear, the breathless hour when even the animals seem to pause and ponder, the universal hour of reverie. A golden halo of light bathed the grassy ridge tops, but the forest and the river below were still cast in heavy shadow. Our sleeping bags were covered with frost, and inside them we were lightly dressed. We awaited the benediction of the sun.

It was a long time in coming, as something anticipated always is. When it appeared, we wriggled out of our bags, shook the frost from them, put on our boots and our hats, and went down the ridge toward the river. The slope was long and astonishingly steep, so steep that we had difficulty in keeping our footing as we eased down it on all fours. We did not have, that morning, adrenaline-powered feet with which to clamber. They felt leaden and clumsy again, as one's feet do in the first and last hours of the day. We had known, briefly, fleetness, and now we were back to putting one foot forward at a time.

We felt, too, a kind of shyness as we crossed the trail and entered the grove where we had begun what seemed an eternity ago to make a camp. I suppose it was not shyness but a sense of trespass, of having presumed to claim a place that was not, after all, ours.

We found the tatters of our things scattered for fifty feet in every direction. It was peaceful and sunny there, like the morning after a storm. We poked through the rubble, looking for what we might salvage: our rain jackets, the binoculars, our spoons and cups, our jackknives, a few feet of rope. What we could not salvage and had no means to carry, we collected, stuffed into the remnants of our packs, and set along the trail to be hauled out later. It took us the better part of an hour to clean up the mess. When we had finished, we gathered the few items that were still useful, wrapped them in the rain covers for our packs, tied them into bundles with the pieces of rope, and slung them over our walking sticks.

We headed down the trail like a pair of hoboes. In a mile, we joined the tracks of the bears. By and by, we met an outfitter, long and lanky and looking dashing in his silver spurs and broad-rimmed Stetson, who was leading twenty-one heavily laden mules upriver in advance of a party of vacationers. He surveyed us with unconcealed contempt. Just as he passed, he leaned toward us. "Making a lot of progress that way, boys?" he drawled.

We let the remark pass. We were filled that morning with the meekness of angels.

Buffalo Winter

WINTER IN WESTERN South Dakota usually begins with a blizzard in November or early December. One day everyone drives into the Black Hills to look at the vivid colors of the leaves; the next, snow whirls the leaves into piles, drifts them under. Some alert newspaper photographer usually takes a picture of a buffalo looking calm and warm in the storm's eye, and some of us think longingly of the pioneers' buffalo-hide coats.

Often, the first nasty blizzard is followed by warm weather, until weather forecasters begin to worry about a brown Christmas. Weeks of warmth may last until early January, with temperatures in the seventies, but cold and snow almost always return. February can be unpleasant, with long gray days, snow, and sleet, but our record snowfall depths have come in March, April, and even May, when ranchers are calving. The all-time record for a swift change in temperature is held by a northern Black Hills town. Any discussion of weather in Dakota or on the Great Plains requires terms like "usually," and "almost," because the only consistent weather pattern is variety.

In my buffalo winter, the blizzards began in November; for two months, the snow rose higher and temperatures sank lower. In late December, snowdrifts stopped tumbling from the sky and froze solid on the ground, and the thermometer hung at thirty degrees below zero through New Year's Eve. The first ten days of January brought chinook winds; tropical air swirled around us, even though the weather people said it was only forty or fifty degrees above zero.

49

Piles of snow that seemed permanent on the landscape crumpled and collapsed, melted and gurgled down the draws. Except in the ranch yard. Our trucks had packed the snow hard as we hauled hay to the cattle, and tropical days just melted the top layer enough to make it slippery. I had fallen down so many times my thighs were interlocking bruises, blue and green paisley. I was sick of wearing heavy boots and long underwear, weary of wrenching muscles as I tried not to fall.

I lived then in an apartment built at the side of my parents' house, a fifteen-by-twenty space with two levels. My first husband and I built the addition as a quick and practical shelter when we returned to the ranch. I expected our stay to be permanent, that someday we'd manage the ranch, build a house nearby. For temporary housing, we poured concrete for a bedroom in the basement, and a bathroom partitioned off under the stairs. A crude plywood door led to the crawlspace under my parents' house; when we opened it to store something, the earth smelled ancient.

On the upper level, a table was tucked into an **L** formed by a handrail on the basement steps. Four tall windows wrapped around that end of the apartment; I suspended plants in front of them to interrupt our view of the snowdrifts. We hung coats above my parents' chest-style freezer. At the other end of the room were kitchen cupboards we'd salvaged from an old house, and a long counter over trunks of antique dishes and clothes. Evenings, we read in two overstuffed chairs before the fireplace in the east wall.

During our marriage, my husband had zigzagged between graduate programs from religion through philosophy to literature, and finally decided he was a writer. When we first returned to South Dakota, he worked at a crude desk and bookshelves built against the bathroom wall, next to the wood stove that heated the space. I helped my father, kept house, and wrote at the upstairs table, where I could feel the warm air flowing away from me, even after we installed a fireplace liner with glass doors. At mealtime, we pushed my typewriter aside to eat at the table, or balanced plates on our laps in the easy chairs.

This winter, the buffalo season, the rooms looked the same, but a new cat slept on a cushion on the typewriter, and my husband was gone for good. "For good." Yes, that's the right phrase.

We'd started a literary magazine, cut wood, fed cows, and lived an artistic ranching life for nearly a year before poverty and his inability to meet support payments convinced me to teach at a college eighty miles away. We moved into a rented house, and came back to the ranch on weekends. My husband got a job with the state arts council, traveling to teach poetry in the schools, and cheered up right away. Before long, he was getting phone calls from women whose voices I didn't recognize, buying new shirts, a new car: the usual story. My ranch-raised cat disappeared into the town, perhaps run over; maybe she found someone with more cash for cat food. My husband took the dog and moved to Montana. I retreated to the ranch, put my typewriter back on the table, published the magazine in the basement, ate all my meals in front of the fireplace, and tamed a barn cat who couldn't believe her luck. She enjoyed visiting the barn, where she no doubt boasted to her old companions.

On this particular night, I'd put my feet up on the hearth and read until nearly midnight. Country people go to bed early because we use so much physical energy during winter days. But misery made me feel even worse by stealing my sleep. Instead of resting so I could tackle a problem with a refreshed body and an alert mind, I paced the floors, read a chapter in one book, a page in another, dusted useless objects—wedding presents packed a dozen times during our marriage. I washed dishes, stepped outside to look at stars and listen to owls. I hadn't slept alone for seven years. I found some grass we'd brought back from graduate school, and smoked a joint. In spite of being sick of ice, I poured gin over some, and downed it; as usual, the liquor woke me, set my nerves on edge, sent me speeding around the room.

After performing these rites of sleeplessness for several hours, I realized I didn't have to stay in the cramped apartment. The warm spell had cleared snow from most roads; by a shortcut, the Black Hills was a half-hour away. In the house, I kept seeing jobs, books I should read, mud I should wash away. Driving relaxes me, makes me think in innovative ways. The winding trails would be deserted and challenging; if the booze made me dangerous, I wouldn't hurt anyone but myself.

When I went outside, I stepped into floodlights: a full moon was just rising, swollen and dull gold. The pickup started at once; the thermometer read twenty degrees. The moon and air were mild, without the chilly paralysis of the past month and a half. No other car moved on the highway; once I turned onto the dirt road—a back way into the state park I use to evade the toll booths in summer—I pushed the headlight button in and drove by moonlight. Slowly. Savoring.

The moon catapulted blue-black tree shadows across the road, so thick and dark I expected a bump when the pickup nosed into them, thought the hood might crumple, my face snarl in windshield cracks. Houses and barns were murky blocks; when I lifted my foot from the accelerator, the pickup drifted quietly, unseen, past my sleeping neighbors.

Turning into the park, I began to watch for reflected light from animals' eyes, more subtle by moonlight than headlight. Pink flashes made my eyes focus on deer raising their heads. Apparently a pickup without lights was no threat, and they grazed again. The pickup eased up a slope with little pressure on the gas pedal. I turned off the road, floated up the hill through the hissing grass.

Humped shapes repeated the shape of the mound in miniature. Rocks. No.

Buffalo.

I'd found the herd, in the instant of looking for it. I braked tenderly, turned the ignition key. When the door opened, the inside light made me squint; I closed it quietly. Stepped up on the road bank, to a dry clump of buffalo grass. Sank down, folding my legs, back straight, inhaling deeply.

Breathing moonlight. Blue light flashed from an eye that seemed big as a dinner plate, flickered on a black horn as a head turned. Another. They lay like soldiers awaiting a dawn attack, mute sword blades gleaming. As my eyes adjusted, their acre of curled hair lay like a plateau of moss on the surface of a sea before me.

The pointed horns were everywhere, aimed at the sky, a soft blue glitter in the moonlight. My ears seemed to expand; I pictured them stretching, opening like flowers, sensitive enough to catch a coyote howl a mile away, hissing grass, an owl's glide. Breathing seemed to shake the ground, make the trees quiver, as if I was inside earth's lungs: the breath of fifty buffalo, a hundred, inhaling my scent.

For the first time, I realized my position. When alarmed or angry, buffalo make a huffing sound, blowing air from their nostrils in quick bursts. When a horse does it, we say "he has rollers in his nose," and settle into the saddle, ready for the buck. The herd was making its collective decision even as I grasped my danger.

I sat two pickup lengths, perhaps four strides, from the foremost animal. Bison are easily annoyed and unpredictable. They can run faster than a horse, spin with the speed and agility of a bucking rodeo bull even though they may weigh a ton at maturity.

How many lay there? Fifty tons of meat, or more, one buffalo leap away from where I sat.

Buffalo are fickle; even those raised in captivity have gored their owners to death; an angry bull can demolish a car, tumbling it as a child might kick a ball. A galloping mass of buffalo, stampeding, minces anything for which they choose not to turn aside. I've seen a bull disembowel another with a turn of the head that looked as casual as a high school girl tossing her hair out of her eyes.

Now, in early January, the cows must be heavily pregnant, enormous with the weight of calves. Do buffalo become edgy during pregnancy? Are they irritable, easily upset? I didn't know.

Movement would do me no good; I wasn't fast enough to untangle my legs, and get inside the pickup before a buffalo could be upon me. Animals can sometimes sense fear. I relaxed, breathed deep of buffalo musk, warm air rising from the hulking forms. Thought hard how I admire them, tried not to think how they were once shot by the thousands, butchered only for their tongues, or hides. The hunters shot until the gun barrels were too hot to touch, left carcasses so thick on the plains earth, men said they could have walked from Texas to Canada without stepping on the ground.

To some Indian tribes, the buffalo represented both prayer and abundance, worship made tangible, perhaps because the buffalo supplied so many of their needs. The last remnants were saved in a roundup directed by a descendant of French trappers and the Lakota tribes native here, to whom these hills were sacred. When the herds grew, some were penned here where tourists could drive among them in relative safety. "Buffalo are Dangerous. Stay in your cars," say the signs. But the animals look massively slow, plodding along dusty trails to water. Every year a few tourists in the West get too close, try to pet one, perhaps, and die from goring, or being crushed by hooves or head.

I'm not one of those folks, I thought. I respect you; possibly even worship you. Here, with moonlight pouring from the scimitars of your horns, worship seems like a particularly good idea.

A few years ago, a large part of the buffalo pasture in this park was consumed in a fire that began with a logger's bad luck, and ended by burning several thousand acres of trees and buffalo pasture. The smoke hung over my prairie home for days, and neighbors fighting fire told horrendous stories of animals singed by flames, horses refusing to be caught and rescued, and one scarlet buffalo apparently hit by a load of the red fire-retardent slurry dropped by airplanes.

But modern fire fighters don't just stop fire, they plan ahead, and the slurry which smothers flames also contains fertilizer and seeds. Rains followed the fire, and it wasn't long before a nervous tourist reported seeing a buffalo that was—ah—er—bright green. Rangers checked out the story because the tourist seemed sane and sincere. Rain on the bull hit by slurry had sprouted a nice coat of grass.

After the fire was out, I drove the back roads of the park to see if some of my favorite spots had been damaged. It was late fall, and I saw several solitary buffalo bulls in meadows ringed with aspen turning gold, lying in state on green grass. When I emerged from the trees, I drove in blackened prairie until I reached a spot where the red earth of the southern Black Hills outcrops. Floods gash red wounds in the tan prairie grass, and in one of those I saw two buffalo bulls standing with their heads nearly against a red, eroded bank. They seemed to be licking the earth. Even with the binoculars, I couldn't be positive, so I drove to within fifty feet of them, and slowly walked closer. Both bulls were fat, ready for winter, their hair spiraling and glossy, their horns polished to gleaming bronze. Eyes shut, heads close together, they stood facing the red bank, nudging it. I was only twenty feet away when one of the bulls turned slowly and looked at me. His nose and mouth were stained brilliant red from the soil, and as I watched, he slowly extended his tongue up into his crimson nostrils, and licked until they turned brown. Then he grunted, and turned back to the bank, slurping up the earth eagerly.

Red earth is rich in iron; perhaps the buffalo sensed a special need for it after the tumult of the fire, or perhaps they were storing minerals for winter. But as I watched, it struck me that a buffalo eating red earth was a powerful symbol: the Lakota emblem of abundance was literally eating the blood red earth from which he sprang and to which he would return. A bit farther down the road, I saw piles of buffalo dung of a delicate rose color, pretty enough to be ice cream.

On that winter hillside, tranquility flowed like a current from the massed bodies before me. I was soothed, serene. Time shifted, or perhaps I fell into a trance, or hallucinated, or dozed. Some might say I was influenced by the drug or the alcohol I'd ingested three hours before. Samuel Johnson remarked, "Depend upon it, sir, when a man knows he is to be hanged in a fortnight, it concentrates his mind wonderfully." Facing the buffalo may have been my soberest moment alive. Yet while my body remained in place, I was not aware of it, or of anything outside it, for some time. Finally some change, more fragile than sound, focused my eyes on the herd again.

Soundlessly, the bulls had materialized. Perhaps they were lying in a protective ring around the cows and older calves when I drove up, and merely stood. At the time, I wondered if they were capable of teleporting—transporting themselves from one spot to another instantly—by thought. Of course not.

They stood before me, a massive curtain of lowered heads, moonlit eyes, level with mine. The curved horns all pointed my way. Bronze statues of buffalo. My hands rose from my lap, palm up, open, in a gesture so old and instinctive I didn't know I moved: *peace. I have nothing to hide.*

Murmuring mixed with grumbles and rhythmic panting, like a distant crowd beginning to grow impatient. In a corner of my brain, a screen lit to show me how I might look if they all advanced upon me. I switched it off.

Nothing happened. After a while, I inhaled deeply, starved for oxygen. The buffalo seemed to vibrate, whispering, shifting the air gently against my face. One by one, the great bulls lay down with soft grunts and sighs, joints creaking as they folded their legs, still screening the cows and calves with their bodies. Like old, wise dogs.

Eventually I noticed the moon settling into the spiky trees. My legs were numb. The bulls still lay close; some slept, heads lowered. I leaned on one haunch, got the opposite foot flat on the ground, and forced myself up, locking my knees. Blood surged through my veins.

I turned my back on the bulls without concern. Once inside, I rolled the window down. Several heavy heads turned when the engine caught, and the truck began creeping along the road. A hundred yards away, I shut the door firmly. The sound, loud as a gunshot, startled me into realization.

I was leaving a holy place, inhabited by philosophers who were also friends. Illumination washed through me; my brain seemed to bubble with wisdom; I could see myself working for years to understand.

I'd rather not write what happened next, but I can't avoid doing so, because it happened; it's part of that night, and this is nonfiction. To me, that means I stick to the truth. If it's not fiction, it's truth, and I'm stuck with it.

Just as I was soon stuck in a snowdrift. Still in that hushed dream of moonbeams and enlightened buffalo bulls, I drove down the dirt road so inattentively the pickup slid into a snow bank on a curve.

No other feeling quite matches the realization, among people who habitually drive deserted roads: the pickup shimmied into the ruts like a nightclub dancer, almost flirtatiously. It wiggled playfully along the frozen track for a moment while I still had hope, struggling to turn it away from the drift. Then it dived to the side like a dancer leaving the stage at intermission: finished with the set, no longer smiling seductively.

By reflex, I gunned the engine, hoping weight and momentum would carry the truck through the drift. At the same time, I felt the truth in my buttocks and hands. Simultaneously, I tried to picture the pickup's box; had I put the shovel back after the last time I got stuck?

I sat still, quickly cold, remembering that every time I'd gotten stuck during my marriage, my husband managed to be somewhere else. I got pneumonia one winter with a hundred cows to feed and water every day, but he drove cheerfully away to teach more than poetry to high school girls. Fury drove me; I chopped ice and pitched hay until my clothes were soaked through with sweat, then sat in a hot bath until I slept. In the morning, I was fine; either my anger or the water boiled the germs to death. Now, while I was stuck in this drift, he was probably stuck in some Montana cowgirl.

When I stepped out of the truck, I left the engine running, heater on. The buffalo were less than a half-mile behind me, but the night had changed. The gnarled trees looked menacing. I examined the track ahead, buried for thirty feet in hard-crusted snow. Under the truck, the pickup's gear box and springs were jammed with ice; if I tried to go ahead, I'd be pushing a growing drift. The shovel lay across two bales of hay and six sacks of cattle cake I'd loaded in November for weight.

Behind the truck, my tracks were straight; perhaps I could back out, following them. I got in the seat, straightened the wheels, and gently shifted into reverse. The pickup moved an inch; the tires caught, and then began to whir, whining in falsetto.

When I hear that whine for more than five minutes, I sneer at a driver who's angry, stupid, or both; the truck isn't going anywhere while tires make that sound. Instead the snow beneath will turn to ice from the friction of futile rotation; miles of future travel will disappear into the air. A friend told me about an old man who drove into his pasture one winter day to check his cattle; when he got stuck, he spun the tires until they burst into flames. He burned to death in his truck. The family will never know exactly what, if anything, he was thinking.

I shut off the engine and got the shovel. Without haste, I dug straight smooth tracks behind the rear tires to the spot where I'd driven into the drift. My numb hands grew clumsier as I worked; I felt like curling up to sleep in the road. The night around seemed to throb with strange noises. Pausing to breathe, I felt the eyes of a malicious watcher. Once I heard a car motor idling nearby, and looked hopefully up the road for headlights. Then I thought again: I was a woman alone on a back road, unarmed, at four in the morning. No time to be hoping for passersby. Just about the time my ex used to get home, in fact. I shoveled harder.

When I'd dug a broad track nearly to bare ground, I got back in the truck, whimpering with cold, and held my hands to the heater vents until I could bend my fingers. Then I shifted gently into reverse, applying a light kiss of accelerator. The engine murmured, grew louder; I was sweating, trying to feel the angle of all four wheels—keep them straight in the track—through my hands. I knew the moment when the gearbox began dragging snow, the pile building. Then the truck lurched sideways, and settled again.

All four tires had slithered out of the track, deeper into the angle between the frozen road surface and the bank. I began digging a new set of tracks beside the first.

Nearly two hours passed before I finally backed free of the drift. My eyeballs felt gritty; I had nearly forgotten the buffalo, but I'd be able to recall the shining images from a small blue space inside my brain. The shovel clanged as it struck the tailgate; I turned the heater on high, and drove wide around the drift. I had gone no more than a half-mile when headlights appeared in my rear view mirror.

I nearly drove into another drift. I had crossed no other trails; the other vehicle must have come from behind me. What was anyone doing in the buffalo pasture at this hour?

The thought made me laugh aloud, a demented sound after my silent night. But it was strange, in this country, if he saw I was stuck without offering to help; most of us help strangers in dangerous weather.

I headed for the main road instead of the shortcut, and the other pickup caught up with me as I drove down a hill to the highway. When I stopped, it rolled up nearly to my bumper, headlights catching me like a spotlight. I was tempted to get out, confront him.

Fear of the kind only women feel on lonely roads at night stopped me. I locked my door and drove on. The county seat town was the other way; in my direction lay nothing but dark ranch homes for thirty miles. Stiff with tension, I drove precisely at the speed limit until the road forked again, and I could head toward home. Surely, I thought, if he were a forest official, or someone going to work early, or even a poacher, he would go the other way, glad to be rid of me.

He followed. No matter what speed I drove, even when I drove nearly on the shoulder through straight stretches enticing him to pass, the glaring lights remained five feet from my bumper. I began to be afraid, to consider and discard wild schemes for evasion. Alone in my truck, I explained to the other driver about my sleeplessness, my drive, how I'd gotten stuck, urged him to go somewhere else.

Then I remembered the motor I'd heard; perhaps he'd been hiding near me for two hours, while I dug. I found the thought more terrifying than facing the buffalo. On a curve, I leaned out my window and looked back at him instead of watching for oncoming traffic, and saw a Forest Service insignia.

By the time I reached the highway junction, I'd figured it out. He lived in one of the cabins the Forest Service maintained for the men who regularly work with the buffalo herd. Sleepless himself, he'd heard the pickup, and driven out to investigate. He may have noticed my truck while I drove with my lights off, cause for suspicion; he had no reason to think anyone drove by moonlight for entertainment. Had he known I was a woman, he might have helped me, but the government didn't pay him to help idiots who got themselves stuck in the middle of the night, especially not unidentified people who might be armed and nervous poachers.

So he waited, sitting comfortable and warm in his pickup, perhaps listening to the radio, dozing. He wanted to see my truck, its license plates, the bed, see if I was hauling a deer or buffalo carcass. No doubt my license number and description were scribbled on a note pad; I'd cooperated by sticking my head out the window. Blonde female, orange Ford pickup, licensed in the same county. He might already know who I was, if he had a cb radio to call a Highway Patrol or Sheriff's dispatcher, or be following me home to arrest me.

When I turned south on the highway leading to the ranch, his pickup drifted across the highway, turned around on another county road, and went back toward the park. Relieved, I concentrated on getting home, thinking of the rumors if I met any of my neighbors on the highway. Yeah, I saw her coming home at sunrise; she must be leading a wild life in town since she got divorced. No one would believe the truth even if I told it.

Later, I considered the contradiction between the two parts of the experience: the unexpected gentleness of the buffalo and the grueling ordeal of being stuck, of being followed. I remembered a zen-like line: "Before enlightenment, haul water, chop wood; after enlightenment, haul water, chop wood." I could not truthfully forget either part of the night—or even the restless misery that had sent me outside.

The yard was utterly black as I put the pickup away; sunrise was an hour away, at seven-thirty. After a hot shower, I slept until nine, dreaming of buffalo bulls with gleaming horns and a glowing language that was not words; of lifting shovels filled with snow, and breathing deeply of moonlight as I drove dark highways. Always, something secret pursued me.

Later that spring, I drove through the buffalo pasture often; whenever my truck appeared, the animals would move toward it in a body. Once, when I spent the day hiking up French Creek, the herd was lying close around the pickup when I returned near dark. I had to wait until they moved off to water, grunting to themselves, before I emerged from the trees and drove away. When I asked a Forest Service official about their behavior, I learned that they were accustomed to receiving feed from trucks of a similar orange. The ranger grinned; I wondered if he'd been the one following me.

I didn't tell him why I asked, or about my encounter with the buffalo in the moonlight. Many incidents in my life have become material for essays or poems; I write partly to understand, and partly to record. I might tell a story dozens of times before I consider writing it down. I don't always understand what it means until after the writing. Sometimes long after. Sometimes never.

Buckeye

Years after my father's heart quit, I keep in a wooden box on my desk the two buckeyes that were in his pocket when he died. Once the size of plums, the brown seeds are shriveled now, hollow, hard as pebbles, yet they still gleam from the polish of his hands. He used to reach for them in his overalls or suit pants and click them together, or he would draw them out, cupped in his palm, and twirl them with his blunt carpenter's fingers, all the while humming snatches of old tunes.

"Do you really believe buckeyes keep off arthritis?" I asked him more than once.

He would flex his hands and say, "I do so far."

My father never paid much heed to pain. Near the end, when his worn knee often slipped out of joint, he would pound it back in place with a rubber mallet. If a splinter worked into his flesh beyond the reach of tweezers, he would heat the blade of his knife over a cigarette lighter and slice through the skin. He sought to ward off arthritis not because he feared pain but because he lived through his hands, and he dreaded the swelling of knuckles, the stiffening of fingers. What use would he be if he could no longer hold a hammer or guide a plow? When he was a boy he had known farmers not yet forty years old whose hands had curled into claws, men so crippled up they could not tie their own shoes, could not sign their names.

"I mean to tickle my grandchildren when they come along," he told me, "and I mean to build doll houses and turn spindles for tiny chairs on my lathe."

So he fondled those buckeyes as if they were charms, carrying them with him when our family moved from Ohio at the end of my childhood, bearing them to new homes in Louisiana, then Oklahoma, Ontario, and Mississippi, carrying them still on his final day when pain a thousand times fiercer than arthritis gripped his heart.

The box where I keep the buckeyes also comes from Ohio, made by my father from a walnut plank he bought at a farm auction. I remember the auction, remember the sagging face of the widow whose home was being sold, remember my father telling her he would prize that walnut as if he had watched the tree grow from a sapling on his own land. He did not care for pewter or silver or gold, but he cherished wood. On the rare occasions when my mother coaxed him into a museum, he ignored the paintings or porcelain and studied the exhibit cases, the banisters, the moldings, the parquet floors.

I remember him planing that walnut board, sawing it, sanding it, joining piece to piece to make foot stools, picture frames, jewelry boxes. My own box, a bit larger than a soap dish, lined with red corduroy, was meant to hold earrings and pins, not buckeyes. The top is inlaid with pieces fitted so as to bring out the grain, four diagonal joints converging from the corners toward the center. If I stare long enough at those converging lines, they float free of the box and point to a center deeper than wood.

I learned to recognize buckeyes and beeches, sugar maples and shagbark hickories, wild cherries, walnuts, and dozens of other trees while tramping through the Ohio woods with my father. To his eyes, their shapes, their leaves, their bark, their winter buds were as distinctive as the set of a friend's shoulders. As with friends, he was partial to some, craving their company, so he would go out of his way to visit particular trees, walking in a circle around the splayed roots of a sycamore, laying his hand against the trunk of a white oak, ruffling the feathery green boughs of a cedar.

"Trees breathe," he told me. "Listen."

I listened, and heard the stir of breath.

He was no botanist; the names and uses he taught me were those he had learned from country folks, not from books. Latin never crossed his lips. Only much later would I discover that the tree he called ironwood, its branches like muscular arms, good for axe handles, is known in the books as hophornbeam; what he called tulip-tree or canoewood, ideal for log cabins, is officially the yellow poplar; what he called hoop ash, good for barrels and fence posts, appears in books as hackberry.

When he introduced me to the buckeye, he broke off a chunk of the gray bark and held it to my nose. I gagged.

"That's why the old-timers called it stinking buckeye," he told me. "They used it for cradles and feed troughs and peg legs."

"Why for peg legs?" I asked.

"Because it's light and hard to split, so it won't shatter when you're clumping around."

He showed me this tree in later summer, when the fruits had fallen and the ground was littered with prickly brown pods. He picked up one, as fat as a lemon, and peeled away the husk to reveal the shiny seed. He laid it in my palm and closed my fist around it so the seed peeped out from the circle formed by my index finger and thumb. "You see where it got the name?" he asked.

I saw: what gleamed in my hand was the eye of a deer, bright with life. "It's beautiful," I said.

"It's beautiful," my father agreed, "but also poisonous. Nobody eats buckeyes, except maybe a fool squirrel."

I knew the gaze of deer from living in the Ravenna Arsenal, in Portage County, up in the northeastern corner of Ohio. After supper we often drove the Arsenal's gravel roads, past the munitions bunkers, past acres of rusting tanks and wrecked bombers, into the far fields where we counted deer. One June evening, while mist rose from the ponds, we counted three hundred and eleven, our family record. We found the deer in herds, in bunches, in amorous pairs. We came upon lone bucks, their antlers lifted against the sky like the bare branches of dogwood. If you were quiet, if your hands were empty, if you moved slowly, you could leave the car and steal to within a few paces of a grazing deer, close enough to see the delicate lips, the twitching nostrils, the glossy, fathomless eyes.

The wooden box on my desk holds these grazing deer, as it holds the buckeyes and the walnut plank and the farm auction and the munitions bunkers and the breathing forests and my father's hands. I could lose the box, I could lose the polished seeds, but if I were to lose the memories I would become a bush without roots, and every new breeze would toss me about. All those memories lead back to the northeastern corner of Ohio, the place where I came to consciousness, where I learned to connect feelings with words, where I fell in love with the earth.

It was a troubled love, for much of the land I knew as a child had been ravaged. The ponds in the Arsenal teemed with bluegill and beaver, but they were also laced with TNT from the making of bombs. Because the wolves and coyotes had long since been killed, some of the deer, so plump in the June grass, collapsed on the January snow, whittled by hunger to racks of bones. Outside the Arsenal's high barbed fences, many of the farms had failed, their barns caving in, their topsoil gone. Ravines were choked with swollen couches and junked washing machines and cars. Crossing fields, you had to be careful not to slice your feet on tin cans or shards of glass. Most of the rivers had been dammed, turning fertile valleys into scummy playgrounds for boats.

One free-flowing river, the Mahoning, ran past the small farm near the Arsenal where our family lived during my later years in Ohio. We owned just enough land to pasture three ponies and to grow vegetables for our table, but those few acres opened onto miles of woods and creeks and secret meadows. I walked that land in every season, every weather, following animal trails. But then the Mahoning, too, was doomed by a government decision; we were forced to sell our land, and a dam began to rise across the river.

If enough people had spoken for the river, we might have saved it. If enough people had believed that our scarred country was worth defending, we might have dug in our heels and fought. Our attachments to the land were all private. We had no shared lore, no literature, no art to root us there, to give us courage, to help us stand our ground. The only maps we had were those issued by the state, showing a maze of numbered lines stretched over emptiness. The Ohio landscape never showed up on postcards or posters, never unfurled like tapestry in films, rarely filled even a paragraph in books. There were no mountains in that place, no waterfalls, no rocky gorges, no vistas. It was a country of low hills, cut over woods, scoured fields, villages that had lost their purpose, roads that had lost their way.

"Let us love the country of here below," Simone Weil urged. "It is real; it offers resistance to love. It is this country that God has given us to love. He has willed that it should be difficult yet possible to love it." Which is the deeper truth about buckeyes, their poison or their beauty? I hold with the beauty; or rather, I am held by the beauty, without forgetting the poison. In my corner of Ohio the gullies were choked with trash, yet cedars flickered up like green flames from cracks in stone; in the evening bombs exploded at the ammunition dump, yet from the darkness came the mating cries of owls. I was saved from despair by knowing a few men and women who cared enough about the land to clean up trash, who planted walnuts and oaks that would long outlive them, who imagined a world that would have no call for bombs.

How could our hearts be large enough for heaven if they are not large enough for earth? The only country I am certain of is the one here below. The only paradise I know is the one lit by our everyday sun, this land of difficult love, shot through with shadow. The place where we learn this love, if we learn it at all, shimmers behind every new place we inhabit.

A family move carried me away from Ohio thirty years ago; my schooling and marriage and job have kept me away ever since, except for visits in memory and in flesh. I returned to the site of our farm one cold November day, when the trees were skeletons and the ground shone with the yellow of fallen leaves. From a previous trip I knew that our house had been bulldozed, our yard and pasture had grown up in thickets, and the reservoir had flooded the woods. On my earlier visit I had merely gazed from the car, too numb with loss to climb out. But on this November day, I parked the car, drew on my hat and gloves, opened the door, and walked.

I was looking for some sign that we had lived there, some token of our affection for the place. All that I recognized, aside from the contours of the land, were two weeping willows that my father and I had planted near the road. They had been slips the length of my forearm when we set them out, and now their crowns rose higher than the telephone poles. When I touched them last, their trunks had been smooth and supple, as thin as my wrist, and now they were furrowed and stout. I took off my gloves and laid my hands against the rough bark. Immediately I felt the wince of tears. Without knowing why, I said hello to my father, quietly at first, then louder and louder, as if only shouts could reach him through the bark and miles and years.

Surprised by sobs, I turned from the willows and stumbled away toward the drowned woods, calling to my father. I sensed that he was nearby. Even as I called, I was wary of grief's deceptions. I had never seen his body after he died. By the time I reached the place of his death, a furnace had reduced him to ashes. The need to see him, to let go of him, to let go of this land and time, was powerful enough to summon mirages; I knew that. But I also knew, stumbling toward the woods, that my father was here.

At the bottom of a slope where the creek used to run, I came to an expanse of gray stumps and withered grass. It was a bay of the reservoir from which the water had retreated, the level drawn down by engineers or drought. I stood at the edge of this desolate ground, willing it back to life, trying to recall the woods where my father had taught me the names of trees. No green shoots rose. I walked out among the stumps. The grass crackled under my boots, breath rasped in my throat, but otherwise the world was silent.

Then a cry broke overhead and I looked up to see a red-tailed hawk launching out from the top of an oak. I recognized the bird from its band of dark feathers across the creamy breast and the tail splayed like rosy fingers against the sun. It was a red-tailed hawk for sure; and it was also my father. Not a symbol of my father, not a reminder, not a ghost, but the man himself, right there, circling in the air above me. I knew this as clearly as I knew the sun burned in the sky. A calm poured through me. My chest quit heaving. My eyes dried.

Hawk and father wheeled above me, circle upon circle, wings barely moving, head still. My own head was still, looking up, knowing and being known. Time scattered like fog. At length, father and hawk stroked the air with those powerful wings, three beats, then vanished over a ridge.

The voice of my education told me then and tells me now that I did not meet my father, that I merely projected my longing onto a bird. My education may well be right; yet nothing I heard in school, nothing I've read, no lesson reached by logic has ever convinced me as utterly or stirred me as deeply as did that red-tailed hawk. Nothing in my education prepared me to love a piece of the earth, least of all a humble, battered country like northeastern Ohio; I learned from the land itself.

Before leaving the drowned woods, I looked around at the ashen stumps, the wilted grass, and for the first time since moving from this place I was able to let it go. This ground was lost; the flood would reclaim it. But other ground could be saved, must be saved, in every watershed, every neighborhood. For each home ground we need new maps, living maps, stories and poems, photographs and paintings, essays and songs. We need to know where we are, so that we may dwell in our place with a full heart.

Where He Is Now

BECAUSE OF ALL the hills around which any journey has to be negotiated, there are usually three or more ways to get from anywhere to anywhere else in Cincinnati, not counting up and over. This is a city of villages connected over time in all the odd and angled ways villages connect, not unlike, say, London, in its conglomerate structure. No urban plan was ever laid over it because there never was, until much too late, any "it" to subject to the grid of a Chicago or Manhattan. Its multitude of parts just grew together as they grew individually over the decades, the centuries. Some of them never did get incorporated into the city proper that now surrounds them, leaving them islanded, a Norwood or St. Bernard, inside its municipal boundaries. And others that did join the city still retain their own clear identities, of which they have become increasingly proud of late, posting decorative signs along their thoroughfares announcing their names and in some cases the dates of their original founding: Columbia-Tusculum, 1788. They are what they are, and, for the most part, proud of it. No one, not even a stranger, would ever mistake Mt. Adams for Mt. Auburn, Price Hill for Bond Hill, Paddock Hills for Walnut Hills, though there is no more a walnut to be found in the one than a paddock in the other. Nor would even a visitor from another country, or another world for that matter, mistake old Porkopolis, the once-upon-a-time Queen City of the West, for either of her shabby Kentucky handmaidens across the river, Covington and Newport.

The roads, anyway, follow the hills—or the limits the hills impose upon them—and more: they follow the banks of streams that have long since gone into hiding in underground conduits; they follow old wagon roads that once wandered from one village to the next; they follow trails the Miamis laid down centuries ago and long-abandoned deer runs and, who knows, maybe even the paths the mastodons trampled through these once-forested hills on their way down to the big river. Today the roads scurry between the hills, wrap themselves around the hillsides, leap across the little valleys on slender bridges, or plunge right down into them. They end abruptly at heavily wooded ravines, suddenly change direction and sometimes even names as the topography dictates, and in a few cases meander up the valleys and around the hills and through the former villages until at last they find their way out of the city. But the one thing no Cincinnati street ever does for long is to run straight and true, and that might even be taken for a significant indigenous trait, not to be separated from the complexities of the city's service as a way station on the underground railway, its German-Jewish-Black-and-Appalachian ethnicity, its conservative-leaning-toward-right-wing political mentality, the northern consciousness that informs its southern exposure as it looks across the river to the Kentucky bluffs on the other side, the fact that people in the east think of it as a midwestern city while those to the west consider it eastern, and maybe, too, the great meandering Ohio itself as it snakes its wide way under the shadow of the city's hills along the course of an itinerary that carries its waters all the way from the Allegheny Mountains to the Gulf of Mexico, a lengthy, muddy, and indirect journey by any measure.

I begin with this tedious and undramatic analysis of the city's meandering ways because it seems to me that all stories are stories of travel, all fiction fiction of place, of the setting down of a body, or bodies, in some familiar place—or perhaps equally often, some quite unfamiliar place—wherein a way has to be found, for the traveler to go, often by indirection after many struggles with misdirection. Everything happens somewhere, and everywhere has its idiosyncrasies of passage: its Dead End streets and One Way alleys, its Do Not Enter thoroughfares and No Trucks parkways, its Private lanes and Children At Play neighborhood streets, its School and Hospital and Traffic Checked by Radar zones. We do not walk around in a daze among the bazaars of Old Delhi, in the midst of the buses and bicycle rickshaws, the vendors of bangles and spices and copper pots, stunned into confusion simply because we have left our familiar place behind. At home, too, the traffic seeks to engulf us and the hucksters flash their gaudy wares in our faces. And though we travel out daily rounds on a kind of automatic pilot, only marginally attentive to our surroundings—sometimes arriving at our destination with no awareness of how we got there, so accustomed are we to every stop sign and freeway exit that we no longer even see them—there is still a kind of mystery to it all: the secrets buried in geology, in history, in weather, in flora and fauna and longitude and latitude and, yes, even in human behavior, that *are* the place in ways we will never fully come to understand, no matter how many of its streets we travel, or for how long. It matters not where we are, we are still and always displaced persons, embarking on journeys whose destinations are only poorly understood, if at all, seeking somehow to find our way around. And the roads are winding, the names confusing, the unexpected barriers everywhere.

What I really ought to be giving you here is a map. But the only map I have is words, those never-quite-adequate guides to the terra incognita of consciousness that are as likely to get us lost as to help us find our way. Only later, perhaps, do we figure out that we were trying to read the map upside down, and never, never, can we get it folded back up the way it came. The brain itself is a landscape of hills and valleys, an intricate network of freeways and dirt paths, access ramps and traffic lights, its routes poorly understood, its road conditions always at the mercy of external forces, its infrastructure forever deteriorating. And the mind, that tangled metropolis, that conglomeration of prehistoric village sites, buried middens, ancient aqueducts, and abandoned temples . . . well. . . .

Let the journey begin. Let it unfold maplike here on your lap or tabletop. "Endings are nowhere to be found," Donald Barthelme warns us, "middles are hopeless, but oh to begin, to begin. . . ." To take that first step into a place we only think we know.

It begins with a young man making his way up an old street en route to the purchase of a pair of cheap shoes. He will find what he's looking for, but it's not an auspicious way to begin a journey because they will hurt his feet. Terribly. They will cause blisters to blossom on both of his big toes and under both heels, which will soon after lead to bleeding, though not before serving their purpose of getting him successfully through a job interview. It will all stop short of infection, fortunately; at some point he'll come to his senses—or the pain will bring him there—long enough to recognize a bad investment for what it is.

In the meantime, though, he's in the right place for what he's shopping for: Vine Street, upper Vine to be exact, in a Cincinnati neighborhood traditionally known as Over-the-Rhine because of its long-since-lost connection to its early German inhabitants. Nearby, in the last remnant of that heritage—one lost, lone, free-standing, immaculately-maintained German restaurant a few blocks further north—the sauerbraten and kartoffel laden oak tables are already sagging into bankruptcy. Now it's a neighborhood of cheap and dingy. He passes pawn shops, grimy tenements, discount furniture stores that promise to provide him with an entire apartment full of furniture for only $29.95 per month, the boarded-up shells of abandoned buildings, drug stores with windows full of trusses older than he is, and, though he's not familiar enough with the neighborhood to be aware of it, a couple of the last free-lunch bars in the entire midwest. He wouldn't be welcome in them anyway.

But he's not interested in any of this scenery. He's no tourist. He's on his way to his uncle's shoe store, a cheap shoe store, or a store of cheap shoes. Actually, he's on his way out of town, or so he hopes, never to return, or so he's determined. This is, he's sure, a city he never needs to see again. Enough is enough. Some places, he's convinced, are places best left behind. Not that he's ever been maltreated here, it's just . . . what? . . . the familiarity? It's all known. It has, he's sure, nothing for him, nothing new at least, nothing . . . possible. He's out of here. And, appropriately enough, though he's not thinking about this at the moment, he knows, has always known it seems, that this particular street he's on is one of the few Cincinnati streets that continues on in one twisting but unbroken line north from the river through neighborhood after changing neighborhood and even through one of those islanded cities within the city until at last, many miles from where he's walking now in his old and comfortable but unpresentable sneakers, it passes out beyond the city limits, changes its name from a street to a state route, and enters the world. A suburban world at first, but of course it doesn't stop there.

Some day, a pleasant early summer day not too many years off, he'll come driving back the opposite way on Route 4, taking the old state highways and avoiding the interstates that have been gouged through the city since his departure, in part because he doesn't know the ways in which the freeways have chopped up his old home town into unfamiliar segments but mainly because he's stalling. He's not happy about this return journey. He's coming back for a funeral, but that's the least of it, for him. He'll realize as he passes the sign announcing the exact size of Cincinnati's dwindling population—wondering, in fact, how they can be that precise about it on any given day, right down to the last digit; aren't there deaths, births, taking place at this very moment?—that this city, within whose corporate limits he now finds himself for the first time in the several years since he left, still has some mysterious, vaguely uncomfortable hold on him, something to do with his growing up here.

He'll have read by then, as part of his on-the-job training, much current psychology—family of origin drama and all that—and now he will be thinking: Place of origin? What about that? Are you forever a child of the place where you grew up? And even: *Did* I grow up here? Was he, he'll wonder, being rushed into adulthood—all those relatives and family friends demanding to know what he was going to be when he grew up—even while he was still attempting to clutch his childhood to himself like a bowl of sweet water . . . without the bowl?

Oh, he understands that people did grow up here, unavoidably—and even that he was one of them—and that they did, most of them, the usual things that people did in the process of growing up. But he'll also have the vague sense that somehow, even while they were growing up here, even in the very midst of their having their childhoods here, something about the very nature of the place—something not unlike the murky creek he spent his childhood summers fooling around in, that sometimes jade green, sometimes orange or purple tributary of the Mill Creek that poured its odd, industrial concoctions into the muddy, meandering Ohio—was conspiring to take their childhoods away from them. Without making them adults, however.

His heels and big toes will twinge when he thinks about that; long since healed, they have nonetheless remained a little sensitive ever since, as a young adult beginning to make some important decisions on his own, he bought that pair of cheap black shoes. Though he's once again wearing a pair of sneakers—old running shoes, actually—for driving comfort, he also has, in his suitcase, a pair of shiny, black, thin-soled, calfskin-lined Italian dress shoes, polished to a high shine, wrapped in a clean old t-shirt, and ready to wear to the funeral. But he still feels like a kid coming back here, still feels like he hasn't quite arrived at the adulthood he was supposed to have set up residence in by now. There was, he thinks, no compensation for the childhoods that were taken away; just as we were children without childhoods, so we've become grown-ups without an adulthood. Without a childhood, he has come to understand, you cannot easily become an adult. Where, he wonders, did my childhood go? How was it taken away from me? Was I too busy doing my homework and playing baseball to notice?

For just a moment, pausing at a traffic light to make a left turn off Vine and head crosstown to an eastern suburb, he has the odd notion that it may still be lying around here somewhere, his old childhood. Unless his folks threw it out when they moved from their big house into a small apartment. When was the last time he saw it, he wonders. He knows, of course, that it wouldn't be of any more use to him now than the old, beat-up, and also missing baseball glove that he couldn't even get his grown-up hand into. What he doesn't know is that it is, in fact, still waiting for him here, right across town at his aunt's house where he's on his way to meet up with the family and change for the funeral, where they will hug him and smother him with kisses and talk about how he's grown and call him by that embarrassing old nickname which, thank god, no one in his current life even knows he once had.

But all that's at a point somewhat further along on his journey, when he succumbs to his several cousins' urging to stay on longer after the funeral—their father's, in fact, an uncle, not the shoe store uncle, he'd always felt close to—and when he has no reason to rush back to the small town in southeastern Wisconsin where he lives—he's an academic now, well, not exactly an academic, but he works at a small academic institution that shuts down in the summertime—and when he meets this woman, who lives in what he once thought was a totally inaccessible part of town that, thanks to the freeway's reconfiguration of the territory, now appears to be practically next door to his oldest cousin's house where he's staying, and. . . . But it'd be a cliché to make note here of what unexpected detours life takes. Especially considering where we left him, having given himself strict marching orders and committed himself to heading straight out of town as directly as possible. Straight? Direct? On those streets? In this town?

And in those shoes? His uncle still has one of those old shoe store fluoroscope machines, probably the last one still in use, where you step up on a small platform, slide your feet into a slot, and then look down through the viewer to see your bones, wiggle your toes, inside your new shoes.

"Unc," he says, watching his toe bones wiggle around inside a pair of stiff black wingtips, getting a funny, out-of-synch feeling as he remembers how he did this as a little kid, taking turns looking through the viewer with his mother, "are these things still legal? Don't they give you cancer?"

"You ever know anyone die of cancer of the foot?" says his uncle. "My customers love it. My real customers," he adds.

His uncle squeezes in beside him. "Look at that fit."

That fit doesn't actually feel so good, but his uncle, who's the expert after all, assures him that it's just a matter of breaking them in, then sits him back down, slips the wingtips off and the sneakers back on, boxes the new ones up, walks his nephew to the cash register at the front of the store, and rings them up at the marked price.

"I'd give you a break on these," his uncle explains, "but I'm already selling them for less than wholesale."

"Here," he says, apparently to show he's really a generous guy after all, "take this." And he reaches to the shelf behind him without looking and tosses his nephew a small can of shoe polish. It's oxblood, not black, but would a properly brought up young man ever complain about a gift?

"Always keep a good shine," his uncle advises him as he walks him to the door. "People see that. A man is judged by his shoes. See these?" In the doorway he turns toward his nephew, his feet making a dark V on the warped pine floor, and together they both look down.

He sees the tasseled black loafers his uncle is wearing. They shine like polished obsidian, but they look like something soft and amazingly comfortable and possibly alive, ready to scurry along some devious route into their hidden burrow at the slightest provocation. They definitely don't look like anything that ever came from this store.

So how shall he judge this man? In fact, he won't have to, not for

long. The courts will, and not by his shoes either, but by his failure
to live up to his financial obligations. And his uncle will not shine in
court. He will whine and grovel and plead, though his nephew won't
be there to see it, nor will any of the rest of the family, either, hiding
its collective head in embarrassment. But it's a real question, all the
same, for a young man headed back down the street toward the center
of town with a shoe box, like a loaf of bread, under his arm: How is
he to judge this man, these people, this place, that adult world which
he seems to be entering but feels vaguely suspicious about and certainly doesn't feel a part of? By its shoes? By the way those who
wear them wear them scuffed or shined, by the way they walk, stroll,
stride, saunter, shuffle through their lives? They never taught him
that in college. Where, exactly, do you learn these things? He struggles to remember what kind of shoes his father wears. Something
large and heavy and thick-soled, he seems to recall. Why hasn't he
been paying attention to this sort of thing? And his mother? Well, it
depends on where she's going, what she's doing. High heels, yes,
sometimes, but are they in style? How would the world judge them?
Judge her?

He looks down at his scruffy sneakers. The laces are frayed, there
are loose threads around the seams, the canvas is wearing through
over his toes. He's had them since high school. He looks up and
sees a stunningly beautiful woman staring at him from a tenement
doorway he's passing. She has fine, fair, smoothly brushed hair down
to her waist, a long face, smooth and pale, and almost translucent
blue eyes. She's wearing a thin cotton print dress, faded but clean
and neatly ironed. She looks to be about his own age, and only a
lifetime of intense socialization, the payoff for all those years of his
mother's hard work, prevents him from stopping and staring at her.
But he does glance sideways at her in passing, long enough to take in
two more things. First, her initially expressionless face takes on a
look of enormous amusement, as if she has never seen such a comic
spectacle passing down her own street before; a flurry of lines whips
across her smooth skin like a sudden wind over calm water, her lips
part, revealing crooked, mocking teeth, and the straight line of her
mouth twists sharply upward at each corner. It is not, he knows, a
welcoming or seductive smile, but a smile that renders him the object
of ridicule; it is the look of experience that drives him, like a stake

through his heart, right back out of his pending grown-upness into the deathly humiliation of childhood; it is an expression of ownership, of a claim to a place that, though he has lived here all his life, is somehow still not wholly his. And second, at the last moment a little child, her exact duplicate in miniature, peeks out from behind her. Also, he realizes by the time he reaches the end of the block, she was not looking at his sneakers.

Well, there's more to life than foot coverings—as if he didn't know that. But what was she wearing? Thongs? Sandals? Nothing? He seems to have an image of long, pale toes, tipped with painted nails, red, but maybe he's just sketching in the rest of the portrait now. Obviously he can't go back, especially after that look. He's got to start paying more attention to the world as it goes by. Or as he goes by it. Otherwise, he's beginning to learn—but what a long way he has to go yet!—there's a danger of missing so much. Things go by so fast, and you never get more than a passing glance at them, and then they're gone. They might as well not have been there. (Oh, but they were!) And you find yourself stranded somewhere, as he'll eventually be in spite of the little object lesson he's just been granted, in the darkness of mid-life, in some place where you never imagined yourself being, and you wonder how you got there and what you left behind and how much you missed on the way that might have been just what you needed now.

But, you object, he's just a kid. Indeed. A kid on his way to his first job, where he'll have his own office and his own salary and pension plan and his own title, Assistant to the Dean of Students, and where he'll wear a coat and tie and, for a while yet, a pair of painfully appropriate shoes to work every day. What a relief to get home at the end of the day to his own little apartment, just a block from campus, and take off his wingtips and slip into his brand new pair of Adidas. He hits the road with them almost every evening, just before twilight, loving their smooth fit and bouncy feel. In less than a mile he's out of town, cruising a country road, his mind a total blank, glancing left at black and white spotted cows and right at a field full of . . . something. The smells of the country have quickly become familiar to him, but he's not yet up on the names of things: holsteins, alfalfa. But look how far he's come already!

He deals with the problems, the academic more than the psychological ones, that the kids have—that's what everyone calls them, "kids," though he still feels like one himself and would look like one, too, if he took off his office outfit. In fact he's regularly mistaken for one, is often carded at the local bars and the liquor store, and was mildly insulted just the other day when his boss, the Dean, said, "I saw a kid out on County Road Twenty Seven yesterday evening who looked just like you." He wanted desperately to say, "That *was* me," but he's still so new on the job he worries about how that would affect the way the Dean sees him. Maybe he needs to—what do they call it?—change his image? He had friends back home who were already starting to lose their hair, but his is still thick and dark. Maybe he needs to put on some weight, grow a beard, grow, he thinks, up, somehow.

In the meantime, he helps students find new advisors when their old ones let them down, intercedes on their behalf with the Registrar and the Financial Aid Office, directs them to the remedial help they need at the Study Skills Center, settles disputes between roommates, organizes fall orientation sessions and spring Honors Day programs, represents the administration on the Student Judicial Board and the Student Publications Committee, escorts visiting Convocation speakers around campus, serves on the Ad Hoc Committee to Select the New Chaplain, the Student Services Committee, the Building and Grounds Committee. . . . His days are scheduled up weeks in advance with student appointments and committee meetings, but he always finds time, even on the spur of the moment, to squeeze in a kid with a problem, even if it means giving up his lunch hour. His evenings, however, except when there are campus events he feels obligated to attend, are empty. That's why, by the middle of his second year at the college, he's taken to hanging out, after his daily runs, at the Cap & Gown.

He's been delighted to discover that in spite of its academic name, the Cap & Gown discourages a student clientele—as best it can without violating civil rights laws. The hamburgers are cheap and juicy, and the bartender, Billy, has quickly learned his name and has never carded him since the first time. In this dark bar, with its wood paneling and the framed diplomas—fake, he's sure—from Ivy League colleges hanging on the walls, with the occasional male professor with whom he has a nodding acquaintance nursing a dark beer at the long bar, with townspeople dressed in work clothes, in Oshkosh coveralls and butter-yellow waitressing uniforms from the cafe down the street, sharing pitchers in the booths, he feels like he's entered a grown-up world. And it is not Cincinnati; it is, he begins to think, a place of his own, the very thing he most needs.

And he knows the town. It's so easy, laid out in a simple grid, numbered streets crossed by streets with the names of trees, mostly, plus some flowers on the north end of town where they seem to have run out of trees. His own apartment is at the corner of Seventh and Elm, though there are, of course, no longer any elm trees in town— or, for that matter, any of the firs or live oaks or palms that have given their names to other streets. The college sits in one quadrant, and in the diagonal quadrant are the feed and seed store, the hardware store, the farm equipment store, and half a dozen auto body shops, as if repairing wrecked cars were a major local industry. Outside of town, the county roads run straight on into the distance, following the section lines, with only the rolling landscape to break up their monotony. Back in town, on the handful of downtown blocks, people park diagonally, in unmetered slots, in one of which, directly in front of the Cap & Gown, his own rusting Toyota Corolla sits this evening.

It's been sitting there for four days, since last Friday night when he drove the six blocks from his apartment because it was raining so hard and then walked the six blocks home because somehow, in between arriving and leaving, he had managed to lose his keys. There are small signs posted on every downtown block forbidding overnight parking, but it's a regulation he presumes no one enforces, since he hasn't been ticketed yet. That's one of the things he likes about this town: no one bothers you, no one is looking over your shoulder to see what you're doing with your life, there's none of the sense he grew up with that an entire community is monitoring your every act.

He has his office and apartment keys on a separate ring, fortunately, but no extra set of car keys, as often happens when you buy a used car. So for the fourth day in a row, he's asking Billy if they've turned up yet.

"Did ya look in the can?" replies Billy, shaking his head.

He nods: "Even in the Ladies'."

Billy shrugs: "Got somewhere to go?"

He shrugs too, but then he says, "That's not the point."

He's drinking his first ever Molson's, straight from the bottle.

Billy offered him a glass, but he turned it down. For several weeks now, though of course he's not in here every night, he's been in the process of working his way, bottle by bottle and can by can, down the bar's impressive list of foreign beers, most of which he's never even heard of, to say nothing of tasted. So far he's made his way from Beck's, both light and dark, through Foster's and Grolsch, among others, to Heineken, which he's at least seen his friends order in the past; Watney's is still a long way off, but, he figures, the way his life is going, or not going, these days, he's got plenty of time. And besides, it's a nice straight line from one end of the beer list to the other.

What he's brooding about this misty spring evening as he sits there sipping his Molson's on a Tuesday night in an almost empty bar is not so much where his keys are—with all those auto repair shops across town, he's sure someone will be able to solve this problem for him—as where *he* is. And how he got there. It is in the midst of such grim thoughts that Sapperstein, a youngish assistant professor in the Humanities Department—whom he knows slightly both from their service together on the Building and Grounds Committee and from the fact that his advisees are always asking to be transferred to someone else, anyone else—comes in and takes the stool at the bar next to him.

"How's it going?" says Sapperstein, who then turns without waiting for an answer and orders a Blatz from Billy.

When he turns back, after taking a long swallow from the bottle, which he still clutches in one hand, he says, "Jesus, man, I've got to get out of this place."

"Wish I could help you," he says, his mind still on his own concerns, "but I can't find my car keys."

Sapperstein guffaws, spewing beer onto his own lap. "I mean," he says, mopping off his jeans with a couple of bar napkins, "waaay out. Long gone. Adios. Ciao. Sayonara. Parting is such sweet sorrow, with the emphasis on *sweet.*"

What can a young man who's not sure where he himself wants to, ought to, be say to such professorial passion? He tries, "That bad, huh?"

"Are you kidding?" says Sapperstein. "I'm dying here. My kids are dying here. My wife is dying here. Do you know where she is tonight? She's at the Lutheran Ladies Book Club! Mrs. *Sapperstein!*

If you find me on this campus next year, you'll find me with a bullet in my brain. This place is *nowhere*."

When Sapperstein has gulped down the rest of his beer and trundled out, the word *nowhere* remains behind, suspended in the air between their two stools, Sapperstein's and his, glowing, blinking like the yellow DON'T WALK lights flashing on street corners in downtown Cincinnati. Now he knows where he is. And with that recognition the word turns liquid and seems to melt, the letters flowing together and spilling in one bright stream down between the two bar stools, where, following their flow, he sees, hooked on the end of a nail protruding from a cross rung on Sapperstein's stool, his car keys.

So he has a way out. Not just four wheels, either; unlike Sapperstein he has no family to tie him down, no professorial ladders to watch his step while climbing. He actually likes his job, and was surprised and delighted by the most recent annual evaluation his boss, the Dean, gave him. Already, though, he's not sure how he found his way into it, with just a BA degree and a major in Classics. *Sursum ad sumum*, he thinks, quoting neither Cicero nor Virgil but the motto of his old high school. Here I am, he thinks, but where am I? And he doesn't mean ZIP code. And what am I going to do during this summer vacation, he wonders, which is practically upon him now? Last summer he carpentered, badly, for a local contractor—the company was even called Local Contractors—who never seemed to care about his lack of skills. The occasional splinter is still surfacing. But he got a great tans, ended the season in the best physical shape of his life, learned a few things beyond just pounding nails, and even finished with some extra money in the bank, though a sizeable chunk of that went quickly in the fall for transmission work. Staying mobile is always costly, but what choice do they have, those who are slowly becoming aware that they still have a long way to go?

But why should he be in a rush go anywhere? There's a long journey to make, as always, but what's the hurry? This is, in fact, an ideal job for him. The students identify with him and he with them; the administration seems to find him reliable, and he manages to find that something he can work with, though he doesn't understand why those greyhairs would trust someone like him; the result is a sort of human suspension bridge between one segment of the campus community and another, graceful to observe, pleasant to travel across, something of an engineering marvel when you stop to think about it. On the other hand, there's not a lot to be said for his private life; he hears talk at lunch in the Student Union Grill that the college is a veritable tropical island of romantic liaisons, but he's never discovered where to apply for the requisite tourist visa.

All in good time, however; he has worked his way to the end of the international beer list and is making good headway through the micro breweries. In two more years he finds himself Associate Dean; people he doesn't even know are approaching him at national conferences about his availability; the college is providing summer stipends for him to attend student services workshops around the country. To play it safe, of course, he still keeps his nonunion hand in at Local Contractors, where for some reason they always find something for him to do whenever he shows up.

High up on roofing jacks one blistering July day, pounding nails into cedar shingles on what he figures will turn out to be the most expensive single family dwelling ever built in the county, it dawns on him that his wages haven't changed since the first day he picked up a hammer. All these years, and he's still, in effect, an apprentice. When either of the other guys on the job needs something, they holler for him, and it doesn't matter what else he's doing at the time. Nails, plywood four bys, bundles of shingles, a jug of water. "Hey, kid!" they shout to get his attention. They're not that much older than the students he deals with from September to June. Don't they know they're talking to an Associate Dean? "Hey yourself," he wants to yell back at them, "do your own dirty work. I'm no different than you." But he is, and he knows it. Still, he thinks he ought to ask the boss for a raise. But the boss is a boss; he's got a two-day growth of beard and a pot belly tucked into new jeans; he rushes from one job to the other in his mud-splattered pick-up. How's a guy even to get his attention?

It takes, the following summer, to make him lay his hammer down and cancel his plans for flying to El Paso to attend the annual conference of Directors of Student Services, a funeral. He packs for the drive to what he still thinks of, though he hasn't the slightest notion why, hasn't been there since he left, as "home." State Route 4, Vine Street's northern extension, the Cross County Highway—he's already been there, and so have we. Likewise the funeral itself, poor dear uncle, the postinterment feast at his aunt's, all those cousins and their subtly pressured invitations to stay on a while longer. Where is he, after all, they ask, and what is he doing, and where has he been all these years? How's life?

Is it possible that these people here, these very loving aunts and uncles and cousins who coo over his presence and call him . . . well, let's spare him that sort of high dive back into the truly murky waters of his childhood. But is it possible, he wonders, that they, who have stayed put in his old home town, have something to tell him or show him about where that childhood went that will enable him to leave it at last behind and finally make the journey into a real life, into the adulthood that they, with their suburban homes and sturdy toddlers and stock portfolios and country club memberships, seem already to have made? Is this worth succumbing to their invitations and staying around for? Is this indeed the place for him to find out . . . whatever it is he needs to find out?

In the evening, when they are sitting in his aunt's elegant living room after the last of the nonfamily guests have departed the funeral feast, he stretches himself and crosses his skinny legs in front of him. Sprawled in this unintended pose in which no one can miss his glorious Italian shoes, he asks of his oldest cousin, the one exactly his own age, "So, you're sure you've got room for me? It won't be any trouble?"

She assures him that there is room to spare; they have just added an extension to the house, a guest bedroom for her in-laws when they come to visit the grandchildren. For now, it's his.

Also, she mentions, when they're standing in the driveway later and her husband is trying to make sure that he remembers how to get to their house, which he is quite sure he does—didn't he grow up here, after all?—there's someone she'd like him to meet, someone she thinks *he'd* like to meet. As long as he's here, that is. If he doesn't object.

He doesn't see any reason to object, as long as he's here, but it's hours before he finds their house. The new freeway intervenes: the street he's following, certain he remembers the route exactly—this is his city, after all, he knows these streets—dumps him unceremoniously onto the freeway, and when he escapes at the next exit he hasn't the slightest idea where he is, doesn't know whether to turn east or west. It's dark already, and he's in a residential neighborhood that doesn't look like anything he's ever seen before: tall, narrow, stucco houses with pointy roofs and minuscule, fenced-in yards.

There are no gas stations, no people on the streets. And the streets, of course: there's no telling what direction they're likely to loop in next or what changes of name they're likely to undergo at each cross-road, not that he recognizes any of them. He learned long ago that this is not a city where directional orientation will do you any good, because the hill-strewn streets stand ready to baffle you at every moment. You either learned it, straight out and early on, or . . . or what?

Or you were like a child again, and the world was too wide and wholly incomprehensible and maybe a little bit magical, a mystery just beyond your grasp, a wondrous place that had its own strange ways of pulling you forever into its tangled heart, something that perhaps adults understood, being, of course, adults, but *you* . . .

He's sitting at an intersection, not another car in sight, and he's crept ahead a bit while waiting for the light to change so that he can read the street signs. He sees that each of the four ways the roads lead from this point bears a different name. How remarkable, he thinks, forgetting for the moment that he has been driving around for hours already, that there are people waiting up for him, probably worrying about him: how absolutely remarkable. This is a point from which one could go in any direction and be somewhere totally different. Something about that notion, this situation, strikes him as immeasurably silly. He's tempted to get out of his Toyota and do something totally inappropriate—and yet, in some way, totally appropriate, childlike—here in the middle of the street: cartwheels, maybe. Here, in Cincinnati, the very town he grew up in, or so he thought, is a place he never knew. He might as well be in some foreign country. What next? he thinks. Why, this is like starting all over. Who knows where the next turn might take you? And out there somewhere, in which direction he hasn't the slightest idea, are not only his cousin and her family, people who will continue to call him by that old nickname no matter what he says, and the comfortable bed awaiting him in their new extra bedroom, but some woman whose name he doesn't even know.

Oh, but he will, he will.

The Bluest Water
or
Getting to the
Bottom of Things

IN MAY 1993, I spent nine days riding a couple of enormous inflatable rafts down the Grand Canyon of the Colorado, traveling with twenty or so others, including guides.

We put in at Lee's Ferry, a few miles below the abominable dam which holds the abominable Lake Powell. Soon we were deep in cold shadows, sliding through rapids and getting used to the silences in the narrow depths of Marble Canyon, four- and five-hundred-foot red rock rims on either side seeming straight above us at times, and the sky perfect blue.

It took me days and days to get onstage and beyond the bookish boy of myself. What, I wondered, as we drifted, was I supposed to be thinking, and who should I be?

If this was play, which was the game? Or if it was theater, as it so clearly in ways was, how to get outside our run of continual prerehearsed routines?

What I managed was turning my attention to layers of time—we were making our way down, the river gradually falling through depth after depth of colored, textured stones, eventually half-way to the beginning of things on earth (such parenthetical long-winded thinking is of course another way of staying semi-abstract and out of the moment). I was counting layers.

Or so I thought. It is likely more accurate to say I was tranquilized in the presence of infinities suggested by the movement of sunlight over the glazed or fractured, shadowed and then glowing surfaces of reddish rock, stack on stack.

We camped on a sandbar below a stonework granary some very ancient people (Anasazi) had constructed in a rocky overhang just where the long jumble of scree slope above us met with sheer cliff. According to archeologists who have dated the tiny deerlike figures (made of driftwood and reeds) which have been found in caves near the river, people lived in those canyons more than four thousand years ago.

In a poem called "Seeing Things," Seamus Haney wrote "the stone's alive with what's invisible." The canyon of the Colorado, when we were quiet, echoed with voices of the dead. The world seemed alive.

In the clarity of the next morning we stopped at a place called Vesey's Paradise (named by John Wesley Powell, who first traveled down the river, for a botanist who accompanied him—so much of any exploration is naming, mapping, thus claiming, making ours). And it was a paradise—an abundant spring of bright water splashing out from cracks in the cliffside after making it's unimaginably complex way down to us through four thousand feet of fractured stone under the snowfields of the Karapowits Plateau—the sandstone vividly red in the morning air, and greenery flowering brilliantly: ferns, mosses, thick-tasseled grasses, looking much like the elaborately reconsructed grottos to be found in various romantic, sumptuous and so-called natural European gardens since at least the Renaissance. In gardens of the Farnesea family on the Palatine Hill, overlooking the helter-skelter marble ruins of the Roman forum, for instance, at the heart of what we understand as civilization. (Our ideas of paradise so often resemble a place to camp).

The next cliffside spring was finer, tiny, its water falling inside a sheath of luminous travertine (a reddish porous calcite deposited from solution in the water—of the sort which drips down to form stalactites and stalagmites in caverns). This was absolutely new to me, a beauty not imagined, out in morning sunlight as it warmed, built up over millenia, like porcelain, gleaming, the water splashing down inside like a secret, a story about the goodness of things.

Water springing from stone: Why do we respond so powerfully and positively to certain natural constructs? Perhaps because they so clearly remind us. For a thoughtless instant we are the old animal in the playground of our true situation, a place where we can build up the fire and dance and sing and tell stories and love ourselves and one another like the children we always were, safe against the tiger of the night.

Before noon of the third day we stopped on a sandy beach at the place where the Little Colorado flows into the big river. While we seemed to be below the surface of earth in the depths of that canyon, the shallow water of the Little Colorado was pale lurid blue, nothing subterranean but rather like water come from the sky, having painted the rocks in the riverbed vivid limestone white. This, again, I had not imagined.

Some miles upstream on the Little Colorado, so I am told, an enormous uplifted travetine bowl has accumulated over the great spring where the blue water of the Little Colorado comes surging up from the earth.

The Hopi understand it as the place where humans (themselves) emerged from the earth. The infinities of sky, the stonefall walls of the canyon, at the bottom a river of blue soft water, elegant white rocks—it's easy to understand how the Hopi came to think of the great spring as the place where their people, which is to say life (significance) came forth.

I don't know if they believe that literally, or as a metaphor, or both. It doesn't matter. What matters is that they in some distant time located a place which was for them worth all reverence they could muster, an act which was sustaining to them in the sense that it made their lives more coherent, and that over generations they have been willing to come over long distances to visit and acknowledge their reverence.

(We didn't need to go see that blue-water spring rising inside its tavertine bowl; it meant nothing to us but spectacle; that place should belong to the Hopi; the story of their existence as a communal people resides there.)

Just upstream on the Little Colorado some of our party sported in mud baths like creatures in paradise. I was reminded of mud-head figures in Hopi ritual who hang around sacred doings, mocking and hooting, playing foolish. Without frivolity we are stuck in the mud of ourselves, and less than ourselves; play is maybe our most central way of learning.

Others in our party tied orange kapok life perservers under their asses like pontoons and coasted through blue water rapids, sort of new-born, which was of course the major point of things right then, at least for the moment trying to get healed inside the moment.

But I sat on a white rock like a sunning turtle, my feet in water, listening to my companions, unable to get out of my mind, to some degree resenting the ease with which my friends found their pleasure, trying to console myself by thinking high intellectual thoughts about pilgrims, and the degree to which they are a lot of time acting out, playing.

What we most ardently want seems at times simple, home for our creature, where without regret we can go ahead and feel healed together with our various selves and each other and the configurations of life on the playground, and not have to think about it. Locked in my mind and listening, I was busy fighting my old self as despite me it worked at untying knots.

That night I lay on the sand, studying configurations of stars we never see from inside the ambient light of cities. I thought, Well, out there you got your infinity and today we were swimming in sacred water, and at least I smiled. My body and mind were trying to be parts of the same fellow.

In what is called the inner canyon we drifted between close walls of water-polished, two billion year old Vishnu schist, fluted and black, convoluted and half the age of the earth since it cooled from its molten stage and hardened, at the bottom of things.

Clarence Dutton, a nineteenth-century scientist and explorer who took it upon himself to name geologic features in the canyon, tried to capture the mystical grandeur of what he saw, at least to European sensibilities, with names from Eastern religions—thus the Vishnu schist and equally primeval Zoroaster granite that is alongside.

Travelers have complained of ominous clastrophobic feelings in those enormous depths of the canyon with the primal mass of the earth crowding around them. The cure for irrational dis-ease, as always, probably, is willingness to progress toward emotionally inhabiting our old animal's actual situation rather than metaphoric territory of the soul's own making, which is to say make-believe. With the help of my friends, I had discovered the pleasures of looking down to examine tiny green beetles in their irridescent splendor; with the help of good fortune I had looked up to find my self eye to eye, as we drifted by, with a bighorn mountain sheep that had come to the river for water.

For such reasons, maybe, those walls of blackish water-polished stone seemed to me simple and gorgeous, not there to remind me not of my own ominous mortality but, rather, if I'd only look around, that I was always, everywhere, surrounded by precisely elegant phenomena.

Finding ways to locate ourselves in new territory serves our need to think we are secure in the lands of forever. For that while in the canyon I was at ease inside intricacy, but in the end I was glad to quit the river. Too much encountering complexities in actuality might make us crazy. We are nothing if not mystified amid glories.

From "A Mountain"

A SMALL CABIN STANDS in the Glacier Peak Wilderness, about a hundred yards off a trail that crosses the Cascade Range. In midsummer, the cabin looked strange in the forest. It was only twelve feet square, but it rose fully two stories and then had a high and steeply peaked roof. From the ridge of the roof, moreover, a ten-foot pole stuck straight up. Tied to the top of the pole was a shovel. To hikers shedding their backpacks at the door of the cabin on a cold summer evening—as five of us did—it was somewhat unnerving to look up and think of people walking around in snow perhaps thirty-five feet above, hunting for that shovel, then digging their way down to the threshold. Men from the Chelan County Snow Survey use the cabin in winter while they measure snow depths and snow densities, and figure how much runoff to expect at the time of thaw. Because of the almost unbelievable amount of snow that can accumulate in that part of the State of Washington, what they do there is a vital matter to the people below and even far beyond the mountains.

What we were doing there was something else again. We were tired. We had walked seven and a half miles uphill since three that afternoon. One of us was in his sixties, another in his fifties, and all of us saw the cabin as a haven from what obviously would have been very cold ground. Until midsummer, the trails had been impassable, and to make the trip we had had to wait for the winter snows to melt. An entry in the register in the cabin said that snow had fallen one week earlier, August 5th. But we had been drawn to the Cascades in part because a great many people believed that they were the most beautiful mountains in the United States. A somewhat smaller and, on the whole, more parochial group felt that these huge, conical peaks, raised in volcanic fire and later carved by moving ice, were the most beautiful mountains in the world. In 1964, the United States Congress set aside this region and others as permanent wilderness, not to receive even the use given a national park, not to be entered by a machine of any kind except in extreme emergency, not to be developed or altered or lumbered—forevermore. Within the structure of this so-called Wilderness Act, however, was a provision known as "the mining exception": all established claims would remain open to mining, and new claims could be made in any wilderness until 1984. At the foot of Glacier Peak, in the center of this particular wilderness, is a copper lode that is half a mile from side to side. The Kennecott Copper Corporation has a patented claim on this deposit and could work it any time. We wanted to have a look at the region while it was still pristine. The others left it to me to add their names to the register in the cabin: Charles Park, geologist, mineral engineer, who believes that if copper were to be found under the White House, the White House should be moved; David Brower, who has been described by Steward Udall as "the most effective single person on the cutting edge of conservation in this country," leader of a conservation organization called Friends of the Earth; and Larry Snow and Lance Brigham, medical students from the University of Washington, who were along to help with the logistics of the trip and perhaps incidentally to give first aid.

A mouse ran out from under the cabin, made a fast move among the packs, and went back under the cabin. We collected firewood and water. There was a cascade, white and plummeting, beyond the cabin. We changed into warmer clothes and lighter shoes. Brower, who hiked in twill shorts and a T-shirt and soft gray Italian boots, put on a long plaid shirt, trousers, and a pair of basketball shoes. Although he was out of shape, Brower was a prepossessing figure. He was a tall man. He had heavy bones, thick wrists, strong ankles. And he had a delicate, handsome, ruddy face, its features all finely proportioned but slightly too small, too refined, for the size of his frame, suggesting delicacy. His voice was quiet and persuasively mellifluous. He had an engaging smile and flashing white teeth. He was in his late fifties, and he had a windy shock of white hair. Brower had dropped out of college when he was nineteen, and disappeared into the Sierra

Nevada. He had spent his life defending mountain ranges and what, by extension, they symbolized to him, and one of the ironies of his life was that his love of the mountains had long since drawn him away from them and into buildings impertinently called skyscrapers, into congressional corridors, into temporary offices in hotel rooms, into battle after battle, and out of shape. (In the idiom of conservation, "battle" is the foremost term for what conservationists do, and conservationist publications are "battle tracts.") Brower's skin was pink from the work of the climb, and when he was taking off his soaked T-shirt he had revealed a fold across his middle. The mouse ran out again from under the cabin, looked around, its nose vibrating, and retreated.

Lance Brigham said, "Stick your head out once more, mouse, and it's curtains for you."

Brower said softly, "It's we who are the intruders."

Park had been taking off his boots—made in Canada, of heavy leather—and was putting on a pair of sandals. He grinned cryptically. He, too, had a shock of white hair. He was in his sixties, and he was as trim and hard as a college athlete, which he had once been, and nothing about him suggested that he had ever been out of breath. From his youth to the present, he had spent a high proportion of his life in the out-of-doors, and a high proportion of that in wilderness. Going up the trail that afternoon, with his geologist's pick in his hand, he whacked or chipped at half the boulders and rock faces we passed, and every once in a while, apparently for the sheer hell of it, he rapped the pick's hammer end on the stump of a tree that had been taken to clear the trail.

"That's a habit I developed long ago—banging on rocks and stumps," he said.

"Why?"

"Kodiak bears. I never wanted to take one by surprise. The same is true in Africa of leopards and gorillas. In other words, never take an animal by surprise."

Park spoke slowly, not because he was hesitant but simply in a measure that seemed compatible with geologic time. He had an almond face, alert gray eyes, and a mobile smile that tended to concentrate in one or the other corner of his mouth. He was even taller than Brower, and he wore khaki from head to foot. He had a visored khaki cap.

Not far into the mountains from their eastern extremity, at Lake Chelan, we had come to an oddly formal landmark. It was a sign that said, "You Are Now Entering the Glacier Peak Wilderness Area." In other words, "Take one more step and, by decree, you will enter a preserved and separate world, you will pass from civilization into wilderness." Wilderness was now that definable, that demonstrable, and could be entered in the sense that one enters a room.

Park said, "Will they let me carry my pick in there?"

"Until 1984," said Brower.

We stepped across the line. I said, "If we get lost in here with that pick, we may discover a new copper deposit."

Brower said, "If you make a new discovery, I'm here to see that you don't get out."

We moved on into the wilderness. The trail was dusty. It was covered with a light-brown powder too fine to be called sand. Park said it was glacial flour—finely ground rock coming out of the ice, ice of the past and ice of the present. Far above us in the high cirques were glaciers—the Lyman Glacier, Isella Glacier, Mary Green Glacier, and, perhaps prophetically, the Company Glacier on Bonanza Peak. The sky was blue and cloudless, a day to remember in the Cascades. Brower said he was disappointed that it was not raining. He explained that he did not like dry duff but preferred the feel and the beauty of a wet and glistening forest, vaporous and dripping. He said that he hoped we would be fortunate enough to have a good rain before the trip was over. He labored slowly up the trail, taking it conservatively, eating thimbleberries and huckleberries as he moved along.

"There are no really old rocks in the Cascades," Park said, nicking a rock in passing. He picked up and admiringly turned in his hand a piece of pistachio-green epidote. Two hundred yards up the trail, he rapped at an outcropping with his pick and said, "That is volcanic." Minutes later, he swung again, sent chips flying, and said, "That is contact rock." This in some way entertained Brower, who laughed and shook his head. I remembered once driving through the Black Hills with Park, and how he would stop his car from time to time and just sit there looking at rocks. As a boy in Delaware, Park used to collect rocks and think about the West. While he was still in Wilmington High School, he had fifty ore minerals in his collection—

hematite, malachite, galena, chromite. "I wanted to study mining, not particularly geology—mining," he said. "I just wanted to get into rocks. Mining has always appealed to me. It's in the out-of-the-way places."

A serrated ridge several miles from the trail had a reddish glow in the late-afternoon light. "See that color? That's pyrite," Park said, pointing. "Copper often comes with it. If I were in here looking for copper, that's where I'd head." The copper terrain we wanted to see was still more than ten miles away, however, and we stayed on the trail.

We passed a big Douglas fir, at least six feet in diameter, that had crashed to earth in the recent past, and Brower said how nice it was to see it there, to know that some lumber company had never had a chance at it, to see the decay stage of a natural cycle—the forest reclaiming its own. If dead trees are not left to rot, he said, the ecology of the wilderness is disturbed. Park kept his reactions to himself. His eye wandered to a square hole in a cedar stump. He waved his pick in the direction of the stump and said, "Pileated woodpecker." We moved on.

After a series of switchbacks had lifted us seven hundred feet in less than a quarter of a mile, we stopped to rest by a stream that was alternately falling through the air and racing down the mountainside. Everywhere, from every slope, the Cascades cascade. Water shoots out of cracks in the rock, it falls over the edges of cliffs, it foams, sprays, runs, and plunges pure and cold. Enough snow and rain fall up there to irrigate Libya, and when water is not actually falling from the sky the sun is melting it from alpine ice. Down the dark-green mountainsides go streamers of white water, and above the timberline water shines against the rock. In every depression is a tarn, and we had passed a particularly beautiful one a little earlier and, from the escarpment, were looking back at it now. It was called Hart Lake and was fed by a stream that, in turn, fell away from a high and deafening cataract. The stream was interrupted by a series of beaver ponds. All around these free-form pools were stands of alder, aspen, Engelmann spruce; and in the surrounding mountains, just under the summits, were glaciers and fields of snow. Brower, who is an aesthetician by trade and likes to point to beautiful things, had nothing to say at that moment. Neither did Park. I was remembering the words of a friend of mine in the National Park Service, who had once said to me, "The Glacier Peak Wilderness is probably the most beautiful piece of country we've got. Mining copper there would be like hitting a pretty girl in the face with a shovel. It would be like strip-mining the Garden of Eden."

Park wiped his forehead with his hat. I dipped a cup into the stream and offered him a drink. He hesitated. "Well, why not?" he said, at last. He took the cup and he drank, put the cup down with a smile, wiped his lips, and said, "That's good stuff."

"It's melted glacier ice, isn't it?"

Park nodded, and swallowed a little more.

Brower drank from a cup that was almost identical to mine—stainless steel, with low, sloping sides, a wide flat bottom, a looped wire handle—with the difference that in raised letters on the bottom of Brower's cup were the words "Sierra Club." Brower for seventeen years had been the executive director of the Sierra Club—its leader, its principal strategist, its preeminent fang. In the mountains, a Sierra Club mountaineer eats and drinks everything out of his Sierra Club cup, and in various wildernesses with Brower I had never seen him eat or drink from anything else. In the past, in the High Sierra, he had on occasion rubbed pennyroyal-mint leaves over the embossed letters in the bottom of his cup and added snow and whiskey for a kind of high-altitude julep, but he rarely drinks much in the mountains, and there was no whiskey at all on this trip. That night at the snow cabin, we ate our dinner from our cups—noodles, beef, chocolate pudding—and hung our packs on high rafters and were asleep before nine. We slept on bunks that had been tiered in the improbable cabin. At two in the morning, we were all awake, with flashlight beams crisscrossing from various heights in the compact blackness.

"What the hell is going on?"

"What is it?"

"What's there?"

"Four very beautiful little tan and white meadow mice," Brower said.

"Aw, for heaven's sake," Park said, and he went back to sleep.

Park, throughout his career, had not made a religion of camping out, and he had been particularly pleased when we found the cabin and its bunks, although they were little more than stiffly woven wire in frames. His general practice of trips of exploration for minerals had been to sleep in a bed if there was one within five miles, so he had managed to keep his lifetime total down to something like nineteen hundred nights on the ground. On foot and alone, he had hunted for copper in the Philippines, in Cuba, in Mexico, in Arizona, in Tennessee. He had hunted for silver in Nevada and Greece, for gold in Alaska and South Dakota, and—on one curious assignment for the United States Geological Survey—gold in Alabama, Georgia, South Carolina, North Carolina, Virginia, and the District of Columbia. He had found what he was looking for. During the Second World War, there was a working gold mine in Rock Creek Park in Washington, D.C. Such is Park's feeling for where ore bodies are that some of his friends think he has occult powers. For fifteen years or so, he used his skills in the name of the Geological Survey. Then, in the late nineteen-forties, he began to teach geology and mineral engineering at Stanford University, where he eventually became Dean of the School of Earth Sciences. From one base or the other—Washington or Palo Alto—he has never stopped hunting the earth for metal, sometimes as a consultant to various companies. He has looked almost everywhere for iron and manganese. He once set up a base camp at fifteen thousand feet in the Chilean-Bolivian Andes and, working up from there, found iron at seventeen thousand feet. In 1956, he was taken in a pirogue up the Ivindo River, in Gabon, to a point from which he took compass bearings and walked for two weeks through jungle. On relatively high ground, elephant trails were so wide and hard they were like roads, but in swamps the elephants' footprints were like postholes. The canopy was so thick it obscured the sky. Park had had serious back trouble for some time, and one day he fell to the ground and could not get up. He lay there for two hours until something jelled, and he got slowly to his feet again and moved on. He was hunting for iron, and he found a part of what is now called the Belinga Deposit. Even in the United States, he usually stayed out, alone, for about two weeks at a time. He went light, eating out of his frying pan and drinking from a small tin cup. He has used the same pick for twenty years. He speaks of the rootlessness of the life of an exploration geologist and says that many people tend to be discouraged by it. "You're just wandering. You're on the loose." He has planted gardens spring after spring and never seen his plants in bloom. Instead, he has drawn from the earth its mercury, lead, zinc, uranium, fluorspar, phosphate, nickel, molybdenum, manganese, iron, lithium, tin, copper, silver, and gold.

In the morning, soon after we were again on the trail, we went around the north edge of a lake that had a surface of at least ninety acres and was almost as big as the glacier that was dripping into it from fourteen hundred feet above. The effect of glacial flour in still water is to turn it green. As we moved uphill, and looked back, we saw that there were three other green lakes, closer to the glacier. In them, small icebergs were drifting. Ahead of us, and far above, was a ridge that ran north-south and dipped at one point to form a shallow notch. This was our immediate destination, and it had been named Cloudy Pass, because the most distant view a person usually has there is of his own groping hands. On this day, though, the sky was without clouds anywhere. The climb was steep toward the pass, and we tended to string out. Brower, in the lead, said again that he wished it were raining.

I asked him if, by his own standards, he would describe the terrain we were in as wilderness. "Yes, it is wilderness," he said. "The Sierra is what I love, but these mountains are perhaps the most beautiful we have." Then he accelerated his pace and was soon far ahead. He seemed to be feeling good, getting into rhythm with the mountains.

A mosquito bit Park on the wrist, and he slapped it. "They follow the snow," he said. "The higher we get, the more mosquitoes there are."

We climbed on in silence for a while, and then he asked why Brower had gone on so far ahead.

"I don't know. He seems to want to be alone," I said.

"He certainly is—let's say—reserved," Park said. "I don't see how anyone could ever break through it. I almost called him yesterday when he said the big trees ought to be left to rot in the forest. Long before they fall, they are dying from the inside out. It's a shame not to use big trees like that." He waved his pick at a stand of spruce. "I am not a member of the Sierra Club," he went on. "I don't approve of their policy. To me, they are preservationists, not conservationists. You can't avoid change. You can direct it, but you can't avoid it. I like Sierra Club books, though."

In 1960, in Yosemite Valley, Brower helped put together an exhibit of landscape photographs and accompanying swatches of prose. Then he developed the idea of circulating the exhibit in book form. The result was the Sierra Club's Exhibit-Format series—big, four-pound, creamily beautiful, living-room-furniture books that argue the cause of conservation in terms, photographically, of exquisite details from the natural world and, textually, of essences of writers like Thoreau and Muir. Brower was editor and publisher. He selected the photographs. He wrote the prefaces. In this way, as in others, he brought the words "Sierra Club" into the national frame of reference. He published Exhibit-Format books on everything from the Maine islands (*Summer Island—Penobscot Country*) to the Grand Canyon (*Time and the River Flowing*), the region of his own youth (*Gentle Wilderness—the Sierra Nevada*), and the mountains we were now crossing (*The Wild Cascades*). Within nine years, people had paid ten million dollars for Exhibit-Format books, and Brower said he had been surprised to find that people were willing to pay that much for beauty. Brower himself was certainly willing to spend money on it. Once, a set of picture proofs did not look quite right to him, and he had ten thousand dollars' worth of plates thrown out. Udall gave *Time and the River Flowing* to Lyndon and Lady Bird Johnson for Christmas, 1964. At twenty-five dollars a copy, the books were, in a sense, investments, and rich conservationists bought them in round lots. Struggling conservationists could buy them in compacted form as three-dollar-and-ninety-five-cent paperbacks.

With Brower as its executive director, the Sierra Club grew from an organization of seven thousand members to an organization of seventy-seven thousand members. The figure seems both large and small. There are more people in Cedar Rapids than there are in the Sierra Club. Nonetheless, under Brower the club became a truly potent force, affecting legislation that had to do with the use of the land, the sea, and the atmosphere. Brower was not the leader in every battle. He concentrated on certain foes, and many were in the Department of the Interior. To the Bureau of Reclamation, he is the Antichrist. They say there that Brower singlehandedly prevented the construction of two major dams in the Grand Canyon for at least two generations and possibly for all time. On the Green River in Utah, Brower stopped cold a dam that would have inundated parts of Dinosaur National Monument. In the cause of mountains, he and lieutenants in the State of Washington fought loggers, miners, and hunters, and won a North Cascades National Park. For nearly twenty years, Brower has crossed and recrossed the United States campaigning for conservation before every kind of audience. The federal government's Outdoor Recreation Resources Review was his idea. He was a primary force in the advancement of the Wilderness Act. His counterparts in other conservation organizations long ago acknowledged him as "*the* spokesman for protected wilderness." Once, when Brower had driven for several hours through wretched fog and rain to attend a meeting and make a speech in Poughkeepsie, I asked him if he could say why he did all this, and he said, "I don't know. It beats the hell out of me. I'm trying to save some forests, some wilderness. I'm trying to do anything I can to get man back into balance with the environment. He's way out—way out of balance. The land won't last, and we won't."

Having moved above the trees into a clear area, Park stopped to look back over the forest, the green lakes, the glacier, the snowfields, and the white peaks beyond. I asked him if, from his experience, he would call this wilderness. "No," he said. "Not with this trail in it." He agreed that what we were looking at was almost incomparable, and he said he doubted if Brower saw anything he didn't see. "That is a beautiful view," he went on. "And these are magnificent mountains. They remind me of the Chilean Andes. But how is a mining company operating a pit on the other side of this ridge going to hurt all this? I don't see it. My idea of conservation is maximum use. I think preserving wilderness as wilderness is a terrible mistake. This area is one of the few places in the country where copper exists now in commercial quantities, and we just have to have copper. The way things are set up, we can't do without it. To lock this place up as wilderness could imperil the whole park system, because in ten years or so, when copper becomes really short, people will start yelling and revisions will have to be made. Any act of Congress can be repealed." Park was speaking slowly, and we were making our way up through open alpine meadows that were splayed with streams and full of heather, lupine, horsemint, daisies, and wild licorice. "I'm in favor of multiple use of land," he continued. "Have you ever been in the Harz Mountains? With proper housekeeping, you can have a mine and a sawmill and a primitive area all close together. When the Kerr-McGee Corporation wanted to mine phosphate on the coast of Georgia, conservationists howled. A hearing was held, and twenty-six people, most of them representing groups, testified against Kerr-McGee. *No one* testified for them. This shocked me. It was like people standing around watching a man get beat up. When Texas Gulf Sulphur drilled three holes and found an ore body in Ontario, people accused them of hiding information. I testified before the S.E.C. on their behalf. The image of copper companies is bad today, with all this conservation poop. There's a Clark's nutcracker!" The nutcracker, in flight, was a hundred feet above us.

We were now about to top the final rise to Cloudy Pass, where Brower was waiting. We looked back again over the eastward view—lakes, peaks, beaver ponds, cascades, snow, ice, white-ribbon streams, and dark green forests. Again Park said, "I don't see it. I don't see how a mine on the other side of this ridge is going to affect that." Park lives in a trim, attractive, solid-looking one-level house on a dead-end street in Palo Alto, and beside his front door is a decorative grouping of green rocks—copper ore—and an old pick with a broken handle. With his present pick, he swung at an outcropping with what seemed to me to be unusual curiosity and force.

"What are you looking for?" I said.

A grin came into the corner of his mouth. "Nothing," he said. "I just haven't hit one in a long time."

Most of the pass was covered with snow, but there were some patches of bare ground, and these were blue, green, red, yellow, and white with wild flowers. The air felt and smelled like the first warm, thaw-bringing day in spring in Vermont, and, despite the calendar, spring was now the season at that altitude in the North Cascades, and summer and fall would come and go into the few weeks remaining before the first big snow of September. Brower had dropped his pack and was sitting on a small knoll among the flowers. Park and I and Brigham and Snow dropped our own packs, and felt the sudden coolness of air reaching the sweatlines where the packs had been—and the inebriate lightness that comes, after a long climb, when the backpack is suddenly gone. The ground Brower was sitting on was ten or fifteen feet higher than the ground on which we stood, and as we went up to join him our eyes at last moved above the ridge-line, and for the first time we could see beyond it. What we saw made us all stop.

One of the medical students said, "Wow!"

I said slowly, the words just involuntarily falling out, "My God, look at that."

Across a deep gulf of air, and nearly a mile higher than the ground on which we stood, eleven miles away by line of sight, was Glacier Peak—palpable, immediate, immense. In the direction we were looking, we could see perhaps two hundred square miles of land, and the big mountain dominated that scene in the way that the Jungfrau dominates the Bernese Alps. Glacier Peak had originally been a great symmetrical cone, and that was still its basic shape, but it had been monumentally scarred, from within and without. It once exploded. Pieces of it landed in what is now Idaho, and other pieces landed in what is now Oregon. The ice sheet mauled it. Rivers from its own glaciers cut grooves in it. But it had remained, in silhouette, a classic mountain, its lines sweeping up beyond its high shoulder—called Disappointment Peak—and converging acutely at the summit. The entire upper third of the mountain was white. And below the snow and ice, black-green virgin forest continued all the way down to the curving valley of the Suiattle River, a drop of eight thousand feet from the peak. Spread around the summit like huge, improbable petals were nine glaciers—the Cool Glacier, the Scimitar Glacier, the Dusty Glacier, the Chocolate Glacier—and from each of these a white line of water ran down through the timber and into the Suiattle. To our right, on the near side of the valley, another mountain—Plummer Mountain—rose up about two-thirds as high, and above its timberline its snowless faces of rock were, in the sunlight, as red as rust. Around and beyond Glacier Peak, the summits of other mountains, random and receding, led the eye away to the rough horizon and back to Glacier Peak.

Brower said, without emphasis, "That is what is known in my trade as a scenic climax."

Near the southern base of Plummer Mountain and in the deep valley between Plummer Mountain and Glacier Peak—that is, in the central foreground of the view that we were looking at from Cloudy Pass—was the lode of copper that Kennecott would mine, and to do so the company would make an open pit at least two thousand four hundred feet from rim to rim.

Park said, "A hole in the ground will not materially hurt this scenery."

Brower stood up. "None of the experts on scenic resources will agree with you," he said. "This is one of the few remaining great wildernesses in the lower forty-eight. Copper is not a transcendent value here."

"Without copper, we'd be in a pretty sorry situation."

"If that deposit didn't exist, we'd get by without it."

"I would prefer the mountain as it is, but the copper is there."

"If we're down to where we have to take copper from places this beautiful, we're down pretty far."

"Minerals are where you find them. The quantities are finite. It's criminal to waste minerals when the standard of living of your people depends upon them. A mine cannot move. It is fixed by nature. So it has to take precedence over any other use. If there were a copper deposit in Yellowstone Park, I'd recommend mining it. Proper use of minerals is essential. You have to go get them where they are. Our standard of living is based on this."

"For a fifty-year cycle, yes. But for the long term, no. We have to drop our standard of living, so that people a thousand years from now can have any standard of living at all."

A breeze coming off the nearby acres of snow felt cool but not chilling in the sunshine, and rumpled the white hair of the two men.

"I am not for penalizing people today for the sake of future generations," Park said.

"I really am," said Brower. "That's where we differ."

"Yes, that's where we disagree. In 1910, the Brazilian government said they were going to preserve the iron ore in Minas Gerais, because the earth would run short of it in the future. People—thousands and thousands of people in Minas Gerais—were actually starving, and they were living over one of the richest ore deposits in the world, a fifteen-billion-ton reserve. They're mining it now, and people there are prospering. But in the past it was poor consolation to people who were going hungry to say that in the future it was going to be better. You have to use these things when you have them. You have to know where they are, and use them. People, in the future, will go for the copper here."

"The kids who are in Congress in the future should make that decision, and if it's theirs to make I don't think they'll go for the copper here," Brower said.

"Sure they will. They'll have to, if people are going to expect to have telephones, electric lights, airplanes, television sets, radios, central heating, air-conditioning, automobiles. And you *know* people will want these things. I didn't invent them. I just know where the copper is."

Brower swung his pack up onto his back. "Pretend the copper deposit down there doesn't exist," he said. "Then what would you do? What are you going to do when it's gone?"

"You're trying to make everything wilderness," Park said.

"No, I'm not. I'm trying to keep at least two per cent of the terrain as wilderness."

"Two per cent is a lot."

"Two per cent is under pavement."

"Basically, our difference is that I feel we can't stop all this—we must direct it. You feel we must stop it."

"I feel we should go back, recycle, do things over again, and do better, even if it costs more. We mine things and don't use them again. We coat the surface of the earth—with beer cans and chemicals, asphalt and old television sets."

"We *are* recycling copper, but we don't have enough."

"When we knock buildings down, we don't take the copper out. Every building that comes down could be a copper mine. But we don't take the copper out. We go after fresh metal. We destroy that mountain."

"How can you ruin a mountain like Glacier Peak?" Park lifted his pick toward the mountain. "You *can't* ruin it," he went on, waving the pick. "Look at the Swiss mountains. Who could ruin *them?* A mine would not hurt this country—not with proper housekeeping."

Brower started on down the trail. We retrieved our packs and caught up with him. About five hundred feet below us and a mile ahead was another pass—Suiattle Pass—and to reach it we had to go down into a big ravine and up the other side. There were long silences, measured by the sound of boots on the trail. From time to time, the pick rang out against a rock.

Brower said, "Would America have to go without much to leave its finest wilderness unspoiled?"

We traversed a couple of switchbacks and approached the bottom of the ravine. Then Park said, "Where they are more easily accessible, deposits have been found and are being—or have been—mined."

We had seen such a mine near Lake Chelan, in the eastern part of the mountains. The Howe Sound Mining Company established an underground copper mine there in 1938, built a village and called it Holden. The Holden mine was abandoned in 1957. We had hiked past its remains on our way to the wilderness area. Against a backdrop of snowy peaks, two flat-topped hills of earth detritus broke the landscape. One was the dump where all the rock had been put that was removed before the miners reached the ore body. The other consisted of tailings—crushed rock that had been through the Holden mill and had yielded copper. What remained of the mill itself was a macabre skeleton of bent, twisted, rusted beams. Wooden buildings and sheds were rotting and gradually collapsing. The area was bestrewn with huge flakes of corrugated iron, rusted rails, rusted ore carts, old barrels. Although there was no way for an automobile to get to Holden except by barge up Lake Chelan and then on a dirt road to the village, we saw there a high pile of gutted and rusted automobiles, which themselves had originally been rock in the earth and, in the end, in Holden, were crumbling slowly back into the ground.

Park hit a ledge with the pick. We were moving up the other side of the ravine now. The going was steep, and the pace slowed. Brower said, ''We saw that at Holden.''

I counted twenty-two steps watching the backs of Brower's legs, above the red tops of gray socks. He was moving slower than I would have. I was close behind him. His legs, blue-veined, seemed less pink than they had the day before. They were sturdy but not athletically shapely. Brower used to put food caches in various places in the High Sierra and go from one to another for weeks at a time. He weighed two hundred and twelve pounds now, and he must have wished he were one-eighty.

Park said, ''Holden is the sort of place that gave mining a bad name. This has been happening in the West for the past hundred years, but it doesn't have to happen. Poor housekeeping is poor housekeeping wherever you find it. I don't care if it's a mine or a kitchen. Traditionally, when mining companies finished in a place they just walked off. Responsible groups are not going to do that anymore. They're not going to leave trash; they're not going to deface the countryside. Think of that junk! If I had enough money, I'd come up here and clean it up.''

I thought how neat Park's house, his lawn, and his gardens are—

his roses, his lemon tree, his two hundred varieties of cactus. The name of the street he lives on is Arcadia Place. Park is a member of the Cactus and Succulent Society of America. He hit a fallen tree with the hammer end.

"It's one god-awful mess," Brower said.

"That old mill could be cleaned up," Park said. "Grass could be planted on the dump and the tailings."

Suiattle Pass was now less than a quarter mile ahead of us. I thought of Brower, as a child, on his first trip to the Sierra Nevada. His father drove him there from Berkeley in a 1916 Maxwell. On the western slopes, they saw both the aftermath and the actual operations of hydraulic mining for gold. Men with hoses eight inches in diameter directed water with such force against the hillsides that large parts of the hills themselves fell away as slurry.

"Holden was abandoned in 1957, and no plants of any kind have caught on the dump and the tailings," Brower said.

Holden, in its twenty years of metal production, brought out of the earth ten million tons of rock—enough to make a hundred thousand tons of copper, enough to wire Kansas City.

Park said, "You could put a little fertilizer on—something to get it started."

When we reached the pass, we stood for a moment and looked again at Glacier Peak and, far below us, the curving white line of the Suiattle. Park said, "When you create a mine, there are two things you can't avoid: a hole in the ground and a dump for waste rock. Those are two things you can't avoid."

Brower said, "Except by not doing it at all."

We left the trail and went off to the right, toward Plummer Mountain, in order to attempt to find our way to the center of the area of the copper lode, and to see for ourselves—if possible—evidence of its presence. Park took the lead. The problem was to try to stay on a contour and still move in a generally westerly direction in landscape that was full of thick vegetation, ledges, ravines, and cliffs. It quickly became apparent that Brower thought Park had no idea where he was going. Our feet hurt—at least, Park's and mine did. I had developed a bone spur under one heel earlier in the year, and Park had made a bad choice with his new Canadian boots, which were stiff and were beginning to wear away parts of his ankles and feet. This fact emerged later. He said nothing at the time. Picking the shortest or easiest route—and assessing the one against the other—was of obvious importance to all of us. Although Brower seemed to be getting stronger with every added mile, he nonetheless was hardly indefatigable. Park had simply assumed command—aggressive, perhaps, because he was so uncomfortable—and we followed him, but Brower kept craning toward other possibilities, other routes. So close up, and so rough in character, the terrain was hard to read. Two or three times, Brower suggested that we try a gulch or a ridge that Park was having no part of, but Park kept moving and paid no attention, perhaps because he does not hear well. What we all feared was that we would come out onto some impossible ledge or up against a cliff face and have to turn back and add perhaps miles to our day. After a time, we got into the beginnings of what appeared to be a descending, curving cul-de-sac; at least, it appeared that way to me and to Brower. We imagined that if we were to go down into it, we would end up facing cliffs and have to climb back out the way we went in. Brower said he wanted to stay on high ground and go to even higher ground to get around the problem. Park kept on walking, downhill and to his right, around the curve, whacking boulders with his pick. With no trail to keep us threaded together, we had to follow. Around the bend, the "cul-de-sac" came open, and the landscape spread out into broad alpine meadows interspersed with stands of spruce and reaching out in gentle gradients toward the talus slopes of Plummer Mountain.

This place had been named the Golf Course, apparently by explorers for Kennecott—or so we gathered from a crude property map we had with us, the "property" being the corporation's patented claims. With very little bulldozing, the Golf Course could in fact become one of the seven wonders of sport, with the red wall of Plummer Mountain above it, the deep valley of the Suiattle falling away beside it, and the sparkling, spectacular imminence of Glacier Peak in full view from every tee, fairway, and green. Brower's response to this conception was that each and every round would have to be played over his remains.

Park said that we had apparently reached the outermost lens of the copper deposit. He looked up at Plummer Mountain, all rusty and tawny and jagged in the air, and described what he was looking at as intrusive rock impregnated with pyrite and, he assumed, with copper—a porphyry of disseminated copper in granitic intrusive material. He said this mountain glacial topography reminded him of Greenland—sharp peaks sticking up through the ice pack. He could almost see the ice that had been there in the past.

Brower said he could see the hole in the ground that would be there in the future. He said that it would be a man-made crater so large it would be visible from the moon.

"Aw, Dave, it wouldn't be that bad," Park said.

While Brower was executive director of the Sierra Club, the organization became famous for bold full-page newspaper ads designed to arouse the populace and written in a style that might be called Early Paul Revere. One such ad called attention to the Kennecott Copper Corporation's ambitions in the Glacier Peak Wilderness under the headline "AN OPEN PIT, BIG ENOUGH TO BE SEEN FROM THE MOON." The fact that this was not true did not slow up Brower or the Sierra Club. In the war strategy of the conservation movement, exaggeration is a standard weapon and is used consciously on broad fronts. Beneath the headline was an aerial photograph of an open pit that Kennecott has created in Bingham Canyon, Utah. It would be difficult to exaggerate that one. Bingham Canyon is the largest copper mine in the United States. Two miles from rim to rim, it goes down into the earth in some fifty concentric circular terraces, so that from the air it looks very much like a thumbprint pressed into the ground—the thumbprint, it works out, of a man well over a hundred miles tall. The Internal Revenue Service eventually reacted to the Sierra Club ads by declaring contributions to the Sierra Club no longer tax deductible. Organizations that tried to influence legislation could not have tax-deductible status. That didn't slow up Brower, either. He went right on with the ads.

"Well, with a small telescope," Brower said.

We moved up the fairways toward Plummer Mountain, walking through buttercups and vetch. Park said cheerfully, "I wouldn't object at all to seeing a nice open pit here, improving the standard of living."

"Improving the standard of living for a short time," Brower said.

"For a hundred years," said Park. "And fifty years after that it's all covered over. There's a beach in New South Wales where the deep sands have rutile, zircon, and other rare things. National Lead and some Australian companies got permission to mine the beach. There was a hullabaloo. They mined it, and now the beach is *better* than it was before. It's been rebuilt. Swamps and mosquitoes are gone. The shorebird habitats were untouched. The Australian government wants more beaches to be mined elsewhere."

Brower let the beach go. He once wrote and narrated a film about the North Cascades, and, with "America the Beautiful" softly rendered behind his own soft-toned voice on the sound track, he said that these mountains were among "the few surviving samples of a natural world, to walk and rest in, to see, to listen to, to feel the mood of, to comprehend." The narration continued, "There isn't much of it left. What there is is all all men will ever have, and all their children. It is only as safe as people want it to be." That must have been more or less what he was thinking at that moment. At length, he said, "The pit is only a small part of what else they do."

"Every mine in the country has someone objecting to it," Park said. "Where are you going to get your metals?"

"Nevada, Arizona—Bingham Canyon."

"People object *there*."

We stepped around several piles of fresh dung. Brower said he didn't know what it was. Park said, "It's bear dung."

A pluming waterfall, hundreds of feet high, fell from the east face of Plummer Mountain, and, for lack of a more specific goal, we were homing on it.

"This scenic climax is of international significance," Brower said.

"That may be, but as long as you've got copper here, pressure to mine is going to continue."

"Well, I'll give up when copper has to be used as a substitute for gold. The kids will decide then. And I think they'll decide not to mine it."

"A mine would remove the mining area from wilderness—anyone in his right mind would admit that," Park said. "You're going to have people, equipment, machinery. You're going to blast. You're going to have a waste dump. You're also going to get copper, which contributes to the national wealth and, I think, well-being. And all that can't possibly affect Glacier Peak."

"The mine will affect anybody in this whole area who *looks* at Glacier Peak. One of the last great wildernesses in the United States would have been punctured, like a worm penetrating an apple. There would not only be the pit but also the dumps, the settling ponds, the tailings, the mill, machine shops, powerhouses, hundred-ton trucks. Good Lord! The mood would go. Wilderness defenders have to get into abstract terms like mood and so forth, but that is what it is all about. How are the people and equipment going to get in and out of here? A road? A railroad?"

"I think cost would have to enter into that."

"O.K. I put a price of ten billion dollars on the Glacier Peak Wilderness. Actually, that is facetious. There is no price. The price of beauty has never been evaluated. Look at that mountain! What would it *cost* to build an equal one?"

A galvanized pipe rising about a foot out of the earth stopped the conversation, and stopped us where we stood. Only three inches from rim to rim, it seemed somehow, to me, in the surprise of coming upon it, to reach far out into the surrounding wilderness, to be the mine itself. It had been marked as Kennecott's Drill Site No. 3. Park said it probably went down about five hundred feet, and that the core samples that had been removed through it must have been three-quarters of an inch in diameter. The core samples would have shown not only whether copper was there, in that spot, but also the concentration of it in the porphyry. Earlier in this century, if copper ore was not at least two or three per cent copper it was bypassed. Now if it is seven-tenths of one per cent copper it is mined. We sat down, roughly in a circle, around the pipe. We each had a plastic bag full of a mixture of peanuts, raisins, and chocolate, and we opened the bags and ate while we looked at the pipe, although there was so little to see. Around it spread the meadow grass, the vetch, and the buttercups, undisturbed.

"What percent of the world's known copper is under here?" Brower asked.

"I don't know," Park said. "Kennecott hasn't told me."

For a time, the only sound was from the wind and from the waterfall on the mountain. Then Brower said, "We don't know the size of the reserve."

"That's true."

"If you start with point seven per cent and work down, say, to point three five—if that level becomes commercially feasible, then there's no telling *how* big the pit will be."

"That's true."

"The theory of economic growth is doomed on a finite planet."

"It has to be."

"We have to figure out how to cool it. I think a major change in thinking is around the corner."

Park took off his cap and smoothed his hair. "I hope your optimism holds," he said. "I'm a pessimist."

"I *have* to be an optimist. It keeps me in business. Otherwise, I'd open a waffle shop."

Of all the things Brower swallows, the two he seems to like most in the world are Tanqueray gin and whipped-cream-and-strawberry-covered waffles.

"Copper affects the international balance of payments," Park said. "We are net importers of copper."

"I can't get excited about that."

"Again, what you're saying is that you're willing to lower the standard of living."

"Very much so."

"Then you increase ghetto problems in cities."

"There is a gap between a lowered standard and the ghetto," Brower said. "One thing we could do, to begin with, is stop copper roofing."

"That's not a great amount. It's mostly in wiring."

"A lot of copper goes into coinage. Quarters are sandwiches of nickel and copper."

"Yes. We could get rid of that."

"We could use aluminum coins."

"Aluminum coins are horrible," Park said, "They're dirty."

"Well, then, I'd rather have a hole in a coin than a hole in Plummer Mountain. A mine in this wilderness is horrible, too."

"The mine has to come. Population pressure is irresistible."

"Population is pollution spelled inside out."

"I agree. At least, I agree that it is a very real problem."

"Families with more than two children should be taxed," Brower said.

"I agree with that, too. Everything is hopeless without population control."

"How many children do you have?"

"Three. How many do you have?"

"Four," Brower confessed.

They both turned to me.

"Four," I said.

The medical students looked on with interest.

"Seven billion people are going to be on the earth in the year 2000," Park said.

"It is wrong to assume so. Demographers make a projection like that and then we all assume it's inevitable and we go ahead and make it so."

Brower has a metaphysical or perhaps superstitious belief in the idea of the self-fulfilling prophecy. He also has no regard for the extrapolations of social scientists.

"India? Africa? Have you seen the figures?" Park asked him.

"I think there will be a massive pestilence."

"Perhaps so, but meanwhile population pressure is irresistible."

"Central Park and the Adirondacks have resisted it pretty well."

Adirondack State Park is the largest park, state or federal, in the United States. It was created in 1892, principally as the result of the efforts of a group of conservationists in Brooklyn, who put into the constitution of the State of New York this guarantee: "The Forest Preserve shall be forever kept as wild forest lands."

Park put on his cap. "There was a titanium mine in the Adirondacks during the Second World War," he said.

We came to a small stream that ran straight down the steep mountainside. We shook off our packs, removed our boots, and set our feet in the water. "Oh, gad, that feels good," Park said. Our feet were as white as fish flesh in the cold water—so cold that I could barely stand it. This was a way to keep going, though. A cold stream offers a kind of retread. The pain goes away for a while afterward, and miles can be added to a day. Reaching upstream, Brower dipped himself a cupful of water. "Wilderness is worth it, if for no other reason than it is the last place on earth where you can get good water," he said. No one else said anything. We were too tired. We stared into the stream, or looked across the deep Suiattle Valley at the virgin forests on the lower slopes and the snow and ice on the upper slopes of Glacier Peak. Park's attention became fixed on the pebbles at the bottom of the stream, and after a moment he leaned forward and reached into the water, wetting his sleeve. He removed from the water a blue-and-green stone about the size of a garden pea. He set it on the palm of one hand and passed it before us. We have been looking all day for copper," he said. "Here it is."

The beauty of the mountain across the valley was cool and absolute, but the beauty of the stone in Park's hand was warm and subjective. It affected us all. Human appetites, desires, ambitions, greeds, and profound aesthetic and acquisitional instincts were concentrated between the stone and our eyes. Park reached again into the stream, and said, "Here's another one. The blue is chrysocolla—copper silicate. The rest is malachite—green copper carbonate."

All of us, Brower included, knelt in the stream and searched for stones. Brower found one. He was obviously excited by it. Brigham found one. Snow found one. Park found one as large as a robin's egg, mottled blue and green, with black specks of cupric oxide.

"My God, look at that!"

"Malachite and chrysocolla in altered intrusive rock," Park said.

"I've got another one," Brower said. "Good Lord, look at them all!"

"Hey, there are even more up here!" Snow called out.

"The rock is probably monzonite—a granite with equal parts of potash and soda feldspars—altered by hydrothermal solutions. I'd have to take it into a lab to know for sure. The copper came way up out of the earth's core when these mountains were fluid."

Larry Snow was shouting from above. He had a green rock in his hand the size of a golf ball. The slope and the streambed were as steep as a ladder, and ten minutes earlier the thought of going up there would have filled me with gloom and inertia. Now I put on my boots and followed him, scrambling hand over foot for the copper.

The higher we went, the larger were the green rocks—two inches, three inches, four inches thick. On a ledge about a hundred yards above Park, Brower, and Brigham, who were still assembling green pebbles, Snow picked up a rock that he could barely manage with one hand. Others like it were all over the ledge—cuprous green and aquamarine.

I held one high in my right hand and shouted down to Brower, "Dave, look at this! Look at this rock! Don't you think it would be a crime against society not to take this copper out of here?"

"Stay up there! Don't come back down!" Brower shouted. He was a small figure, from that high perspective. He was waving Snow and me away. "Stay up there! We'll send a party for you next spring!"

At the back of the ledge was the source of the copper. A deep, narrow hole had been blown into the side of the mountain, making what appeared to be a small cave—a nick in the wilderness, exposing and fragmentarily spilling its treasure. Snow and I filled a small canvas bag with perhaps twenty pounds of ore and made our way back down the streambed.

No one seemed anxious to move. I again took off my boots and put my feet in the stream. Brower had made an attractive collection of green pebbles. He looked with interest and feigned contempt at the big stones we had brought down. Brower is a collector of rocks. Behind his desk in his office in San Francisco were rocks he had collected from all over, and notably from the canyons of the Colorado— Glen Canyon, Grand Canyon. In most cases, he did not know what these rocks were, nor did he appear to care. He had taken them for their beauty alone.

Park was contemplating Glacier Peak. We were as close to it as we would ever be. It was right there—so enormous that it seemed to be on top of us, extending upward five thousand feet above our heads. "That's the sort of thing that draws people into geology," he said. "Geologists go into the field because of love of the earth and of the out-of-doors."

"The irony is that they go into wilderness and change it," Brower said.

Park appeared to be too tired to be argumentative. "There are some silly things about the mining laws," he said after a time, and he went on to explain that once a mining company or anyone else establishes a patented claim on public land they have complete rights to do anything they want, just as if they—and not the people of the United States—were owners of the property. Within federal law, they can cut down all the trees, they can build skyscrapers. If Kennecott wants to, Kennecott can put up a resort hotel in the Glacier Peak Wilderness. This law, enacted in 1872, makes no sense now to Park. He said he thought that mining companies should be given leases, and that these leases should include strong restrictions on mining practice and use of the land. In his view, something like that would go a long way toward eliminating the dichotomy that currently exists between conservationists and miners. While he was saying all this, he dried his feet in the air. I noticed for the first time that Park's heels were so raw red they were all but bleeding. He pulled on his socks and, with care, his boots. He got up—we all got up—and moved west along the ridge. He was forced to trudge, even after we rejoined the trail. Going to Image Lake would add several miles to the trip, involve an extra climb, and, the next day, a precipitous descent, but when the trail forked, Park headed for Image Lake.

Above Park's desk at Stanford was a picture of a jackass, with the caption "Can I help? Or do you want to make your own mistakes?" Near it was a photostatic blowup of a five-cent postage stamp showing cherry boughs and the Jefferson Memorial over the legend "Plant a More Beautiful America." Park's great-grandfather was a Minuteman. His grandfather was a guide on the Santa Fe Trail. His father had a real-estate and travel agency in Wilmington. His older brother went off and became a cowpuncher for the Bell Ranch, in New Mexico, and this in part established the draw to the West that Park felt throughout his youth. Tall, loose, rangy, and graceful, Park was a basketball player—a very good one—and he loved the game so much that he played not only for Wilmington High School (he was in the Class of 1922) but also, on the side, for various churches. His father told him that he had to worship at any church for which he played basketball, so for a long time he went to church at least twice each Sunday. He says he hasn't been to church since, except on the day that he was married. Also in those days, he made camping trips along the Brandywine, fished with a drop line in Chesapeake Bay, collected rocks that people sent him from beyond the hundredth meridian, and waited for the day when he could go beyond it himself.

When he was eighteen, he went to New York and shipped out in steerage on a Matson Line steamer for Galveston. It was the cheapest way West. He was not sure where he was going. He thought he might go to Golden (the Colorado School of Mines), or possibly to Socorro (the New Mexico School of Mines). "In those days, if you wanted to go to one of those places all you had to do was show up," he once explained to me. Eventually, he showed up at Socorro. He was the captain of his college basketball team, and he learned his mineralogy, and went on to get his master's degree at the University of Arizona and his Ph.D. at the University of Minnesota. In mining camps in those years, he became known as Chas (pronounced "chass"), specifically because the nickname distinguished him from the numerous Chinese in the mining camps, who, to a man, were known as Charlie. For a time, he worked as a mine surveyor for the New Jersey Zinc Company in Hanover, New Mexico, where he met a girl from Colorado—Eula Blair—who eventually became his wife and the mother of his two sons and his daughter. His daughter is a teacher of physical education. His sons are both working geologists—one with Humble Oil, the other with Hanna Mining. Mining geology is not widely taught anymore, and across the years students have come from all over the earth to Stanford because—in term, anyway, when he was not in equatorial Africa or the Andes or the Great Basin or the Black Hills—Park has been there, to teach them courses with names like Ore Genesis 101.

We were about a mile east of Image Lake. Park stopped, picked up a stone, split it in half with his pick, and said, "We are well past the mineral deposit. The mine won't come anywhere near Image Lake. The rock here is not intrusive. It's completely volcanic."

"Of course, it could be a volcanic overburden," said Brower, to suggest the possibility that far beneath the earth's surface the copper might spread to untold dark horizons.

"That's true. It could," Park said, with a tired shrug, and he trudged on.

We were a somewhat bizarre group on arrival at Image Lake. Park and I could scarcely place one foot after the other. The medical students appeared to be as fresh as they had been in the morning. And Brower was yodelling with pleasure. Brower yodels badly. The happier he seems to be, the more and the worse he yodels. He is Antaeus in the mountains, and he was clearly feeling good.

Image Lake is very small—a stock-water pond in size—and it stands in open and almost treeless terrain. Slowly, we went around it, looking for a place to sleep. The sun was just setting, and we had arrived much too late. We walked past tents along the shore—blue tents, green tents, red tents, orange tents. The evening air was so still that we could hear voices all around the lake. We heard transistor radios. People greeted us as we went by. The heaviest shadows were in the northwest arc of the shore, so the air was particularly cold there, and space had been left. We took the space. We had come into the mountains from the east. These people had come in from the west. It had not been an easy trip for them, to be sure. The nearest roadhead was fifteen miles west of us and some four thousand feet below. Nonetheless, the lake that night had the ambience of a cold and crowded oasis. Shivering, I climbed up a slope to witness in the water the fading image of the great mountain. Objectively, the reflection was all it was said to be. But a "No Vacancy" sign seemed to hang in the air over the lake.

A real sign pointed the way to a privy. We collected firewood, which was very hard to find, and when we had something of a blaze going and had all drawn in close around it for warmth, I said to Park and Brower, "Do you feel that you're in a wilderness now?"

"Yes," Brower said. "All these people certainly diminish the wilderness experience, but I've seen crowds in wilderness before. I know that they'll go away, and when they go they haven't really left anything."

Once, on a trail in the Sierra, Brower and I passed numerous hikers coming in the other direction, and because there were so many of them they disturbed him. They weren't riding Bonanza Trail-Bikes and they didn't have transistor radios and they weren't tossing beer cans away. They were disturbing to him only because they were there. Brower kept asking them if we were likely to find "too many" people in Humphreys Basin, which lay ahead of us, and when he concluded that Humphreys Basin—an area of several thousand acres—was going to contain too much of humankind he left the trail and struck off overland for another part of the mountains. Once, also, Brower and I were approaching the Sierra from the west on Route 198, and it happened to be the evening of the final day of a holiday weekend, and a river of cars was coming in the other direction. Brower drove without hurry. "The longer we wait, the more people we'll get out of the mountains," he said.

Now, at Image Lake, Park said, "There is no wilderness to me. My idea of wilderness is not to walk a quarter of a mile to a biffy. There's just too many people here."

Brower said, "It's hard to believe that this many people would walk this far."

"Population pressure," Park said. "You can't stop it. I don't really understand why they come here, though. This is a very ordinary little mountain lake."

We put our dinner into a single pot, boiled the food, ate it; and no one noticed what it was. Park was the first to speak again. "The more I see of this country, the more I fail to see what that copper mine would do to it. When we started, I was under the impression it might do something, but, golly, I can't see that now."

"The excavation would be within a mile of here and would effectively remove even this lake from wilderness. Right now it has more impact than it can bear. The ecosystem is delicate here. Recovery rates are fast, but nonetheless it is getting pounded. And the disruption would go all the way to Suiattle Pass, so the Glacier Peak Wilderness would effectively be cut in half."

"There would be a mining company here on business, and that's what they'd be doing—that's all. The miners would stick to the mine. Some would go off hiking or fishing, sure, but they would be doing that anyway. Miners like wilderness."

"The trouble is they want to dig it up and take it home."

"Awww."

"Logging follows mining."

"You can control that."

"That's what I'm hoping."

"Your idea of control is to keep it out."

"All a conservation group can do is to defer something. There's no such thing as a permanent victory. After we win a battle, the wilderness is still there, and still vulnerable. When a conservation group *loses* a battle, the wilderness is dead."

"It doesn't have to be."

"It's dead by definition."

"I don't agree with that concept of wilderness—to just take a big block of land and say you're going to keep it for the future. I can't see it."

"Wilderness was originally a nice place to go to, but that is not what wilderness is for. Wilderness is the bank for the genetic variability of the earth. We're wiping out that reserve at a frightening rate. We should draw a line right now. Whatever is wild, leave it wild."

"I would take a certain area and make part of it accessible and part of it inaccessible. Taking very large areas out of the country and keeping them as they were a thousand years ago—you can't do it. The population pressure is too great."

"A wilderness is a place where natural forces can keep working essentially uninterrupted by man. If ten per cent is still wild, we should tithe with it. Man has taken enough for himself already. We should pretend the rest doesn't exist. It's there for a different purpose."

"What purpose?"

"Not man's purpose. Man is a recent thing in the time scale here."

The moon had risen, pale and gibbous. We looked up at it. Men had been there recently and were going back in a few weeks. "There may be possibilities in the moon, but I can't see it," Park said.

"Apollo 11 proved the capability, and that was quite enough," Brower said. "Now let's spend the money on something else. We need to save the earth."

"Moon walking is silly," Park agreed. "There are too many things about the earth that we don't know, that would improve our lot, and that cost a lot of money."

"We're not so poor that we have to spend our wilderness or so rich that we can afford to. That kind of boxes it in nicely. Newton Drury said it."

"I don't believe you can stop expansion of the consumption of raw materials."

"You stop when you run out," said Brower. "Meanwhile, you make it less wasteful."

"Waste is criminal."

"If we recycled enough copper annually, we could do without this mine. Now that we know that we ourselves are on a spaceship, we have to get into our heads a concept of limits. Some things must stop or the world will become repugnant. There are limits everywhere, whether we are dealing with an island, a river, a mountain, with people, or with air. Living diversity is the thing we're preserving."

The fire had subsided almost to nothing, and the conversation subsided with it. The air was quite cold. We dispersed and got into our sleeping bags. Brower had arranged his pallet on top of a high promontory above the lakeshore. As a mountaineer, he knew that less dew condenses on high ground, and also that the air is warmer there. Park and I felt too achingly sore in the feet to bother making the climb.

We stretched out below. As Park adjusted himself to the ground beneath him, he said, "I know half a dozen lakes like this that I can drive to and where I would find less people. I'll give you my interest in Image Lake for a piece of a counterfeit penny." Then he fell asleep. It was 8:30 P.M.

In the morning, we went down to the Suiattle River—a drop of three thousand feet from Image Lake down the face of Miner's Ridge on a grassy incline so steep that Brower began telling stories about what happens to people on slopes like that if they fall. They apparently start to tumble, and sometimes can't stop. Park said he didn't care whether he fell or not—he was that uncomfortable. He finally took off his boots and put on his open leather sandals, deciding that bruises all over his feet would be preferable to the pain in his heels. His difficulty notwithstanding, he kept knocking rocks apart all day. After the big drop, the trail, for something like ten miles, ran roughly parallel to the river. The more altitude we gave up, the larger were the trees, the deeper the forest, until we were walking among big Douglas firs six feet thick. The air was warm and sunlit, and even when we could not see the river through the dense trees, the Suiattle was something to hear. It had the overbearing sound of rock sliding in a steel chute. As the afternoon lengthened, the sound grew louder. Park said he had known rivers in Alaska that could be crossed in the morning but by afternoon were unfordable torrents of melted glacier ice. "This one is like them," he said. Coming into view, the Suiattle was a headlong chaos of standing waves and swirling eddies, white with spray and glacial flour. "This one is a really wild river," Park went on. "Look at that rush of glacier milk."

The lower reaches of the trail had been scarred and battered by an improvement project commissioned by the United States Forest Service. Dynamite had torn great rocks apart, and some of the big trees had been felled to make the trail wider and the grade easier. Brower began to say unflattering things about the Forest Service, which he described as a collection of timber engineers who have no concept of ecology and whose idea of selective logging is to select a mountain and cut all the trees down. He said, "We conservationists would like to keep the Forest Service out of wilderness, and, for that matter, the National Park Service, too. They build too many things for their own convenience—for rangers who have forgotten how to range."

Brower had scarcely said this when we came upon a man who had three horses with him and several empty dynamite boxes. He was about thirty-five, strongly built and in excellent condition, solid muscles under his T-shirt, short-cropped hair, pale gray eyes. His name was Don Dayment, and he told us he had been the foreman of the crew that improved the trail. Brower complained bluntly about the desecration of the trail. Dayment looked from Brower to Park to me to the medical students, and he said. "You wilderness-lovers are all the same."

"You foresters are all the same," Brower said.

Dayment cinched his horses. "Wherever man goes, whatever he does, he scars the land," he said. "That's the way things are. We were told to make a ten-per-cent grade here with a two-foot tread and eight feet of clearance. If we had to chop a six-foot fir, too bad."

I asked him where he lived, and he said he had been born twenty miles from where we stood.

I asked him how he felt about the copper mine.

"I don't like it, and I'll tell you why," he said. "I don't like the class of people that would come with it. I've seen their camps—in Wallace, Idaho, and Butte, Montana. They're dirty and run-down, and so are the people. I wouldn't want my children growing up around them."

Over the last five miles, each of us went at his own pace; we gave up all cohesion as a group. I walked with Brower, who was moving fast, because I had the almost drunken, rubber-legged feeling you get toward the finish of a long, long walk, and the roadhead at the end of the trail had become for me a repeating mirage. The trail ran closer and closer to the Suiattle—right beside it in some stretches—and the sound of the water was deafening. Over what proved to be the last thousand yards, though, we became aware of a sound even louder than the sound of the river—a higher-pitched roar, coming in jugular gusts, and increasing in volume as we moved down the trail. We came to the roadhead. There in the river, in the middle of the river, the white torrents crashing over it, was a bulldozer. Half submerged, its purpose obscure, it heaved, belched, backed, shoved, and lurched around on the bottom of the Suiattle as if the water were not there. The bulldozer was stronger than the river.

I took off my boots and sat alone on a ledge where my feet could reach the water. For a couple of hours, I had been able to think of almost nothing but feet. Now the cold milk of glaciers dispelled that, and as I watched the bulldozer my mind went back over the day—all the way back to its beginning. Miner's Ridge, as it extended westward from Image Lake, was a ridge indeed. The terrain fell away as steeply on the north side as it did toward the Suiattle, and we had walked for a mile or so—before beginning the descent—along the ridgeline of a topographical configuration that was like a sharply pitched gable roof. There was no timber up there, and in the early morning the ridge was isolated from the land below by huge bodies of cloud that filled up the river valleys on either side almost to our shoes. Above the clouds, the air was clear and the sky blue, and nothing else broke into that world but Glacier Peak, seven miles away—all ice and snow, and almost too dazzling to look at as it sprayed sunlight in every direction. Big blueberries were growing along the trail, and we began to eat them as if we had had no breakfast. Some were a half inch in diameter. Filling his Sierra Club cup with berries, Brower said, "I'm just taking the renewable crop. Only bears will object."

Park ate his blueberries straight from the bushes. His eyes lifted suddenly and followed a bird in flight above the ridge. He said, "Look at that marsh hawk. What's *he* doing up here?" The hawk canted to its left and soared in the direction of Glacier Peak. Streamers of cloud began to rise from the Suiattle Valley, cross the face of the mountain, and above the summit disappear, sparkling, into the blue. Park said it was a shame that more people couldn't see Glacier Peak—in fact, he thought people had a right to see it—and a nice little mining road would take care of that.

Brower said that a view of Glacier Peak, to mean much of anything, ought properly to be earned, and that the only way to earn it was to get to it on foot.

"What about people who can't walk?" Park said.

"They stay home. Ninety-nine point nine per cent can walk—if they want to."

"The other one-tenth percent includes my wife."

Without hesitating, Brower said, "I have a friend named Garrett Hardin, who wears leg braces. I have heard him say that he would not want to be able to come to a place like this by road, and that it is enough for him just to know that these mountains exist as they are, and he hopes that they will be like this in the future."

"The future can take care of itself," Park said. "I don't condone waste, but I am not willing to penalize present people. I say they're penalized if they don't have enough copper. Dave says they're penalized if they don't have enough wilderness. Right?" He smacked a stone with his pick.

"Right," said Brower. "But I go further. I believe in wilderness for itself alone. I believe in the rights of creatures other than man. And I suppose I accept Nancy Newhall's definition: 'Conservation is humanity caring for the future.' It is the antithesis of 'Eat, drink, and be merry, for tomorrow we die.' "

"These are the best blueberries I've ever seen," Park said. "Here on Miner's Ridge."

Brower's cup was up to its brim, and before he ate any himself he passed them among the rest of us. It was a curious and surpassingly generous gesture, since we were surrounded by bushes that were loaded with berries. We all accepted.

"I just feel sorry for all you people who don't know what these mountains are good for," Brower said.

"What are they good for?" I said.

"Berries," said Brower.

And Park said, "Copper."

DOUGLAS CARLSON

Tide Pools

AT NO TIME HAD so much snow (up to twenty inches) fallen so early (October 4) in the northeast. The *Times* called it a collision of cold and soggy air masses in a weather valley created by a low pressure system. They might have mentioned the glacier that carved and ploughed a topography featuring high elevations where temperatures could stay near freezing in early October. Or they might have mentioned the continents' parting that left the Atlantic Ocean behind as a source of soggy air. Or the 350 million-year-long collision of continents that heaved up the land that became the mountain ranges where the snow fell. Mistakes like the October 4 storm happen even in the most carefully ordered worlds, and I found little to do but drive straight into it. As I drove, I remembered the map on the Weather Channel as I took one last look at it before leaving our motel at York Beach, Maine. I saw North America in powder blue with a chartreuse blob that had taken over the Northeast; our weather person said the blob represented light to moderate showers. Along the western edge, over the Berkshires and Catskills, skulked two sinister, white patches—snow. Outside the motel window, the Atlantic pushed five-foot waves against York Beach. Below in the parking lot, my family waited in the car. And even though I would drive a half-day, spend—thanks to the storm—an extra night in another motel, then drive some more, I wouldn't lose the odd balance I felt at that moment: of fear and joy, of real, imagined, and remembered worlds. Until I saw what the storm had done.

A week before, I had driven eastward through fall leaves near their color peak. Along the north-south river valleys—the Hudson, Westfield, and Connecticut—many trees remained green. Oaks and some maples still hadn't turned, even at 1400 feet. At this height, however, alder, birch, beech, and the remaining maples had become sufficiently spectacular to bring out carloads of leaf peepers from Boston and New York City. Most vividly, though, I remember flames of sumac, the bright yellow of wild grape at the woods' margins, and whole fields of purple or white aster. To this scene, a New England cliché, a foot of wet snow applied some serious change. In the areas hit worst, leaves that had turned color were knocked to the ground and buried; leaves still green clung to trees, supporting wet snow in heavy piles. Aspens and birches bent over or lay flat; even some hemlocks, their drooping branches suited for shedding snow, did the same. While maples and oaks lost primary branches, locusts seemed to have been blown apart. Unbroken white hillsides hid asters and goldenrod.

Commerce would suffer, but to the natural world, the storm offered little that could be called disastrous. Fallen trees open up holes in the canopy, letting in sunlight that slow-growing trees such as hemlocks wait for. A dead limb soon provides a new habitat for fungi and, eventually, contributes nutrients to the soil. Aster seeds fill New England's air each fall. A sense of perspective reveals the storm not accidental at all but rather a sign that things are moving along nicely. Yet the storm unsettled me; mine is a smaller view. I had left the coast with a head full of images about to be fragmented by a freak of nature; only later could I reassemble them, learning what I knew all along.

We had spent the week at York Beach because at the north end of the beach we can turn seaward onto Cape Neddick, follow Nubble Road a mile, then turn seaward again onto Cape Nubble and drive a tenth of a mile to its tip, an accessible universe filled with the worlds of tide pools. At the seaward end of the parking lot that crowns Cape Nubble, we can see, across a narrow channel, Nubble Rock and Nubble Lighthouse, another New England cliché. Skirting the point lies a confused mass of granite boulders, many man sized and larger. Crevasses, depressions, and cavities hold hundreds of tide pools— each a different world, each worth exploring. Without realizing it, I began to fall into a mood of well-being—my family around me, a time of rest, reading, writing, photography, and conversation. I found this contentment reflected in the tide pools as I scrambled over the rocks each day, trying to see into them all.

I jumped from rock to rock, looking deep inside the pools they held, lying on my belly on dry rocks, squatting on algae-slick platforms by the lower pools. Each pool—some washed more, some less, by the waves—held a different community. The sea left some alone for varying lengths of time, some not at all; habitats differed in turbulence, salinity variation, amounts and kinds of food. I looked down and in, occasionally surprising my own face in reflection, looking into my eyes. Sky and clouds below me and above, I dove and climbed at the same time. A gull's reflection filled a mussel pool high above the low tide mark—black-blue mussels; delicate, pink corallina; green cladophora bright in sunlight then in sudden shadow. The gull landed beside me and joined others feeding in small pools under ledges and in shallow crevasses. Unafraid, a dozen herring gulls surrounded me, picking food from the pools. I crawled over; the gulls backed off a bit. Their pools were snail pools. Thousands of periwinkles up to $^1/_8''$ feasted on algae. Gulls feasted on them.

In lower pools, surf came gurgling, flushing foam and, invisibly, food. From one, I scooped a handful of small stones and broken shells and put it on a dry rock. Immediately, the pile came alive with tiny shrimp that wriggled for cover and finding none, curled their transparent bodies and waved their legs in the air. Each time I took a layer off the pile, I saw more shrimp until I pulled all the debris away, exposing a solid, writhing mass of nutrition.

To busloads of tourists in the Nubble Point parking lot, the boulders just above low tide appear covered with brown slime. But up close, among the larger boulders, one can stand in wider crevasses and look, head-on, not into slime but into a vertical habitat of rockweed and the animals it protects. Thousand of individual rockweed plants, each at least a foot or more, cling with their holdfasts to the boulders' sides. Fastened, each plant commands a clear rock area up to a foot. Its fronds divide again until a forest canopy, several feet across, of soft, brown tentacles sways at high tide and hangs heavy, wet, and limp against the rocks after the tide goes out. Underneath this layered drape, communities live hidden from predators, protected from desiccation, and provided with food.

Like a voyeur moving from window to window, I lifted layers of rockweed, spying on communities living in a forest of rockweed trunks. As I examined boulder after boulder, I realized that of all the habitats among the rocks, this seemed the most at rest, balanced and waiting. Here the world turned sideways: top branches dried in the setting sun shining directly on them. Underneath, trunks stayed moist. Animals moved up and down the rock face (back and forth in their world); periwinkles grazed on the algae, barnacles and mussels hid beneath it; immature green crabs, barely an inch across, foraged. Stalking among them all, voracious packs of dog whelks played out their role: bold- or thin-striped predators boring into their victims, consuming them.

Nights I read about the balances in a tide pool—the adaptability, strength, and flexibility of the living things that survive there. I took pleasure in knowing cycles I couldn't verify. Night and day, for example, the animals and plants save each others' lives. During daytime, plants use sunlight to make sugar and starches out of carbon dioxide and water, liberating oxygen needed for respiration. Oxygen makes possible complex biochemical breakdown of organic matter, releasing energy, carbon dioxide, and water in the process. Perfect. Except at night when darkness shuts down photosynthesis while respiration continues more or less unabated. The amount of carbon dioxide in the water diminishes in daylight while oxygen accumulates. But at night, oxygen is used up, and carbon dioxide, which combines with water to form carbonic acid, accumulates. If the imbalance continues without correction the next day, the oxygen depletion and the acidity will kill everything. The balance of the pool—really a series of imbalances being corrected—reveals the true nature of balance among all living things: diatoms, invertebrates, or people.

Similarly, each tide roars in with a sea full of food—plankton for mussels and barnacles, small marine life for the carnivores— renewing as it splashes in white waterfalls over black rock and tears up rock crevasses and through the pools. Like the algae, some organizisms survive the power and rush by being flexible; other, like limpets and barnacles, have strength enough to cling to the rocks, surviving the forces that sustain them. Far from miniature, perfect saltwater aquariums to be carried home and put in the den, tide pools balance on the edge of conflict and change.

Our last night together, we brought chowder back to Cape Nubble and watched the storm build the surf. Inland, the moon set into clouds that held a record-breaking snowstorm, the first winter gale. Seaward, Nubble Light spun into the sky.

Later we walked. In the dark, we helped each other over rocks, slippery with algae in the splash zone (blue-green algae, my brain told me). But the imagination, not the brain, engages on a night for saying goodbye. We watched the surf crash into boulders and counted the seconds the mist took to travel on this new, Canadian air and into our faces. In a tide pool, we saw the lighthouse repeat itself, revolving in its own reflection. I imagined crossing the channel to the island, becoming a silhouette reflected in the same pool.

High tide, storm tide, cuts someone off; someone stays behind. Whichever side we're on at high tide is the one we must live on. Reflections surrounded us: Nubble Light's red, regular; the lights of York Beach reflected on the bay; just offshore a vessel ablaze with light. Lights still reflect off the water; parents still bring their children to the shore. The lights brought me back to the times when our sons were small and young enough for those Cape Cod trips each spring to the cottage on the bay. Wrapped in a blanket, we would sit on the porch at night and watch the light near the target ship blink irregularly and the red one off Billingsgate and the shore lights of Brewster shimmer in the water where the land turned back westward.

The vessel off Cape Nubble, sparkling and gay at night, would float ugly at sunrise like a huge, gray log. Reflections confuse. So I check out my memories. Was it really that great back then? Oh, yes. Four of us wrapped in a blanket, watching lights on the water. They fall asleep: first Jeff, then Donna, then Kevin. I won't wake them up; I won't go inside. I tell myself, I have to keep this going just a little while longer.

But I couldn't.

So I've settled for these forays, brief and intense. I gather everyone together and rush to some point of land and thought that holds past and future, memory and hope. We use the land a day or two until it insists on returning us to the present—high tide returning, storm approaching, night deepening around us. Time to turn from the familiar edges: of land and sea, growth and change, happiness and fear.

In a motel in Springfield, waiting for the plows to clear the Mass Pike of snow, I had a startlingly clear memory of an earlier trip to another edge. I remembered sitting at a picnic table that held oak leaves and three-pronged pine needles pointing contradictory directions into the woods. Lichens, delicate and fanshaped, decorated the table with pale green patches of light. A gray squirrel had left the remnants of his breakfast: acorn shells, broken and chewed. And I watched the table closely, trying to gear my thoughts down to a manageable size, fitting them to the detail of a leaf, an acorn cap.

I had set out, two hours earlier, to the east, the direction of the sea. I began on a small, winding path through the woods, kicking up a covey of bobwhite into a turbulence of feathers and wings. Shortly, just as suddenly, the woods disappeared; Commonwealth Electric had turned them into a bridle path/RV route. Under the power lines, poverty grass turned silver in the low sun; aster and poison ivy shone violet and crimson. I followed the power line slash north until a sand road turned east again. But I left this route of tire tracks and litter at a National Seashore sign. I was eager for isolation, weary of intrusion.

I walked around the barrier with the surf barely audible in the distance and with kinglets, chickadees, and blue jays on both sides. Here moss splotched the trail of nearly white sand. For the first mile, the woods were unremarkable, with trees well spaced and large: oaks to six inches in diameter, pines to ten inches. Occasionally I passed through waves of kinglets, flitting and flipping in the low branches like locust leaves shook loose and falling in a small breeze. Oak leaves crackled under my feet. Then, gradually, the trees became smaller, the surf louder.

The trail turned slightly at a twenty-foot drop that I recalled from my Geological Survey map; I knew I was closer. Here the sunlight broke through more often, shining once on a violent pile of blue jay feathers—the colors of the ocean, the color of the sky. The undergrowth thickened, and small, dead trees littered the ground. All the time, the surf grew louder and I walked faster. Finally I broke into a trot, eager to see what I could already hear.

And then the deciduous woods fell away. I hurried along a row of pitch pine that ran parallel to the shoreline. Through the branches, I could see an area without trees. The path turned, and I walked through a forest eight feet high. For two hundred feet I still only heard the waves, but climbing a swelling in the ground I saw the ocean, one hundred yards away. For over an hour, my field of vision had been obscured and baffled by trees and undergrowth; now I could see as far as my eyes permitted. A new sense of space filled me, and I could only stand, waiting for it to pass. To the left and right, I looked over acres of dark green and brown, but the momentum of my walking seemed to force me straight ahead, into the sea. I fought a wave of confusion, then fear, that finally receded when I looked down and walked slowly. As the vegetation shrank, I felt the northerly wind on my face, then my arms, then my legs. Finally, with the forest at my feet, I stopped at the edge of a fifty-foot marine scarp, the Outer Beach, the Atlantic.

I watched—I don't know how long. Small, wind-formed ripples broke the beach's smoothness. To the north, a piece of driftwood and the wind combined to draw a comet and its tail in the sand. A ring-billed gull strutted near the surf, the only living thing on a long, brown table, endless and flat. The bright sea highlighted whitecaps and gulls. A ragged line of scoters flew by.

So I stood and stared, replacing memory with reality—at the end of my walk but still at its mid point. There ought to be somewhere to go but back, over the same ground. I stood, filled with all of my journeys to this place, with a familiar longing to stop time right there. But nothing remained but to turn my back on what I had come for, preserving the pleasure of turning towards it again. Walking back into the woods—trees and bushes rising around me: at my ankles, my waist, my shoulders—I sank from sight.

Back at the picnic table, I picked up one of the brown oak leaves. Its form lacked precision, uniformity. Its veins, through their branches, once joined the air with the stem, tempting me with an image of a journey back to life's source. But common sense reminds me the source is unattainable; a dead leaf is an isolated event. For answers, I find uncertainties: the irregularity of an oak leaf, disorder of pine needles and dead leaves, intermittent blue jay and chickadee calls, and the sun shining in random shapes on the ground.

Leaves fall; families scatter. Storms obscure at first, disrupting the turns and cycles we depend on. Driving west on the New York Thruway, I saw fields standing green without snow by the time I reached the valley of the Schoharie River. Everything returned to its place: autumn where it belonged, my car headed home, I to sit, alone, in my Lake Erie cottage at a table covered with an oilcloth the color of a Cape Cod fisherman's slicker. Through the window I'd watch another winter coming on—rain turning to snow, water to ice—waves and land calling to mind all the cycles that demand adjustments from me until I run out of ideas—then continue, perfectly, without me.

BETH SIMON

Widows and Dead Men

*I*N THE HOURS surrounding the Banaras sunrise, religious Hindus, and also tourists, come to the River Ganges. About twenty feet before the river bank, the street splits into two forks. The right is a progression of vegetable stalls, antique dealers, and narrow dark shops displaying herbs and powders, dried snake skins, chillum, stone vessels, skulls. The left fork has fruit vendors, cheap cloth, and the lepers. The street then rejoins to form a set of wide concrete steps that descend into the water. This is Dasashwamedh Ghat, the most popular of the bathing docks.

Both sides of the steps are lined with old people, most of them mothers or mothers-in-law, most of them widows. They have come, or were sent by their families, to die in Banaras. They sleep in ashrams, retreat houses, and in the beginning, they give donations to pilgrims, to yogis and renunciates, to the local and virtuous poor. After a year, or after two, the money from home stops, and except for begging, they live on the brief meal the ashram provides.

Each sunrise, they bathe, pray, settle on the steps. Some are knotted by arthritis into terrible shapes. Many are without teeth. Their skin is like rice paper, wrinkled and translucent from the hard light reflected off the river. They appear to be a hundred years old, bewildered, in pain. They wear cloth like winding sheets. Pass by them and their faces, like flowers, turn, and the turning is a breeze that whispers, *Please, Sister. Help, Daughter. Hear your Mother.*

The first few times I went to Dasashwamedh Ghat, I carried my cassette recorder in a shoulder bag with "Free Tibet" woven on one side, and a pool of loose change in my pockets. When I saw the women, I easily gave away every paisa, but got only halfway through the hands.

The next week, I prepared. At Godauliya Crossing, I purchased small items from street vendors and took my change in twenty paisa pieces. At the ghat, I came toward each woman respectfully, my footsteps soft, head bowed, eyes lowered. I distributed the money evenly, two coins per person. I said, "Namaste," to several who wore white widow's saris.

I doubt that anyone ever physically touched me, but there was a brushing, like moths, like clouds of mosquitoes, across the hem of my *kamiz*, across the billowy material of the legs of my *shalwar*.

Day after day, I thought of the widows on the right hand fork, and so I began to approach the ghat from the left. This route led me by the lepers. They sprawled against mounds of dirt and debris dredged up from the annual river reclamation. They looked like large bundles of rags. Their stumps, the nose holes and cheek bones exposed where the flesh had fallen away, were wrapped in cloth strips.

On the left fork, I dropped money onto tin plates and walked away quickly. I tried not to inhale. I had begun to see what was possible in this life. One day, a girl, glossy hair, smooth flesh, fifteen, sixteen years old, pushed a makeshift wheelbarrow so close to me that the edge nicked my calf. I almost fell onto the footless man tied to the wheelbarrow by string around his waist. The girl squatted beside him, took a chappati out of a dirty cloth and tore off a bite. When she fed it into the man's mouth, I saw she was missing two fingers.

I flung coins at them like gravel, yelled "Don't touch me," whipped around. The air was hot, black. I waved my arms like a landlocked bird. I wanted them all, the crippled, the eyeless, the thin bitter dying, to fly into the air like ash, blow away, leave the ghat silent, empty, clean.

I ran back along the left fork, then east along the right. I saw a shop and pushed through the beads.

Inside, the air was cool, the light like green glass filtered through gauze drapes. Two velvet Victorian jackets glowed secretly against the opposite wall. One was a rich garnet color, one a tight-waisted black with jet buttons. Immediately to the right of the door, a rosewood tea chest the size of an infant lay on a spindle-shaped pedestal carved from teak. I put my hand on the chest to steady myself, stroked the chest lid, and wept.

"From the Raj, Memsahib." The dealer glided forward. "The early days." He lifted the chest and held it out toward me. When I opened the lid, the room filled with the perfume of tea bushes in bloom. The dealer glanced out through the curtain of beads, then back at me. "May I send for refreshment?"

I shut the lid and patted it. "Very nice."

"Memsahib, it is beautiful, rare, flawless. The price is three thousand rupees."

I said, "Okay."

"Understand me," he put it back on the pedestal. "I am not one of the touts out there. I do not bargain."

"Good." I picked the tea chest up, and hugged it tightly. "Perfect."

I crossed the ghat. At a fruit stall I bought red bananas newly shipped from the Malabar Coast. I sent a little boy to hire a bicycle rickshaw. I peeled and ate a banana while I waited. I gave nothing to anyone.

When the rickshawallah pedaled up, he recognized me. "Now you do the good thing, my Sister. You are not the people to be walking."

One day my fieldworker, Nagender, was driving me across the Ganges to a town on the other side of the river. We stopped at a tea stall he liked, and he began telling me about a friend's death. The friend had gone to the wedding of a young girl, a sheltered girl of good family, a girl of their neighborhood. At the wedding, the friend had drunk too much. "And then," Nagender said, "he began saying disrespectful things about the bride. Bad things he seemed to think were jokes."

The tea stall owner came over to the jeep to offer me more tea. "He wouldn't leave. He wouldn't shut up. He picked a fight."

"He got beaten up." Nagender grinned. "And cut. He fell on something rusty." He pointed at the blue veins branching under his own wrist.

"What he got was tetanus." The tea stall owner scrubbed his

knuckles across his scalp. "Then lockjaw." He shook his head. "Go figure."

"Wait," I said. "Wait a minute." They both looked at me, as if I might have thought of something clever. "He didn't have shots? No one took him to a doctor?"

Nagender finished his tea and tossed the unbaked clay cup at a pariah dog up the street. "He insulted the bride, the bride's family. Everybody." He squeezed the ends of his mustache, shaping the long coarse hairs on each side into a point thick as a dogtooth. "And perhaps he didn't remember the cut." He hopped back up into the driver's seat of the jeep.

"When was the wedding?" I asked.

"Not so long ago." He started the motor and I climbed into the jeep.

Nagender introduced me to the administrator of a public hospital who escorted me on a tour of his building. One room held sixteen cots, four at each wall. We stood at the foot of the one occupied cot. A man fully clothed, sleeping or unconscious, lay on his back.

"My lockjaw ward," the administrator said. "See how I pity those such as this man?" He pointed up toward the ceiling. High on the walls, like an armada docked in an overcrowded harbor, framed photos and posters of gods and saints and famous teachers rubbed against each other at odd angles. There were the rulers of the universe: Shiva with his trident; Rama, Sita, and muscle-bound Hanuman, the monkey god; Blue Krishna played his flute to melt the milkmaids. Those born human, The Buddha, Swami Yogananda, The Mother, demonstrated the achievement of peace. Those still alive, like the Sikh champion of Khalistan, or a Muslim *Sant* of the district, looked down on us quizzically, and yet not without sympathy. A yellowed, curling print of Madonna with child was wedged in among them.

"You have gathered everyone," I said. "This is very kind."

The administrator shrugged. "What else can I do?" He nodded at the man on the bed. "I have no funds, no treatments. At least the wretches can call on their guru at the time of their crisis."

As if pulled by wires overhead, like a puppet, the man before us rose up involuntarily, howled, and convulsed.

In Banaras, it is easy to see someone die, easy to see them before and after. With the appropriate rags and body, a man can earn a living by falling down on the side of a street and acting out death throes. Sprawled in the dust, grey-faced and bony, he twitches and spits, and religious people who happen to be passing leave alms for the funeral.

Funeral processions come from all directions on the way to the burning ghats. Male relatives hold the stretcher shoulder high, and the mourners chant as they move through the streets. Once, when I was in a bicycle rickshaw, a procession coming the other way stopped for a moment. The stretcher was almost directly below me. On it lay something rolled up in white gauze, a lozenge, a pellet. A body. In Banaras I saw how a body is small. I learned how in death, we shrink.

I never doubted the purity of the Ganges, or the efficacy of bathing. I did not doubt that one can sluice the scales of defilement and knowledge into nothing. In Banaras, I learned what a river could do, and I wanted it, to submerge, rise, free from hope, from language, from this long and helpless series of mistakes.

But eventually, I stopped going to Dasashwamedh. I wanted to follow the others, but I didn't know how, and whenever someone asked me, "Where do you bathe?" I said, "I don't bathe at Dasashwamedh. Too crowded." And yet, I yearn for water, the shedding, like a psoratic skin, of horizon, the waking up, unconfined, finally beyond land.

Home as Eden's Picture Book
The Fiction of Sacred Space

*E*VER SINCE WE WERE banished from Eden, we've had trouble with drawers, closets, picking up socks. Clutter spills over, essentials disappear. *Have you seen my fountain pen?* Strange particulars materialize and mingle with the familiar. *Where did this key come from?* We just don't seem to be at home. Ever since we were cast out of the cozy Garden, we've been living out of a suitcase, taking up a spare room, expecting to go back home, back to the perfection which persistently eludes us. And so, ever since, we have been trying to make order and to begin again, to separate the water from the dry land, to chance upon a Center and—this time around—not eat of it. To locate the mates to our socks, to chance on the spoon for the marmalade, and to find our way Home.

Strangers in a strange land shouldn't be surprised that chaos will break out in a buffet drawer. I happen upon a pack of postcards, as maimed as an old poker deck. Stirring the back of a drawer for a pair of scissors, the rubber band crumbles and the postcards fan into my hand. *In what drawer did the First Couple keep the needle, the thread, the scissors, to sew their figleaves into garments?* The pictures are a commplace wish-you-were-here. I turn them over. The hunched and smudged writing is postcard genre: having-a-good-time-miss-you. Who saved them? Why? They're neither elegant nor rare. They were written to the same address, but they bear no stamps, no postmarks. No one stuck them in the mail. Perhaps Willm, the person who wrote but didn't send the raggedy postcards, was their persistent reader.

Should I snoop in someone else's correspondence, inscribed before I myself had ever licked a stamp?

I read them. Postcards, after all, cannot modestly hide their thoughts.

I'm as wrong about the wish-you-were-here as I am wrong about the having-a-good-time.

I spread them out on the polished wood of the dining room table. *Which of Eden's trees was felled to make a table for the seductive fruit?* Since the postcards are not dated, I attempt a chronology. *Once we left eternal Eden, we've been on the clock.* I try to start at the beginning, which is, of course, in the middle, the omphalos. If we cannot begin in the sacred Garden, then, at least to the heartland, the breadbasket. The beginning of this postcard story is an exile, too: someone had left home. And these were his letters back.

This first card surprises me as it is not about the amber-waves-of-grain on the picture, not about adventure, but about memory. It is nostalgic. Home is where we are not. The paltry news on the card laps over into the space for the address.

> Dear Mom,
>
> Remember how all the time you said we'd be like Doro-thy in that movie, would someday open a door & every-thing would be in color. Made no sense. I am sunburned. Guess you'd say I'm in color now. I'm having eggs in Kan-sas, but the cook says she never heard of Dorothy. Her name's Betty & she fried them with little burnt ruffles the way I always liked them. Betty says she wouldn't call Kansas home because she wants to leave it. She sat down & had coffee with me. Then I left.
>
> X. Willm.

Home, we want to say, is eggs crisp-edged in cast iron and served up on a blue willow plate. Ah, but wait: our hatchling scribe hinted at the *dis*comforts of home. He left Mom gazing into movies and Betty looking down the road. Anyone left at what we like to call home is hollowed out with longing for somewhere else, as lonely as the wanderers.

QUESTION: Is Sacred Place the receptacle for our nostalgia?

Dorothy traveled by tornado and magic slippers and hot-air bal-loon; and Willm was propelled by sunlight and eggs and black-eyed susans lining the road (she by wind and he by sun). Is it any wonder they both—by these atmospheric circulations—found themselves in that state of consciousness which might be called Oz? Oz: the distortion of the familiar into the strange, the disfigurement of the homely into the bizarre, the distention of the self into a character. Dorothy returned to a black & white home, a mundane version of the beautiful, peculiar Oz. But the story's sentimental choice was to put the eternal child back in waking, baking Kansas with pale Auntie Em rather than in her emerald dream of Oz. Willm left behind his childhood, (almost) sending his photochrome postcards back to drab home and gray Mom, the Mom who hoped to turn a corner onto color. *Kansas or Oz, which is more like a postcard of our First Home, Eden?*

The entire planet is Home, but the whole globe overwhelms the psyche. Who can feel at home with the mysteries of so many mansions? We comprehend only a minuscule portion of the planet, and from that circumscribed perspective, construct a Sacred Space. Those little picket fences around divine reality merely show up our resistance to seeing the sacred in unlikely places and our mourning for Eden. And whatever we call Home is a pack of memory's postcards, a picture book of Eden. *Make yourself at home, the God said, wearing his grandmotherly apron and cap, only pay no mind to that cookie jar.*

QUESTION: Is Sacred Place a vision of Home or pause on a journey?

It's not that There's No Place Like Home, rather it's that there are many places *like* home, but there is no place that is Home itself, the great old Garden. Sacred Place is a tabernacle set up by the side of the road, a makeshift tent, an ally-ally-outs-in-free, a circle drawn in the sand, a reminder of Eden, a home away from Home. It should not surprise us that the ancient Israelites built an entire tradition from nostalgia—the anxiety for the home that never was. Sacred Place casts the uncanny back upon the commonplace. Our great mythic images (dis)locate the baby Jesus out back of a No-Vacancy motel and the baby Moses in a soggy backpack. We are in flight or in flux. We reach back for Eden. *God pointed his accusatory finger past the Garden, and the First Couple covered their shamed parts—their faces— with their hands.* And perhaps that tension between the familiar and the strange describes the character of Sacred Place within the western tradition, a fictional garden of fruits and curses. Sacred Place is made up as much of dread as of serenity. Home may be a sentimental concept, but Sacred Space is not merely a repository of sentimentality. Home is where you feel so uneasy you leave, and Sacred Space is where you feel so queasy you draw a circle round it.

Maybe Willm's first postcard was not so chatty as the one he wrote in Kansas, maybe it was a more tentative cry from the wilderness. I choose another card as the beginning point of his quest, a picture of a giant Saguaro cactus with a little bird nesting under one of its elbows. On the back:

> Dear Folks,
> Just to let you know don't worry about me.
> Will write later.
> X. Willm.
> I am sorry I had to leave Billy at home.

When his adventure was nothing to write home about, still he wrote. Back in those literate days people recorded even their sense of nothing, or even their resistance to writing. *Was the Snake Eden's scribe before he lost his fingers to grasp his pencil and his knees to hold the paper steady? Who snatched up the story and carried it out from the Garden?*

QUESTION: Is the naming and marking of sacred space an artificial separation and the beginning of much trouble?

In Western experience sacred places spring up as secret recapitulations of the anxieties of Eden. All these sacred places point homeward, the primal Home from which we were banished. To imagine the perfection of Eden also conjures the Fall. One cannot compass a space as sacred without the double fears of stepping both into it and out of it.

Our vagabond Willm gestured homeward with his postcards. And it was Home, that least accessible place, not the brave new world, that became as vivid as memory, as dream. Home is a nostalgic invention. We can't get there from here. We can only remember it, map it, regret it. Invent it, erase it, pursue it.

> Working for a lady and her old father who gets around pretty good. The old father says you should never go to bed the same day you get up. Don't try to write me here. I'll be moving on one of these days. When I get a good payday.

I see that Willm did make his way to relatives and the comforts of home away from home. On the reverse of the world's largest rose bush (its root came from Scotland in 1885; its arbor covers over 6,000 square feet), he wrote:

> Dear Folks,
>
>> Don't ask me to come home. I know you wrote Mae and Aunt Mae & told them I'd get homesick. Aunt Mae says she got way more homesick when she tried to go back to her home. They had rented out her bed. I know you got word to Ed & told him to watch for me. He tried to give me $20 and ship me home. He did his part.
>
>> Love, Willm.
>
> Take Billy in the house, Mom. Please do.

Mae and Aunt Mae, Billy the dog and Willm the boy, a practical family of few words. The postcard is the eloquence of the reticent, traveling is a way of talking.

New York, New England, New Jersey—colonialist ways of naming place was renaming and may be a cry of homesickness as much as of conquest. Place is a collection of memories—a human imposition— upon the planet. A holy place is often a misremembering of what was there before. When Europeans invaded the Western hemisphere they tangled two myths: their European homes and their biblical home. They explored their "New English Canaan" (as it was designated in 1637) with an intent to reconcile old stories and old places to new hopes. America was (and is) an experiment in the creation of Sacred Space. America is a back door, a forced reentry into Eden. *The God called out, Where are you?*

Maybe Willm's epistles-never-mailed had the same purpose, to see a strange, new place as a counterpart photograph of faraway home, as a negative of Eden. Other, more nested, centered perspectives might not respond to Willm's adolescent-male version of sacred time and space. America is a heroic mounting of the mother, and thus the story of its Sacred Space comes with the taint of the adolescent's blindness. Europeans celebrated the continent as Paradise regained, although this time around they were going to have their way with it. *Eden as terrarium.*

QUESTION: Does Sacred Space conjure reality in the past, in Eden (or project us into the future, in Heaven)? Is it the rabbit-hole escape from our dull but frantic selves?

I look again at the picture postcards. They seem to celebrate and idealize the continent, just as the Europeans did in their early descriptions. Perhaps trivial postcards illustrate the ways in which we sentimentalize, personify, capture and miniaturize, mystify and moralize the world. *Eden as Skinner box—the animal presses the lever for food or to avoid a painful stimulus, a shock. Eden as sinner box.*

QUESTION: Does Sacred Space capture and personify, miniaturize, mystify and moralize? Does it make a holy postcard of place?

Once upon a time pilgrims journeyed from one holy spot to another, gathering up indulgences and bringing home stones, bones, and postcards (little images or prayers) for the cow to swallow when she took sick or Grandfather to keep under his pillow while he napped in the same room with Death. A fragment of a Sacred Place could be plundered to heal an afflicted one. Maybe Willm quested like a grail knight for a cure for the sickness back home. On the back of a field of poppies he had written,

> Dear Folks,
>
> I bet Mom will hang these flowers in the kitchen. It will make you think you are already in Spring and so your knee won't hurt, Pop. Ha Ha. It's always Summer here. It's always everything here, you find flowers and fruits on the same branch. You can walk down the road and a free meal drops right in your hat. Now if I can just find the tree that grows pies.
>
> X. Your son.

Did God or the Serpent tempt Eve with the first recipe for apple pie? Maybe the token floral curative was the first card Willm wrote. *The Man was restless at home in Eden, the God caused a sleep to fall upon him.*

QUESTION: Is it possible that the very concept of Sacred Space, of a set-apart place belonging to divine things, is a field of poppies?

The exclusivist Hebrew prophets, in establishing their pure monotheism, condemned gods, trees, beasts, and stones to oblivion. Jeremiah was the voice of a reform movement to abolish the contaminated authority of 'high places,' making Jerusalem the central and sole holy place. It was a political measure with implications, for all the generations following, to make us doubt the blessings of place. However, there is another iconoclasm, as that of Chuang Tzu, the great Taoist philosopher. He was asked, where is the Tao? He answered the humbug question, in the floor tile. And when his questioner protested, he said, in the shit on the tile. Jeremiah's iconoclasm was to purify, reform, centralize, ridding the sacred center of goddesses and trees, until his efforts were doomed as the Babylonians seized Jerusalem and the Jews had to learn to worship their God in a strange land, in the absence of Sacred Space, their divinely bestowed land. Conversely, we read Chuang Tzu's sensibility of the sacred as expansive or as an iconoclasm of inclusion, in which the absurdity of a special Sacred Space is countered by the joy of the divine, or the Tao, revealed both everywhere and nowhere. The Western delusion of division—that the sacred is found only in my own family narrative, or my own accustomed habits—may inhibit the ability to experience sacred awe, releasing the limitations of what we know and are. If place can be fenced in, then the sacred will mock the fence from outside the boundary.

But Willm's mom never got a chance to pin up the dazzling poppies of his good intentions; Pop's arthritic knee must have kept on aching, right along with their hearts, as they sneaked glances out the window for their son. Willm had taken himself to the South, all the while his head full of home all snowed in, like the glass paperweight he used to shake. *Does God ever revisit the Garden, walking up and down of an evening, missing his chicks, regretting their departure? Is Eden, like any other home, a cracked and emptied shell?*

QUESTION: Is Sacred Space a pit of errors, a place to throw in all our faults and plagues?

Sacred places might be hallowed as zones of renewal and asylum to escape the terrors of ordinary time. And, once in a while, even as a place for nature itself to heal. The area of the Kaaba stone in pre-Islamic times, when it was governed by the tree-clinging goddesses, was a sanctuary where criminals could not be apprehended, a refuge where animals were free from hunters, and a paradise where poets could sing. Had Willm rediscovered the Sacred Place when he scribbled on the back of a view of San Diego's Greyhound bus depot:

> I had a squirrel, a white-tail deer, pigeons, and a crow all
> eat out of my hand. They get as hungry as I do.

Maybe this is his first card, from before the Fall (and much as I am disappointed in the picture), the message is from Adam and the beasts.

No, I am wrong. Willm and the beasts are all hungry, all caught in time and desire. To hunger is to seek, is to be outside of Paradise. Landscape fetishists and phallic adventurers seek after a prelapsarian image, a pristine place which they can adore and celebrate their own conquering footfall in the virgin space. We like the spot where we fantasize we are the first, so that a holy point is more about an explorer than the place explored. The line America drew between civilization and wilderness has left the exiles ever wondering on which side of the divide is the sacred. Our Greyhound bus depots, too, Chuang Tzu would remind us, embody the Tao.

QUESTION: Is a space sacred because it lies where time's arrow does not pierce it?

Sacred Space and Home are alike because Nothing happens there, at Home or at the Sanctuary. Maybe these postcards compel me because they avoided postmarks and hid in a drawer, a small attempt at confounding time. They popped up from *illo tempore*, out of creation's sequence.

I rearrange the cards, letting this Willm tell his own skinny little fortune. Perhaps he began where Dante did, finding himself in the middle of a vast woods. So, I center the postcard with a forest scene. A bear silhouette made of a cutout of rabbit fur is pasted over snowy trees. A rabbit skin as a bear rug. A card made in Germany but labeled from Colorado. A sentiment never sent. Who knows where we are, how we are, who we are if we cannot ask those questions from the sanctified place called Home?

> Dear Pop and Mom.
>
> How are you? I am fine. You ought to be here, talk about excitement, we sure do have it here. Ha Ha. Went poaching with these guys and I brought down a four-point deer. Mountains are full of game. Might stay here, at least while the venison holds out. Ha Ha. Maybe I will come home soon one of these days for a visit. Love, Willm.

Bear. Rabbit. Deer. These were not the three beasts impeding Dante's journey, nor the three figures escorting Dorothy on the yellow brick road. *Adam was in Paradise with the Animals, he named them but found them unfit companions. Do the Animals beyond the gates of Eden remember the slight and keep their distance?* This postcard reminds me, though, how often we kill to consecrate. Which came first? Willm's postcards of the animals eating from his hand, or his eating the animals?

A stone will suffice if it is blood-stained, a mountain or a tree is a point of sacrifice, a chalice holds consecrated blood. We love bloody spots. Battlefields, murder scenes, lovers' leaps, Golgatha. Willm acted out a pageant of peril, like a bunny in a bear suit, like a rifle against a deer. Sacred Spaces often spring from the agonies and injustices of battlefields and disasters; the space is a text of a human drama. Historically, we like the place where blood was spilled. Drawings, likenesses, hides, carcasses, or blood of animals often serve to mark up the human's Sacred Place, paradoxical designators of the old unblemished hang-outs of gods. On the back of a snowy mountain peak, Willm wrote:

> Dear Mom,
>
> I didn't actually get to this place, but I thought you'd like the picture. Happy Birthday. Don't get any older 'til I get back. Ha Ha. I might show up one of these days.
>
> X. Willm

Home betrays us by changing, decaying. Whatever Shangri-la we go toward, we can't quite get there. And the road between Home and Paradise betrays us by failing to resemble closely enough the Kodachrome memory of a postcard.

All these random visions, yet some of these particular images must have compelled Willm as he meditated before spinning postcard racks. His postcards are like stumbling on little paper models of stones of witness. But he never went near a mailbox. *The trouble with Eden, Adam groused, was that there was nobody to send a greeting to, saying having a great time, wish you were here.* Willm meant to send them.

I wonder if Willm made one big circle around the country, or did he criss and cross? A hotel lobby with an expanse of plumed carpet brags, "One of San Francisco's newer fire-proof hotels."

> Mom,
>
> I wore out my shoes. I got some new ones. I stuck my feet in an x-ray machine they had in the store, you look right down at the skeleton wearing your shoes. Been thinking about that skeleton walking with me all day. Ha Ha. The city has everything you want. There's a machine

> for everything, gum, cigarettes, Coke, your Weight and
> Fate. X. Your Son.

The prodigal wrote on the back of a card with a line of "lovely can can girls":

> Dear M & P,
>   Can't believe you figured out how to get a letter to
> me. I got it. But some fella took my notebook & cash
> money and your letter. I guess he can read it awhile. I
> already read it a hundred times. After he spends my
> $50, he might look up your address & write you for some
> more. X. Your son.
>   Sorry to hear of Ed found dead of a Sunday, 3 pm.
> Sorry about your bum knee, Pop. I know the work is harder
> for you now. Sorry to hear the fever took Twila. Sorry
> about the Oldsmobile. Mom, you take Billy in the house
> by the fire when he gets cold.

QUESTION: Does the Western experience of Sacred Space cast a shadow?

That is, does the dualistic imagination of space demand an unholy for every holy? Those who uphold civilization presume a wilderness. Those who hate the city love the country. These boundary lines are a net thrown over the world; whatever we rope off as sacred space is a spurious geometry. Whatever we rope off from ourselves is even more suspect.

> I threw my voice down a well and lost my jacket today.
> X. Willm.

QUESTION: If place is sacred, will the individual self be extinguished there?

Can a place be sacred if it serves the fantasy of ownership? If the river is named for an administrator and the mountain range is labeled with the name of a fur-trader and killer, then is place a projection of ego rather than an apprehension of the sacred? Was Willm's journey sacred? Isn't it possible that part of his discovery of the sacred was of his own fragility and even irrelevance? The adolescent goes out in quest of himself, but the sacred hazard carries us beyond the self and beyond the mere particularity of place. The sacred journey relieves us of the ego self, does not gather up its souvenirs.

In the fictions of creation, can Sacred Space be appropriated by a technique, a strategy for pretending that nature's interest is the human psyche? But the notion of Sacred Space itself requires a human perspective. Currently, our collective psyche fantasizes a sacred that has not been touched by humans, yet sequestered for human meaning. The powers of animism have always allowed a salt lick, a quarry, a spring to manifest the divine. The Western religious tradition has squelched the animistic impulse, has relegated natural phenomena to inferior or evil categories, has looked to escape what it designated as Nature. Yet, the current backlash to the dualistic heritage inadvertently keeps to some of those suppositions by fetishizing nature.

There is no end to the making of sacred places. Sacred Place profoundly disrupts the complacency of its pilgrims. The paradox is this: a space can only be sacred by being named so, but once it is named and therefore becomes sacred, it has the power to eradicate the complacent ego self who has named it. And unless we are eradicated on the spot, then we are mere graffiti artists, fencing, staining, and defacing our own external psyche.

Willm, I see, leaves off from train-hopping and hitchhiking and begins to settle even as he gets wheels:

> Dear Folks,
>
> Plenty of work out here. Don't worry about me. I traded off this watch a gal gave me & by the time I got done I ended up owner of a panel truck with three pretty good tires. X, your son.
>
> If I ever get hold of some stamps, I will stick these in the mail.

He began to participate in the fantasy of ownership, a fall from the encounter with the sacred.

Can we embroider our homily, Home Sweet Home, on Jacob's stony pillow? In Genesis Jacob lay down his head upon an old sacred spot of the Canaanites, and captured it by the Hebraic warfare of storytelling, that is, appropriating a place, renaming, unremembering, making a story go another way. The place had been called Luz (meaning 'almond tree') and he renamed it Bethel (God's house). The place had been Canaanite, the story steals it, making it Israelite. But what was the story of the almond tree? Another sacred tree logged off our collective memory. Jacob oiled the stone upon which he had laid his head, but his dream was a ladder to the realm of angelic beings. Most of the forms of biblical religion hold more firmly to the dream ladder than to oil and stone, foregoing the centrality of place for a trail of disconnected narrative.

QUESTION: Is there is no Home? And therefore, is Sacred Space an illusion of the discontent?

Biblical tradition tells of a nomadic people who are promised the home of someone else—they trash or usurp the old sacred places they come upon. But even more important to the Western scriptural tradition than the claiming and renaming of the Land of Milk and Honey is the story of the loss of that land, more precisely, the terror of the loss of that land's memory. After 586 BCE, when the people of Judah were finding out whether they could worship Yahweh in a strange land, and then especially after 70 CE, when the diasporic Jews had to relocate their lost Jerusalem from land to text, the Western imagination has been camping out in a sleeping bag, the god coming to rest in any tent we put up, expressing an anxiety of place deep as our bones and our alphabet. Our sacred experience has been a double claim, first to build a home in memory, and then to proclaim we do not need to be home in it. As rabbinic sages advised, "If there is a famine in the city, scatter your feet; and if one is unfortunate in one place, let him go to another place."

QUESTION: Is Sacred Place in tension with the concept of Home?

> Dear Mom and Pop,
>
> Your picture got wet. Felt bad. So this lady I stayed with gave me a picture of her folks. Look almost like you. So now be glad you are better dressed. But I remember you. The parents in the picture didn't have a dog, so I drew in Billy Boy beside them. I mean beside you.
>
> X. Willm.

Home is another name for amnesia.

We can't quite recall the Garden's inviting tree and ripe fruit, nor the compelling Mother of All Living, but maybe remember the tempting Serpent, original home-dweller entwined in his tree, born as crafty as we were born naked. *In the center of the Garden, more than ripe fruit, was the tattletale Snake.* The myth of the Garden continues to generate the nature we seek and know, which means we cannot be Home.

QUESTION: Is Home itself perceived as an assault on nature and thus we are always interlopers, ill at ease?

Home may be where the hearth is; if only we can, in time, make home where the earth is. The sacred is a smudge on our fantasy of nature, a text written over a dream place.

> Dear Pop & Mom,
>
> I slept on an ancient burial. There's this guy digging them up fast as he can cause the dam's going to flood them. It's against the law to dig them up but not to drown them. He gave me some beads, so I'll bring you some ghost beads. I wonder if the Indians will haunt me or take care of me. Some people around here say the Indians should never have made their graveyard where the dam's got to go. Willm.

The politics as well as poetics of land is the creating and making (and eradicating) of memory. Between the sacred, the capitalist opportunity, the anthropological site, the law, and the tourist's curiosity, is a labyrinth of one point. Between the grave robber and the holy pilgrim is a fine point.

QUESTION: Does death give life to Sacred Space?

These postcards make me think that Willm wanted to shrink all his discoveries and ship them back home, to slip all the rest of the world into Home's pocket. (What else could a sacred place be, but all the mysteries of the universe folded into the pocket of one's own back yard?) His postcards encapsulated and packaged the world as gifts for the Home he himself had abandoned. Stitched to the end of one card is a doll-size cotton bag of salt "From the Great Salt Lake." On the message side our scribbler had noted,

> I caught a fish in my shirt and cooked the fish over a fire and got a clean shirt in the bargain. X Willm.
>
> No news. Will write later.

From the other end of the country and attached to another a packet of seeds, a "Seeds'n Greetings For Your Memory Garden." POSTMASTER PLEASE HAND CANCEL. "When you grow Mayflower seedlings you will be following the example of the Pilgrims who grew them over 300 years ago." *Did the God who banished the First Couple, the God who sewed clothes for them, tailor pockets into their Animal skins? What stone or seed did we purloin from Paradise?* A scrap of Eden by the side of the road. The Pilgrims reestablished Paradise, which they thought required razing the Garden and transplanting some of the old world by the sweat of the brow. Perhaps this Mayflower card was the first in Willm's series, the maiden in his voyage:

Mom,

I met this girl named Cindy who wanted to go back East to her folks. Car broke down and we broke up. But I kept going East anyway. Cindy got on the train, I never met up with her again. Your loving Willm.

But I see that his broken heart mended. I wonder if this is the card that ceased his wandering:

Mom,

Guess what. I'm engaged. Her name is Sylvia. I told her she'll have to wait for a diamond. She wears a ring her Dad gave her made from a piece of the plane that killed Will Rogers. Her folks live in Point Barrow, Alaska where he went down. Willm.

Suppose Adam had posted a valentine to Eve—'Roses are red, bone of my bones, Wherever you wander will be my homes'—and invented time and space as well as love?

I shuffle the cards again and begin to arrange in reverse order, looking for the last of the series. On the back of a picture of the Chrysler Building Willm wrote what could have been his finale:

I visited the Empire State Bldng. Went right to the top. Had a penny made into a good luck piece for you. This machine squashes a penny into a prayer.

Where is that good-luck penny compressed and metamorphosed into an embossed prayer? Where are the Indian burial beads? Where on Willm's journey did they slip through a hole in his pocket? And when another child found them, did that accidental place become sanctified? Maybe they're all in that buffet drawer. Where's that ring made of Will Rogers's crashed plane?

QUESTION: Can place carry memory? Is place a collection of memories—a human imposition? Then, is Holy Place a misremembering of what was there before?

Sacred Place is an artificial designation, an imposed story upon the eloquence of silence. Home is a false memory. A postcard is a conventional way of satisfying the expected. The road unfurls, sacred space is not a destination, but a network of promises and remembrances, a going to and fro upon dreams. The spring snaps and catapults a child into adult, and puts distance between past and present. Until the child flees from home, there is no time, no past tense. Until we leave home, there is no time. It's always a present tense which has the vaguest past (a before I existed) and a vaguer future (when I get big). Cast out of the Garden, all the adventures begin—sex and death.

> Pop,
>
> You should get a load of this tree. It is older than Jesus. We really drive the car right through, this is not a trick picture. Happy Birthday. Think of me waving to you from there. Made me think of when you said there's nothing you can't do if you put your mind to it. Love, your son.

Willm found the so-called Natural Cathedral with rhyming plaques nailed to ancient redwoods, with souvenirs for sale. "Sink down. Oh traveler, on your knees, God stands before you in these trees." *The God said, lest they make a tunnel through the tree of life and drive through it, I will drive out the man.* If we are so careless with our sacred places, how will we learn to tend the gardens beyond the gates? In some sense the making of Sacred Space gives insidious permission to desecrate the rest of the planet. When no place is sacred then all can be resacralized, then the planet and ourselves can be rescued from our greed and carelessness. Until we turn the myth inside out, our knowledge of sacred space will be misplaced— precisely because it names a place as sacred, thereby betraying the rest of the planet. Sacred Place itself, as western culture has designed it, implies that the rest of space is sullied or inferior. But America is a remythologizing enterprise, knitting together the separate ways of dwelling in the sacred: the exaltation of a walled garden, Paradise, and the inspiration of wandering in the wilderness and sending post-cards back. The fantasy of America lets us wander and pollute like lost souls in the midst of the Tree of Knowledge and the Tree of Good and Evil. Perhaps we can reconsider the drawbacks of nationalism when we consider the varieties of sacred spaces. *The real estate of the Garden is vast. Why are things spilling out of drawers?*

Maybe the last card Willm wrote is this one, oblivious that Death's entrance coincides with the First Couple's exit:

> I went out to the fountain of youth but I am plenty young yet so did not take a bath in it. Ha Ha. Everybody is treating me swell. Plenty work of all kinds.

QUESTION: Is the making of a Sacred Space just another name for subduing the earth and having dominion over it?

If we ever do get back to Eden, we'll start remodeling. We'll need more storage space for all the memorabilia. *Can't leave the socks and magazines scattered among the trees of Paradise; can't have a missing pen fallen among the heaps of ripe fruit.* And when, in the return, Eden is cluttered with memories, where will we keep all the old postcards? But could we be in Paradise if we had a memory—postcards—from our exile, our wandering? Will it, after all, feel just like being on the road, camped in our makeshift homes, drawing circles on the earth? Isn't the return to Eden, the Homecoming, to find that, after all, we never left the Garden and all the earth is sacred?

Well, what if we should return to Eden and find the snake's socks strewn all over the garden, unable to find a use for them since he'd been cursed to crawl? Did everything have its place in Eden? Except for desire, willfulness, cleverness? Is Sacred Space the picture of order? Symmetry, concord, everything in its place, is the creation of place. Our sacred impulse, though, is the meandering of story.

Do we impose order and intention where there is none? The postcards bear seemingly random images . . . a country church in Ohio, the train station in Butte, Montana, generic palm trees, an anonymous coffee shop with red leatherette booths and chrome-legged tables. In Genesis, as in other cosmogonies, creation of space is really the creation of order—of relationship and proportion—lurking in chaos. Willm gathered up brightly-lit city nights, trains, antebellum beauties, a ghost town, bridges, and usually, no news but his own longing:

> It is still drizzling this morning. Feels like I've been here before. But you know I haven't.

QUESTION: Is Sacred Space the illusion of returning Home and "to arrive where we started and know the place for the first time"?

Willm discovered the Tree of Life over and over again on his journey. He collected an image of a tree growing out of solid rock, with an iron fence squaring off the amorphous rock and spindly tree. *Eve looked back over her shoulder and said, If I worry about the Angel with the flaming sword guarding the gates of Eden, it's only that the forest of Eden would be ignited. If Eden's forest burns and we are not there to see it, has anything at all happened to Paradise? If the tree falls is it still Eden?*

Sacred Place is the placing of persons. On the back of a postcard portrait of Saltwater, Navaho Medicine Man, Willm wrote:

Dear Folks,

*I'm staying with a guy who's lived in the same place
for thirty years but kept me up all night talking about
Back Home.*

X. Your Rambling Man.

A place is a layered text—with a Native American name for its river, a murmur of pre-Columbian existence; a French name for a town, an assertion of early interference (called explorers or missionaries); a street map full of English names come to own and govern; a burst of renewed energy with foods offered from semblances of Mexican, Indian, Tai, Italian, and Chinese menus, children spill over the streets trailing remnants of African, northern European, middle Eastern gestures. What is the difference between a tourist stop and a pilgrimage site, between exile and adventure? Each summer my grandmother asks me to come home, although we are separated by two generations of adult households. And she, when I am there with her, speaks of Back Home, a remote but vivid Eden of her memory. Home is spread out upon the earth.

QUESTION: If Sacred Space demands a boundary line, what about the "something there is that doesn't love a wall"?

A silly card of a giant clam with a cartoon smile carries Willm's incongruous message:

*I slept by the sea. The sun went down. Then all the
colors sank and I went with them. The tide woke me up.*

This, I think, must be the last card our reborn boy wanted to send, his mystical experience of singularity and unity. Amidst all the ways we scatter our treasures and heap up our leftovers, once in awhile we come to a place in which all reality converges—the sacred. We might fall into a place which does not need human perspective, name, or honor, but a place which bleeds, weeps, seeps its own presence, a place which gives itself away—the holy. And that place might be anywhere and everywhere. Willm seems not to have run out of luck or continent. He makes it all his home, and all his picture book of Eden.

QUESTION: Does the naming of Sacred Space pretend that all the rest of the universe exists for my sake, even if I defer that arrogance by claiming I am solely for God's sake?

And once Willm settled in and made a home—with Sylvia or Cindy—maybe he pawed through these cards, the ephemera of his memories. And he made a sacred text of wandering in the realm of the sacred, in no place, unattached. Or maybe he recalled the home he abandoned. Or maybe he remembered his encounter with the uncanny, paraphrased in his postcards, in the face of an alligator, a train, a silver-gowned girl reflected in a pond.

QUESTION: Is Sacred Space necessarily in text—in memory and imagination—and all terrafirm versions are imitations?

Any spot at all will do. Place is time's souvenir. Time is place's storytelling. All we have to do is charge admission, or erect the golden arches, or repeat a story there, or X-mark the spot. The sacred is the X, the texting of place.

Willm's postcard confessions pin his heart upon his wanderer's sleeve. Merely garden-variety sentiments, yet they echo that deep longing for the Garden. By means of these flimsy pasteboard pictures any place would channel sacrality for Willm; and any unlikely tabernacle—a courthouse, a haphazard pioneer museum, a petrified forest—is a glimpse into unmediated reality. Any place that is photographed, recalled, even paused before, becomes a Sacred Space.

Perhaps there is a fundamental tension within these points on the map of our cultural psyche. And thus, Home, Sacred Space, and Eden all shadow as well as magnify one another, and wherever we go we could hang our hat, but wherever we sleep we dream of a mysterious place.

I suddenly glimpse a peculiar light in my back yard. I have never before seen the rain fall in such shimmery waves. It is not raining in the front yard. In the back yard it rains in glistening curtains. How strange the familiar can be. How numinous. As Willm once wrote in indelible pencil, "It feels like I've been here before, but you know I haven't."

QUESTION: Does the making of Home and the creation of Sacred Space form a triangle with the unknown point of lost Eden?

QUESTION: Or is it that we well remember Eden and that we recognize our Sacred postal-card Places, both of which might help us find our way back Home?

QUESTION: Or is it that we can know our way Home and our way back to Eden, and that these will compass us toward the holy, and will discover the location of the unknown, Sacred Space?

I get another rubber band, wrap the postcards, put them back in that drawer. We scatter our feet, are not at Home, are no longer in Eden, and in the interim we are unable to keep a boundary on the Sacred.

KATHLEEN NORRIS

Getting to Hope

To GET TO HOPE, turn south off U.S. Highway 12 at Keldron, South Dakota. It's easy to miss, as the town is not much more than a gas station and general store with a well-kept house behind it, and a sign announcing that Cammy Varland of Keldron was Miss Teen South Dakota of 1987.

Turn onto the gravel section-line road and look for a wooden map on your right. Built by the Busy Beavers 4-H Club, it has the mysterious yet utilitarian air of the seashell, twine, and bamboo maps that South Sea islanders once made for navigational purposes. The Keldron map consist of wooden slats painted with names and numerical inscriptions. Peterson 8 s 4 E 1 N indicates that you would drive eight miles south, four miles east, and one mile north to find the Peterson ranch.

The small metal sign for Hope (13 s) may or may not be up. The wind pulls it down and it can be a while before someone notices and reattaches it. But you don't need directions; just follow the road south and turn when it turns 90 degrees west, then another 90 degrees south, and then it's just another mile or so.

Ten and a half miles along the road, at the crest of the second hill, you'll be able to see where you're going, a tiny ark in a sea of land that unfolds before you for nearly fifty miles. At night you can see the lights of Isabel, South Dakota, some forty-five miles south, and Bison, about the same distance to the south-west.

The breaks of the Grand River are visible, land crumpled like brown paper. The river itself lies at the base of the steep cliffs it has carved into the prairie, sandstone glinting in the morning sun. *Paha Sunkawakan Sapa,* or Black Horse Butte, is a brooding presence on the horizon south of the river.

You will pass a few modest homes and farm buildings along the way, some in use, others in disrepair. The most recently abandoned, a classic two-story farmhouse, has boarded-up windows and an extensive but weed-choked corral. A house abandoned years ago is open to the elements, all its windows and most of its shingles gone. A large shelterbelt, planted in the 1930s, is now a thicket of dead trees. Once the trees are gone the house will lean with the wind until it collapses; but that will be a while.

Like the others who have business in Hope, I know who left; I know why. Every time I pass the abandoned houses I am reminded of them. "Hope Presbyterian Church is located by itself on the South Dakota prairie," is what the church history says. But that doesn't begin to tell it. Hope Church, which fifteen years ago had a membership of 46, is down to 25 today, scattered on ranches for thirty miles around. The loss is due to older farmers retiring and moving to town, and younger farmers leaving the area.

Hope Church is an unassuming frame building that stands in a pasture at the edge of a coulee where ash trees and berry bushes flourish; chokecherry, snowberry, buffalo berry. The place doesn't look like much, even when most of the membership has arrived on Sunday morning, yet it's one of the most successful churches I know. Along with Center School, the one-room schoolhouse that currently serves nine children from Grand Valley, Riverside, and Rolling Green townships in south-west Corson County, Hope Church gives the people who live around it a sense of identity.

"It doesn't matter what religion they are," says one longtime member. "The Lutherans and Catholics tell us that Hope is important to them, too, and becoming more so. We're *the church* in the neighborhood." A former pastor said of Hope Church, "It seemed that whatever was going on, a farm sale or a funeral or wedding, Hope was a part of what happened in that community." A measure of this may be seen at the annual Vacation Bible School for children, which is attended by both Lutheran and Catholic children.

The current church was built by its members in 1961 on the cement foundation of an old barn. But its roots go back to 1916, when people gathered for Sunday worship in the dance halls of the small settlements at White Deer and Glad Valley. "Church wasn't awfully regular in the horse and buggy days," says an older member of Hope, the son of one of the founders. "The ministers at McIntosh or Thunder Hawk were circuit riders then, and it could take them half a day to get down to us." Neither congregation ever had a church building. Until they merged in 1950, one congregation met in a one-room school, and the other in a hall that served as a community center where baby showers, funeral luncheons, wedding dances, and anniversary celebrations are also held.

Hope is well cared for. Both the outhouse and the sanctuary are freshly painted. Two small, attractive stained glass windows depicting a cross in the center of a sunburst and a dove with an olive branch flying over a landscape that resembles the fields around Hope Church were recently added to the south wall behind the pulpit, placed on either side of a handmade cross of varnished wood. The elegantly curved oak pews with carved endpieces are hand-me-downs from a church in Minnesota. A member of Hope drove his grain truck more than three hundred miles to get them.

Hope has a noble and well-used upright piano whose sound reminds me of the honky-tonk pianos in Western movies. But when Carolyn plays her quiet-down music at the beginning of a service, "Shall We Gather at the River" or "Holy, Holy, Holy," she's as effective as a Russian Orthodox deacon striding sternly through a church with censer and bells. We know it's time now to listen, that we will soon take our journey into word and song, and maybe change a little along the way. By the time we're into our first hymn, we know where we are. To paraphrase Isaiah 62, it's a place no longer desolate but delightful.

There is no indoor plumbing at Hope, but the congregation celebrates with food and drink at every opportunity. Once, when I arrived on Sunday, I noticed several popcorn poppers in a back pew. That was for after church, to help everyone get through the annual congregational meeting. Once, Hope gave me a party with homemade cake, coffee and iced tea, and Kool-Aid in big coolers that the men carried into the basement.

In the manner of the other tiny country churches I know (United Tribes in Bismarck and Saint Philip's in Maili, Hawaii) Hope is such a hospitable place that I suspect that no matter who you are or where you come from, you will be made to feel at home. But don't get so comfortable that you underestimate the people around you; don't entertain for a moment the notion that these farmers and ranchers are quaint country folk. Most of them have college degrees, though the figure is down slightly from 85 percent in the mid-1980s, a statistic that startled the pastor, who had last worked in Scranton, Pennsylvania, where 3 percent of her congregation was college educated.

Hope's people read, and they think about what is going on in the world. If you want to know anything about agriculture on a global scale—the cattle market in Argentina or prospects for the wheat crop in Australia—this is the place to ask. As one pastor recently put it,"the thing that makes Hope so vibrant is that the congregation is so alive to the world."

Hope's members take seriously their responsibility as members of the world's diverse and largely poor human race. A few years ago, reasoning that people who raise food (and often have a hard time getting a price for it that covers their expenses) should know more about why so many in the world can't afford to feed themselves, they conducted a study of the politics of hunger. To conclude the study they invited an expert on the subject to come from Chicago to address churchpeople in the area. They also studied the ethical issues of raising animals for food. As ranchers who know the life history and temperament of every cow in their herds, they were dismayed to discover the inroads factory farming had made in American agriculture.

In recent hard times, while Hope's membership declined by nearly half, the amount the church donates for mission has increased every year. It now ranks near the top in per capita giving among Presbyterian churches in the state of South Dakota.

One former pastor said, "It can be astonishing how tiny Hope Church makes you feel so strongly that you're part of a global entity." This is a long tradition at Hope. A rancher whose three daughters spent several years in ecumenical church work in Sydney, Paris, Rome, and Brussels says, "Our girls always knew that the world was bigger than just us. They had cousins who were missionaries in China in the 1950s and 1960s. In those days missionaries got every seventh year off, and they'd stay with us on the ranch. Our children grew up hearing stories about other places."

For this and other reasons pastors find the Hope congregation stimulating to work with. One told me if he could sum them up in one word it would be "appreciative." Another said, "Hope was where I realized how much the members of a rural church actually work as well as worship together. They live supporting each other. We'd spoken of such things at seminary, as an ideal, but this was the first time in twenty years of ministry I'd actually seen it done. It made me realize how vital a small country church can be."

Perhaps it's not surprising that so tiny a rural congregation is not often well served by the larger church of which it is a part. For all their pious talk of "small is beautiful," church bureaucrats, like bureaucrats everywhere, concentrate their attention on places with better demographics: bigger numbers, more power and money. The power of Hope Church and country churches like it is subtle and not easily quantifiable. It's a power derived from smallness and lack of power, a concept the apostle Paul would appreciate, even if modern church bureaucrats lose sight of it.

In the manner of country people everywhere (and poets also for that matter) the people at Hope tend to be conservators of language. Once, when I found myself staggering through a benediction provided by the denomination that, among other things, invited us to "authenticate the past," I stopped and said, "I'm sorry, but that's ridiculous English." Laughter became our benediction that morning.

Like most small churches in the western Dakotas, Hope must be yoked to another, larger church in order to afford a full-time pastor. When Hope's sister church in Lemmon, thirty miles away, received memorial money to purchase a new Presbyterian hymnal that includes many contemporary hymns and more inclusive language, Hope decided to stay with their 1955 model. Not because its members aren't progressive. It's a relatively youthful congregation, in fact, with nary a fundamentalist bone among them. But the old hymnal works well for them, and many of their standards are not included in the new book: "I Need Thee Every Hour" and "I Love to Tell the Story" (which, not surprisingly, has been a favorite of mine since childhood), and "Nearer, My God, to Thee." That last hymn was a revelation to me when I first came back to church. Like many people, I couldn't think of it without picturing the band on the Titanic in *A Night to Remember*. I was pleased to discover that the hymn is an evocative retelling of the story of Jacob's dream.

As one pastor of Hope, a graduate of Princeton seminary, said to me, "Church intellectuals always want to root out the pietistic hymns, but in a rural area like this those hymns of intimacy are necessary for the spiritual welfare of people who are living at such a distance from each other." He added, "City people want hymns that reassure them that God is at work in the world, but people in the western Dakotas take that for granted."

The conflict between urban and rural theologies is an old one in the Christian church. Back in fourth-century Egypt, the Bishop of Alexandria, at the urging of intellectuals smitten with Greek philosophy, announced as church doctrine that when you pray you must not have any picture of God in your mind. One old monk is reported to have wept, saying, "They have taken away my God, and I have none I can hold now, and know not whom to adore or to address myself." Some monks took to their boats and traveled the Nile to Alexandria, where they rioted in front of the bishop's palace until he recanted. Hope's people have been more quiet about letting the greater Church go its way.

I find it ironic that the new inclusiveness of the official church tends to exclude people as rural as those of Hope. But I may have been spoiled by the company I keep on the prairie, the Benedictine monks and country people, some well educated, some not, who know from their experience that prayer is important, that worship serves a purpose, that God is part of everyday life, and that singing "Nearer My God, to Thee" may be good for a person. It's a rural hymn: it's the rare city person who can imagine sleeping out in the open, a stone for a pillow and a heaven of stars above.

Maybe we're all anachronisms in Dakota, a bunch of hicks, and the fact that the images in many old hymns, images of seed and wheat, planting and reaping, images as old as the human race and as new as the harvest in the fields around Hope Church, really aren't relevant any more. Twenty-five Presbyterian farmers, or a handful of monks for that matter, don't have much to say to the world.

And yet I wonder. I wonder if a church like Hope doesn't teach the world in the way a monastery does, not by loudly voicing its views but by existing quietly in its own place. I wonder if what Columba Stewart, a contemporary Benedictine, has said about such earthy metaphors, that "the significance of field, vineyard and garden metaphors in biblical and post-bibilical texts . . . lies beyond their relevance to the agricultural economy of ancient peoples," really means that our urban civilization surpasses such metaphors at its peril. As Stewart says, "these images describe the process of human cultivation," and as such they may be an essential part of being human, and of being religious in a human way.

Does the city, any city, need Hope Church? Does America need people on the land? In the last volume of Ole Rolvaag's *Giants in the Earth* trilogy a country pastor, addressing Norwegian farmers in Dakota who are losing their "old country" ways, and in fact are eager to lose them in order to become good Americans, declares that "a people that has lost its traditions is doomed." He adds:

> If this process of leveling down, of making everybody alike . . . is allowed to continue, America is doomed to become the most impoverished land spiritually on the face of the earth; out of our highly praised melting pot will come a dull . . . smug complacency, barren of all creative thought . . . . Soon we will have reached the perfect democracy of barrenness. . . . Dead will be the hidden life of the heart which is nourished by tradition, the idioms of language, and our attitude to life. It is out of these elements that character grows.

The process of acculturation to American life has traditionally been accelerated in cities; it takes more time for rural people to change. But Rolvaag's pastor is as relevant as the contemporary debate about multiculturalism. "If we're to accomplish anything worthwhile," he says, "we must do it as Norwegians. Otherwise we may meet the same fate as corn in too strong a sun."

I wonder if roles are now reversed, and America's urban majority, native born or not, might be seen as immigrants to a world of asphalt and cement, and what they need more than anything is access to the old ways of being. Access to the spirits of land and of place. The image of a democracy of barrenness rings true when one turns on the television and finds bland programs designed for the widest possible audience, or when one drives a busy freeway or walks through an airport parking garage, places that are no place, where you can't tell by looking if you are in Tulsa or Tacoma, Minneapolis or Memphis.

The sense of place is unavoidable in western Dakota, and maybe that's our gift to the world. Maybe that's why most Americans choose to ignore us. Upward mobility is a virtue in this society; and if we must keep moving on, leaving any place that doesn't pay off, it's better to pretend that place doesn't matter. But Hope Church, south of Keldron, is a real place, a holy place; you know that when you first see it, one small building in a vast land. You know it when you walk in the door. It can't be moved from where it is on the prairie. Physically, yes, but that's beside the point.

Hope's people are traditional people, country people, and they know that the spirits of a place cannot be transported or replaced. They're second-, third-, and fourth-generation Americans who have lived on the land for many years, apart from the mainstream of American culture, which has become more urban with every passing year. Hope's people have become one with their place: this is not romanticism, but truth. You can hear it in the way people speak, referring to their land in the first person: "I'm so dry I'm starting to blow," or "I'm so wet now I'll be a month to seeding."

A pastor who was raised on a farm in Kansas said he thought what made Hope special was that the members were "all, or nearly all, totally dependent on the land." He didn't seem to mind that church attendance got sparse at haying time and at calving, which is a round-the-clock operation for most ranch families; every three hours or so someone must check the pregnant heifers. The fact that this often coincides with brutal spring blizzards doesn't help; newborns can freeze to death in a matter of minutes.

"I spent some time on trail rides with Hope's ranchers," the pastor said, "and also helped at lambing. But they were a bigger help to me than I was to them. To touch the earth, the real earth once again, restored my soul."

I once heard Martin Broken Leg, a Rosebud Sioux who is an Episcopal priest, address an audience of Lutheran pastors on the subject of bridging the Native American–white culture gap. "Ghosts don't exist in some cultures," he said, adding dismissively, "They think time exists." There was nervous laughter; we knew he had us. Time is real to us in America, time is money. Ghosts are nothing, and place is nothing. But Hope Church claims by its very existence that place has meaning in and of itself. You're still in America in the monastery, and in Hope Church—these absurd and holy places— you're still in the modern world. But these places demand that you give up any notion of dominance or control. In these places you wait, and the places mold you.

Hope is small, dying, and beautifully alive. It's tribal in a way, as most of its members are related. But it does not suffer from tribalism, the deadening and often deadly insularity that can cause groups of people to fear or despise anyone who is not like them. I find in Hope many of the graces of a monastery, with stability of place and a surprisingly wide generosity in its hospitality.

It was hospitality that allowed the people at Hope to welcome me as a lay pastor. It was absurd for me to be giving sermons to them, the only person in the room who hadn't been to church in the past twenty years. I had little experience of the Bible apart from childhood memories; no training in either scripture studies or homiletics. What could I possibly say to these people about scriptures they had been absorbing all their lives?

I did what I could, and my long apprenticeship as a poet served me well. I didn't preach much, in the traditional sense of the word; instead I stayed close to those texts, talking about the stories I found there and how I thought they might resonate with our own stories. And I got some thoughtful and encouraging response. I followed the lectionary for discipline, but got a laugh one Sunday when I mentioned that I'd chosen to ignore the advice I'd found in a guide for pastors, that one shouldn't try to connect the Old Testament, Gospel, and Epistle texts but concentrate instead on one brief passage. I said that telling a poet not to look for connections is like telling a farmer not to look at the rain gauge after a storm.

Preaching sermons was a new and unnerving experience for me, and having the people at Hope to work with was my salvation. They made it easier for me to do in those sermons what I saw I had to do, that is, disclose myself in ways different from those I was used to, hiding behind the comfortable mask of fiction. The "I" in a poem is never me—how could it be? But the "I" in my sermons came closer to home, and that was risky. "That's why we appreciated you," one Hope member told me.

I got to try out my sermons first at Hope, as the Sunday morning service there is at 9:00 A.M. and the one in town is at 11:00 A.M. More than once I finished at Hope by asking, "Can I get away with saying this in town?" Once a woman replied, "That depends on how much faith you have," which was a good answer, as the Gospel text that day was the story of Jesus hollering at his disciples in the middle of a storm, "Why are you so afraid?" The church in town had been through a stormy period a few years back, and my sermon was an attempt to help put those bad times to rest. I knew that if I had misjudged, I would only stir things up again.

I began to find that Hope Church opened doors for me the way that Benedictine monasteries had, and it offered similar surprises. Every time I read the scriptures aloud in the Sunday service at Hope I became aware of sparks in those texts that I had missed in preparing my sermon, and that was a wonderful experience for a poet to have, as it said much about the power of words to continually astonish and invigorate us, and even to surpass human understanding.

Monks, with their conscious attempt to do the little things peaceably and well—daily things like liturgy or chores, or preparing and serving meals—have a lot in common with the farmers and ranchers of Hope. Both have a down-to-earth realism on the subject of death. Benedict, in a section of his *Rule* entitled "Tools for Good Works," asks monks to "Day by day remind yourself that you are going to die," and I would suggest that this is not necessarily a morbid pursuit. Benedict is correct in terming the awareness of death a tool. It can be humbling, when we find ourselves at odds with another person, to remember that both of us will die one day, presumably not at one another's hands. If, as Dr. Johnson said, "the prospect of being hanged in the morning wonderfully concentrates the mind," recalling our mortality can be a healthy realism in an age when we spend so much time, energy, and money denying death.

But maybe denying death is something people need to do. One might even look at a medieval cathedral as an expression of that need. Those buildings, however, were also made for celebrating life with music and art, with the play of light and shadow on stone and colored glass. They are beautiful in ways that modern exercise machines and lifestyles leading to that tofu-in-the-sky are not.

Tofu is still a novelty at Hope; people there obtain their protein from animals they raise on land that is suitable for nothing else. I learned at Hope Church just how profoundly the activities of farming and ranching, working the land and working closely with animals, affect the way people approach matters of life and death. Preaching in both a town and a country church, I found that the hard texts of Advent—texts about waiting, about judgment and last things—were accepted in the country while in town there was already pressure to start celebrating Christmas.

When the great wheel of the lectionary came round to the text in

Isaiah that begins, "Comfort ye, comfort ye my people," and reminds us that "all flesh is grass," I preached a sermon at Hope that attempted to address the meaning of Advent in terms of the tangle of pain and joy we feel in preparing for birth and death. The town church had opted for no sermon that day. Instead, we sang Christmas carols and listened to sentimental poems from *Ideals* magazine. That text from Isaiah was read aloud during the service, but its meaning was clouded by cheer. We were busy comforting ourselves and had no wish to be reminded of our mortality.

The difference between the two churches on that Sunday confirmed what I had begun to suspect: the people of Hope Church were less afraid than the people in town to look into the heart of their pain, a pain they share with many monasteries, which also have a diminishing and aging population. When these people ask, "Who will replace us?" the answer is, "Who knows, maybe no one," and it's not easy to live with that truth. The temptation is to deny it or to look for scapegoats. The challenge is to go on living graciously and thankfully, cultivating love. Not sentimental love but true charity, which, as Flannery O'Connor said, "is hard and endures."

The people of Hope live far apart from each other on the land: paradoxically, I suspect this is one reason they seem better at creating community than people in town, better at being together while leaving each other alone, as I once heard the monastic ideal defined. How are we to get along with our neighbor in hard times and good? How can we make relationships that last? Those who live in small rural communities, who come to know their neighbors all too well over the years, know the truth of the words of a sixth-century monk, Dorotheus of Gaza: "The root of all disturbance, if one will go to its source, is that no one will blame himself." When I read those words in a sermon at Hope Church, one old farmer forgot himself; he nodded and said aloud, "That right." He was assenting to a hard truth, one confirmed by a lifetime of experience.

"All flesh is grass" is a hard truth, too, and it has real meaning for people who grow grass, cut it, bale it, and go out every day in winter to feed it to cows. They watch that grass turning into flesh, knowing that they in turn will eat it as beef. They can't pretend not to know that their flesh, too, is grass. And they know that grass dies, not just in the winter, but in summer's dry heat. "All flesh is grass, and its beauty is as the flower of the field." That image comes alive in the West River of Dakota, and also an image from Psalm 90 that speaks of "grass that springs up in the morning" and "by evening withers and fades."

It's hard for me to imagine Hope Church dying, almost impossible to picture it abandoned or falling into ruins, as human constructions inevitably do. Absurdly, I think of its death the way I think of our sun dying. Eventually, long after anyone is around to see it, the sun will grow redder and perhaps more beautiful before it finally burns out. The Grand River will have turned to ice by then, and Black Horse Butte may be stripped of its skin of grass and soil.

It's absurd, too, that I find a Benedictine monastery and a tiny Presbyterian church in the middle of nowhere to be so absolutely and perfectly complementary. I am not showing due respect to religion as I was taught it: as a matter of the fine points of who's in, who's out, who's what as defined by dogmatic and denominational distinctions. But then, I don't have to. This is the Wild West. Out at Hope, in the summer, bellowing cows at a nearby watering tank sometimes join in the call to worship; one year baby rattlesnakes showed up for Vacation Bible School.

One former minister at Hope who had come from the urban East told me that her strongest memory of Hope Church was of an evening service in July. Standing in the pulpit she could see down the length of the church and out the open door to a large round hay bale catching the last rays of sunlight. "It was dark on one side and pure gold on the other," she said, "and I thought, that's a measure of the wealth here, that will help make things come out right this year."

She also told me that she couldn't imagine what was happening at the first funeral service she conducted for a member of Hope Church when, as people gathered for the graveside service, the men, some kneeling, began studying the open grave. It was early November, and someone explained that they were checking the frost and moisture levels in the ground. They were farmers and ranchers worried about a drought. They were mourners giving a good friend back to the earth. They were people of earth, looking for a sign of hope.

DOUGLAS BURTON-CHRISTIE

INTERLUDE

The Literature of Nature and the Quest for the Sacred

O<small>N THE EVENING OF</small> 16 June 1979, a group of forty-one sperm whales inexplicably beached themselves on the central Oregon coast. It soon became apparent that the whales were doomed—"they were haemorrhaging under the crushing weight of their own flesh and were beginning to suffer irreversible damage from heat exhaustion."[1] Thus, saving the whales was out of the question. Still, as they lay dying, a steady stream of the concerned and the curious—scientists, police, local residents, media representatives, naturalists and environmental activists—poured onto the beach to see this astonishing sight for themselves. Each came with a particular interest in the event: scientists wanted to gather as much data as possible before the corpses decayed (even if it meant applying chain saws to the jaws of the great animals); many of the local residents came simply to "see history"; the media was there to get the story; the Oregon Parks Department was concerned to keep order and to keep the threat of disease from gaining ground; for some, the stranding of the whales was a 'numinous event.'

How to account for these diverse responses to the stranding? One response is to consider the varied questions that witnesses brought to the event. Some asked simply what should be *done* about the whales, immediately. Others wanted to know what could be learned from the whales. Still others had questions less easily answerable: who *were* these mysterious creatures? How should they be treated? In some ways the questions and root impulses behind them were in basic conflict with one another. It soon became clear that it was not possible

simultaneously to carry out scientific experiments, facilitate an im-
promptu tourist attraction, maintain law and order, contemplate
these mysterious beings in wonder and ensure that they died with
dignity. As the days unfolded, practical exigencies and no-nonsense
scientific research gradually came to dominate the proceedings. The
event became reduced to a problem to be solved. Engineering pre-
vailed over reflection. This did not come without a cost. As one of
those present observed, it "interfered with the spiritual and emotional ability of people to deal with the phenomenon."[2]

Why did this happen? How did such a numinous event come to
be so reduced, so impoverished? One witness of the event, writer
Barry Lopez, offers this telling explanation: "As far as I know, no
novelist, no historian, no moral philosopher, no scholar of Melville,
no rabbi, no painter, no theologian had been on the beach."[3]

The absence of such witnesses (and the possibility of their presence) raises important questions about how we perceive the natural
world, about what language and categories are most appropriate for
describing our diverse experiences in nature and about whether it is
possible to speak meaningfully of a spirituality of nature. It is precisely the capacity to see and describe the natural world on many
levels at once and to invite the human observer to become implicated
in its mystery that characterizes the contemporary literature of nature and marks it as significant for spirituality. In particular, one
finds in this literature a deft synthesis of science and art, a sensitivity
both to empirical observation and to aesthetic creation. The result is
a richly textured vision of the natural world that opens out new paths
for exploring the sacred and provides new impetus for cherishing the
living cosmos.

Spirituality and the Literature of Nature

Rooted in the tradition of Ralph Waldo Emerson and Henry David
Thoreau, the literature of nature in the North American tradition
has in our own time come to be associated with the names of Annie
Dillard, Edward Abbey, Loren Eiseley, Barry Lopez, Mary Oliver and
many others. This literature is characterized by an acute attention to
the particular, by its local character, by a focus on experience, by its
valuation of imagination, by an implicit, oblique evocation of the

transcendent, and by an enduring ethical impulse. As such, it holds immense promise for helping us to understand the shape and texture of the diverse, emerging spiritualities of the natural world arising in contemporary experience.

Still, it is not easy to describe the spirituality or spiritualities that emerge from this literature. As Catherine Albanese has noted in her book *Nature religion in America*, this particular expression of religion has tended to arise outside of the bounds of conventional religious structures and ideas. There is no listing for nature religion in the yellow pages, no consensus on what might comprise the spirituality and theology of such a religion.[4] Yet it is alive and well in our midst. The growing popularity of the literature of nature is one important indication of this. In the part of the world I come from, the western United States, readings by these poets and writers draw interested readers and listeners by the hundreds, even thousands. There are writing workshops and festivals throughout the west— cowboy poets gather annually in Elko, Nevada, to declaim their verse, while an "Art of the Wild" conference held each summer in Squaw Valley, California, draws writers and poets seeking to hone their craft. On a national scale nature writers have been honoured in recent years with the Pulitzer Prize (Annie Dillard's *Pilgrim at Tinker Creek*) and the National Book Award (Barry Lopez's *Arctic Dreams*). Although it is difficult to calculate the breadth of appeal or influence of all of the literature of nature, the depth of response it evokes is undeniable. At least some of its appeal, I would suggest, is rooted in its evocation of nature as numinous and transcendent.

What precisely is nature writing and in what sense does it have anything to do with spirituality? Thomas Lyon, in his masterly discussion of American nature writing in the book *The incomperable lande*, argues that the literature of nature has three main features, "natural history information, personal responses to nature, and philosophical interpretations of nature." He suggests that it is "the relative weight or interplay of these three aspects" that "determines all the permutations and categories within the field."[4] Lyon has developed a provisional "taxonomy of nature writing," distinguishing seven main approaches or types which he situates along a "spectrum." On one end are those works mostly concerned with information about the natural world and on the other end those taken up with more personal, philosophical reflection.

Beginning on one end of the spectrum, we find "field guides and professional papers," whose primary role is to convey precise information about the natural world, though they can also speak with literary grace and poetic force, as in the case of Roger Tory Peterson's *A Field Guide to Western Birds*. The "natural history essay," such as Rachel Carson's *The sea around us*, also provides an expository description of nature, although it is often fitted into a literary design so that the facts give rise to some sort of meaning or interpretation. The focus moves from the natural world itself to the author's experience in the natural world in the essay form known as the "ramble," exemplified by Annie Dillard's luminous *Pilgrim at Tinker Creek*. Moving still further away from the primacy of natural history facts to a clear emphasis on the writer's experience, one encounters the "solitude and back-country living essay"; Edward Abbey's *Desert Solitaire* is one of the most vivid examples of this form in contemporary literature. The "travel and adventure essay," such as Barry Lopez's lyrical *Arctic Dreams*, often draws a contrast between the too-safe habituated existence left behind and the vivid life of discovery. The "farm essay," of which Wendell Barry's *A Continuous Harmony* is a good example, raises questions about whether it is possible to find a thoughtful way of fitting into the natural patterns of a farm rather than always imposing some sort of abstract order upon them. Finally there are the analytic and comprehensive works on "human beings and their role in nature," such as Thomas Berry's *The Dream of the Earth* or John Hay's *In Defense of Nature*. Here, interpretation predominates and the natural history facts or the personal experiences are decidedly secondary.[6]

In what sense are any of these works about spirituality? To answer this, it will help to consider briefly some recent discussions among scholars of spirituality regarding the meaning of the term and the shape of the field. In a recent article, Bernard McGinn distinguished three main approaches to the study of spirituality—"historical-contextual," "theological," and "anthropological." The historical-contextual approach, McGinn suggests, "emphasizes spirituality as an experience rooted in a particular community's experience rather than as a dimension of human existence as such."[7] The theological approach to spirituality emphasizes the ongoing importance to spirituality of central theological categories without which it is difficult to conceive of spirituality at all. This approach need not be characterized by the subservience of spirituality to categories arising from systematic theology (as was characteristic of much of what was known as "spiritual theology"). Rather, it recognizes that there is an ongoing, reciprocal, dynamic relationship between expressions of the experience of God (spirituality) and systematic, conceptual formulations of belief (systematic theology).[8] Finally, the anthropological or hermeneutical approach is the one that seeks to understand spirituality as a fundamental element in human experience. As Sandra Schneiders defines this approach, it is "the experience of consciously striving to integrate one's life in terms not of isolation and self-absorption but of self-transcendence toward the ultimate value one perceives."[9] For the purposes of this discussion, I want to focus my attention on this last approach, for it is here that literature of nature and the spirituality evoked there can best be situated.

One of the benefits of an anthropological or hermeneutical approach to spirituality is precisely its inductive, phenomenological, open-ended way of apprehending and describing spiritual experience. Without prejudging where and in what form spiritual experience ought to be found, such an approach attends first of all to the wide variety of phenomena that might reasonably be considered as evoking a transcendent or depth dimension to existence, seeking to describe and interpret the phenomenon as it presents itself. This does not mean that such experience is conceived of as contextless (and therefore inaccessible to historical study) or as lacking in cognitive content (and therefore inaccessible to theological reflection). However, if it is true, as Sandra Schneiders argues, that "the experience of the spiritual life includes more, much more today, than religion, and religion includes much more than theology, and theology includes much more than specifically Christian content," then we must be prepared to look for spiritual experience in new places and to pose new questions about that experience.[10] It is in this sense that the literature of nature is relevant to the current discussion. It represents one of the new expressions of spirituality emerging in contemporary experience that, although not easily accessible to either the historical-contextual or the theological approach, can be examined through an anthropological or hermeneutical approach. To understand the spirituality evoked by this literature means beginning not with certain a priori theological assumptions, but with a willingness to *listen* to the patterns of symbolic and metaphoric language found there.

DISCERNING THE SPIRIT IN NATURE

In the literature of nature, discerning the spirit means above all cultivating an ever deepening sense of relationship with the natural world, a relationship that is rooted in mystery. As ethnobotanist Gary Nabhan has noted, ". . . natural history writers are really students of relationships. They are more interested in the dynamics between two living beings than in a single living organism as a *thing*."[11] This literature is respectful of the mystery inherent in these relationships, especially the human relationship with nature. Nature writers take great pains to suggest, in Robert Finch's words, "a relationship with the natural environment that is more than strictly intellectual, biological, cultural, or even ethical . . . they sense that nature is at its very heart, *an enduring mystery*."[12] This involves a careful integration of poetic and scientific sensibilities. By attending carefully both to the natural world itself and to the poetic process through which observations are transformed into art, writers in this genre create an aesthetic climate hospitable to mystery.

Both scientific and artistic sensibilities are required in nature writing because the goal is to probe the mystery of nature and to describe accurately what is there. One might even say the aim is to probe mystery *by* describing accurately. Here, science and art co-operate with one another to construct a complex web of meaning from the experience of the natural world. There is a desire, as Thomas Lyon puts it, to "harmonize fact knowledge and emotional knowledge." Edward O. Wilson and Barry Lopez, approaching the same subject from two different vantage points, that of a scientist and an artist respectively, agree that "science and aesthetic-emotional-intuitive knowledge not only coexist in nature writing, but conspire to suggest something greater, as it were, than the sum of its parts."[13] Such an approach requires a revision of our conventional assumptions about the respective domains of the scientist and the artist.

The artist-naturalist is called upon to take seriously the study of the limitless minutiae and variation of the natural world, to cultivate the careful habits of observation and the deductive methodology of the scientist. This is one of the reasons why there is so little tolerance among contemporary nature writers for vague, uninformed, romantic ruminations on nature. Note Barry Lopez's intimate familiarity with Arctic biology in *Arctic Dreams* and *Crossing Open Ground*,

Annie Dillard's carefully acquired grasp of entomology in *Pilgrim at Tinker Creek,* John McPhee's detailed understanding of plate tectonics in *Basin and Range.*[14] In each case, precise scientific knowledge informs and deepens a larger literary, spiritual sensibility. The metaphors and symbols arise not only from the writer's imagination, but from the natural world itself.

Barry Lopez describes the intricate pattern emerging from close observation of the landscape along the Charley river in Eastern Alaska.

> What is stunning about the river's banks on this particular stormy afternoon is not the vegetation (the willow, alder, birch, black cottonwood, and spruce are common enough) but its *presentation.* The wind, like some energetic dealer in rare fabrics, folds back branches and ruffles the underside of leaves to show the pattern— the shorter willows forward; the birch taller, set farther back on the hills. The soft green furze of budding alder heightens the contrast between gray-green willow stems and white birch bark. All of it is rhythmic in the wind, each species bending as its diameter, its surface area, the strength of its fibers dictate. Behind this, a backdrop of hills: open country recovering from an old fire, dark islands of spruce in an ocean of labrador tea, lowbrush cranberry, fireweed, and wild primrose, each species of leaf the invention of a different green: lime, moss, forest, jade. This is not to mention the steel gray of the clouds, the balmy arctic temperature, our clear suspension in the canoe over the stony floor of the river, the ground-in dirt of my hands, the flutelike notes of a Swainson's thrush, or anything else that informs the scene.[15]

Here careful, spare description of what is "presented" by the land yields insight and understanding. The individual species of trees come alive and speak as a whole, their subtle variations in color and form comprising a rich, complex vision. The metaphoric evocation of this vision emerges as a gradual unfolding and is inseparable from Lopez's hard-won knowledge of the place: it is only after several days on the river and increasing familiarity with its rhythms that a pattern finally emerges.

Cooperation between science and art also requires the scientist to abandon the myth of objectivity toward, detachment from, or comprehensive knowledge of the subject matter. It means that the scientist must develop the aesthetic, interpretive sensibilities of an artist. Here consider the elegant aesthetic quality of the writing of Loren Eiseley, E. O. Wilson, Rachel Carson and Richard Nelson. Steeped in careful scientific research, their work also reflects an uncommon level of imaginative, emotional engagement with the subject matter and graceful literary expression. The style and form of the work are significant. Loren Eiseley, trained as a scientist, became frustrated with the conventions of scientific discourse and was increasingly drawn to articulate his vision in what he called "the personal essay" or "the concealed essay." Here, the personal anecdote "was allowed gently to bring under observation thoughts of a more purely scientific nature."[16] Eiseley developed this into a fine art, weaving together personal insight and scientific understanding to create a resonant vision of the natural world.

The possibility of deep imaginative interaction with nature means paying attention to the utterly subjective and personal character of one's interest and inclinations. "You start," says E. O. Wilson,

> by loving a subject. Birds, probability theory, explosives, stars, differential equations, storm fronts, sign language, swallowtail butterflies—the odds are that the obsession will have begun in childhood. The subject will be your lodestar and give sanctuary in the shifting mental universe.

Sometimes these inclinations have their origins in something as basic as physical make-up. Wilson tells how the great metallurgist Cyril Smith was drawn to the study of alloys by the fact that he was color blind. His impairment led him to turn his attention at an early age to the intricate black-and-white patterns which are found everywhere in nature, "to swirls, filigree, banding, and eventually to the fine structure of metal."[17]

The creative value of one's personal inclinations and orientation does not always sit easily with the assumptions about acquiring knowledge prevalent in western science. Anthropologist Richard Nelson's early training in biology exposed him to a kind of science from which the self and its wider interests were a priori excluded. Its emphasis on quantified data, controlled experiments, technological monitoring devices, and theoretical analysis left him with the sense that it would never be able to teach him what mattered about nature. Thus his pleasure at finding a refuge in anthropology "where the descriptive approach had persisted like an orphan child, and where the study of Native Cultures revealed traditions of natural history that seemed richer than anything accessible in Western science." During his long years spent with the Koyukon people of Alaska, he absorbed an entirely different attitude toward the natural world. It was their humility that struck Nelson most deeply: "I never heard them speak of how much they knew, but of how little, and of how much there was to learn, how difficult it was to understand even the smallest mysteries surrounding them."[18] This attitude of humility creates the mental atmosphere, Nelson suggests, for approaching nature respectfully, with openness, for seeing deeply into its heart.

Careful attention to the intricate patterns in nature and to the language appropriate to them means cultivating a fresh vision of the natural world which only the eye of the poet, the clash of metaphors, can produce. That eloquent chronicler of the Southwest, Joseph Wood Krutch, suggests that the cultivation of a poetic sensibility is indispensable if we are to have any chance of even *noticing* the natural world, much less taking it into ourselves: "It is not easy to live in that continuous awareness of things which alone is true living . . . the faculty of wonder tires easily. . . . Really to see something once or twice a week is almost inevitably to have to try . . . to make oneself a poet."[19] Rachel Carson speaks in similar terms to describe the predicament she faced in writing her acclaimed book, *The Sea Around Us*. When asked why this book about the sea, based on close, scientific observation of the underwater world, was so "poetic," she responded: "If there is poetry in my book about the sea, it is not because I deliberately put it there, but because no one could write truthfully about the sea and leave out the poetry."[20]

Poetry here means paying attention to metaphors, whose tensive force enables us to experience the natural world in a new way and to uncover the significance—the "truth" in Carson's words—of this experience. It also means learning to open ourselves to the unexpected, learning to use our imaginations to discern previously unforeseen relationships. There is the suggestion here of the need for an emotional involvement with the subject matter, a quality that Edward Abbey contends is necessary for any authentic engagement with the natural world: ". . . sympathy for the object under study, and more than sympathy, love. A love based on prolonged contact and interaction. Intercourse if possible. Observation informed by sympathy, love, intuition."[21] The cultivation of such an attitude can help open us to encounter the transcendent in nature.

Nature writing suggests endless possibilities for genuine encounter with the natural world, for entering into relationships of mystery. This is especially true of what might be called "narratives of conversion" which convey, sometimes directly, more often obliquely, the place and manner in which an author was beckoned, even seized by the sense of mystery in the natural world.[22] Such narratives suggest both the revelatory power of natural epiphanies and their capacity to transform those who experience them. Moreover, their effects often pass beyond the immediate subject to open up new horizons of understanding for countless others. One such narrative, which has taken on extraordinary significance in the American conservation movement, concerns a turning point in the life of Aldo Leopold, who discovered to his surprise both the immense cost of waking to a sense of relationship with the natural world and the endless possibilities it engendered.

Travelling as a young man through the canyon lands of Arizona, he and his companions stopped one day to eat lunch on a high rimrock. Gazing into the canyon below, they suddenly caught sight of what appeared to be a doe fording the river. Only when she had crossed the river and had begun climbing toward them did they realize their error: they were watching a wolf. Following behind her were a half-dozen others, grown pups who "sprang from the willows and . . . joined in a welcoming melee of wagging tails and playful maulings. What was literally a pile of wolves writhed and tumbled in the center of an open flat at the foot of our rimrock." Leopold and his friends did not hesitate: "In a second we were pumping lead into the pack," bringing the old wolf down and scattering the others. He reached the old wolf in time "to watch the fierce green fire dying in her eyes. I realized then, and have known ever since, that there was something new to me in those eyes—something known only to her and to the mountain."[23]

Reflecting on this bloody epiphany many years later, Leopold noted with chagrin how disjointed his own relationship with the natural world had been at the time, how shallow his judgment and perspective. Not only had he callously assumed the right to kill the wolf, but he had completely misunderstood the delicate ecological balance he was disturbing—"I thought that fewer wolves meant more deer, that no wolves would mean hunters' paradise." The systematic application of this principle during the subsequent years in state after state throughout the west had caused deer populations to explode and vegetation to be decimated. The result? "Starved bones of the hoped-for deer herd, dead of its own too much . . . dustbowls, and rivers washing the futures into the sea." All this because we had not learned, as Leopold put it, to "think like a mountain," to consider the implications of our actions from the perspective of the earth. The birth of Leopold's new sense of relationship with the natural world and the land ethic he helped to articulate emerged from that chilling moment when he glimpsed "the fierce green fire" dying in the eyes of the old wolf. This unexpected epiphany removed a veil from Leopold's understanding and revealed to him a heretofore unimagined dimension of reality. It would nurture his lifelong search for a balanced, respectful relationship with the natural world and become a touchstone for the modern ecological movement.

CONCLUSION

In Leopold's narrative we have a vivid reminder of the intimate connection that exists between the encounter with mystery, the emerging sense of relationship with other species and the growth of a sense of responsibility for the natural world. If we are to respond in a meaningful way to the increasingly rapid ecological degradation of the planet, we will need to rethink many of our most cherished assumptions about the natural world and our place in that world. The literature of nature can help us to do that. By attending carefully to the texture of the natural world and its endless capacity to illuminate and transform our existence, nature writers help us to recover a genuine sense of belonging to the living cosmos. Those of us who study and teach spirituality can learn a lot from these writers and poets about where we need to be and how to think about the deepest challenges facing us. Perhaps they can help lure us, as Barry Lopez suggests, "onto the beach" where together with the scientists, novelists, historians, painters, poets, we can learn to listen carefully and give imaginative voice to the elusive traces of the spirit in nature.

Notes

1. Barry Lopez, *Crossing Open Ground* (New York: Scribners, 1988) p 120.

2. Lopez, *Crossing Open Ground*, p 127.

3. Lopez, *Crossing Open Ground*, p 146.

4. Catherine Albanese, *Nature Religion in America: From the Algonkian Indians to the New Age* (Chicago: University of Chicago Press, 1990).

5. Thomas J. Lyon (ed), *This Incomperable Lande: A Book of American Nature Writing* (Boston: Houghton Mifflin, 1989), p. 3. For a further indication of the breadth of the genre, see also: Thomas Lyon (ed), *Witness: New Nature Writing* III: 4 (1989); Daniel Halpern (ed), *On Nature: Nature, Landscape, and Natural History* (San Francisco: North Point Press, 1987); Stephen Trimble (ed), *Words from the Land: Encounters with Natural History Writing* (Salt Lake City: Peregrine Smith Books, 1989); Robert Finch and John Elder (eds), *The Norton Book of Nature Writing* (New York: Norton, 1990); John A. Murray (ed), *Nature's New Voices* (Golden CO: Fulcrum, 1992); Peter Sauer (ed), *Finding Home* (Boston: Beacon, 1992).

6. Roger Tory Peterson, *A Field Guide to Western Birds* (Boston: Houghton Mifflin, 1961); Rachel Carson, *The Sea around Us* (New York: Oxford University Press, 1950); Annie Dillard, *Pilgrim at Tinker Creek* (New York: Harper and Row, 1974); Edward Abbey, *Desert Solitaire* (Tucson: University of Arizona Press, 1988); Barry Lopez, *Arctic Dreams: Imagination and Desire in a Northern Landscape* (New York: Charles Scribner's Sons, 1986); Wendell Berry, *A Continuous Harmony: Essays Cultural and Agricultural* (New York: Harcourt Brace Jovanovich, 1972); John Hay, *In Defense of Nature* (Boston: Little, Brown, 1969); Thomas Berry, *The Dream of the Earth* (San Francisco: Sierra Club Books, 1988).

7. Bernard McGinn, "The Letter and the Spirit: Spirituality as an Academic Discipline," *Christian Spirituality Bulletin* 1:2 (Fall 1993), p 6.

8. On this question, cf Bradley Hanson, "Theological Approaches to Spirituality: A Lutheran Perspective," *Christian Spirituality Bulletin* 2:1 (Spring 1994), pp 5–9; Philip Sheldrake SJ, "Some Continuing Questions: The Relationship between Spirituality and Theology," *Christian Spirituality Bulletin* 2:1 (Spring 1994), pp 15–18.

9. Sandra M. Schneiders, "Spirituality in the Academy," *Theological Studies* 50 (1989), p 684.

10. Sandra M. Schneiders, "A Hermeneutical Approach to the Study of Christian Spirituality," *Christian Spirituality Bulletin* 2:1 (Spring 1994), p 10.

11. Trimble, *Words from the Land*, p 5.

12. Robert Finch, "Being at Two with Nature," *The Georgia Review* 45:1 (Spring 1994), p 101 (emphasis mine).

13. Thomas J. Lyon, "Introduction," in Edward Lueders (ed), *Writing Natural History: Dialogues with Authors* (Salt Lake City: University of Utah Press), pp 3–4.

14. Barry Lopez, *Arctic Dreams: Imagination and Desire in a Northern Landscape* (New York: Scribners, 1986); Annie Dillard, *Pilgrim at Tinker Creek*

(New York: Harper and Row, 1974); John McPhee, *Basin and Range* (New York: Farrar, Strauss and Giroux, 1981).

15. Barry Lopez, *Crossing Open Ground* (New York: Scribners, 1988), pp 78–79.

16. Loren Eiseley, *All the Strange Hours: The Excavation of a Life* (New York: Scribners, 1975), p 177.

17. E. O. Wilson, *Biophilia: the Human Bond with Other Species* (Cambridge MA: Harvard University Press, 1984), p 65.

18. Richard Nelson, *The Island Within* (New York: Vintage, 1991), p 161.

19. Joseph Wood Krutch, *The Desert Year* (Tuscon: University of Arizona Press, 1985), pp 37–38.

20. Trimble, *Words from the land*, p xiii.

21. Edward Abbey, "Down the river with Henry Thoreau," in Trimble, *Words from the Land*, p 62.

22. On this question, cf also: Douglas Burton-Christie, "A feeling for the Natural World: Spirituality and the Heart in Contemporary Nature Writing', *Continuum* 2:2–3 (Spring 1993).

23. Aldo Leopold, *A Sand County Almanac and Sketches Here and There* (New York: Oxford University Press, 1949), pp 129–130.

PART II

THE GNAWING

There is a great pole somewhere, a mighty trunk similar to the sacred sun dance pole, only much, much bigger. This pole is what holds up the world. The Great White Grandfather Beaver of the North is gnawing at that pole. He has been gnawing at the bottom of it for ages. More than half of the pole has already been gnawed through. When the Great White Beaver of the North gets angry, he gnaws faster and more furiously. Once he has gnawed all the way through, the pole will topple, and the earth will crash into a bottomless nothing. That will be the end of the people, of everything. The end of all ends. So we are careful not to make the Beaver angry. That's why the Cheyenne never eat his flesh, or even touch a beaver skin. We want the world to last a little longer. (Cheyenne)

The story/legend is quoted in its entirety from: *American Indian Myths and Legends,* selected and edited by Richard Erdoes and Alfonso Ortiz. Pantheon Books. 1984, 484–85.

Alfred Jacob Miller

PORTRAITS OF THE AMERICAN WEST

EL PASO MUSEUM OF ART

First of all you find an acorn.
Or the squirrel.
Perhaps something you hold from the past
beyond memory
into heritage
or ancestral levels
of God's thought
and you're following the long haul of fuel
heated on old campfires.

It's somewhat disappointing after a while.
This guy's stilted in the direction
of the sunset
overrimmed with too much of a 19th century eye
I mean
Indians holding their ears
and the title *Waiting for the Locomotive*

the curly hairs of buffalo
horses
all too arabesque and harem-like

could be more of a caravan to Egypt, yes
biblical
there's Joseph on a camel
just sold

like a treaty.

Asylum in the Grasslands

He commanded them to sit down on the grass
Mark 6:39

When some adjustment occurs
not in the actual circumstances
no they seem to stay the same
but in one's attitude
or way of viewing as aperture

that small squeak of passage into acceptance
or at least liveability
so one is not assumed to be in a lock
that can't be stepped beyond

it's a fragile gate
the opening of faith
the letting of anotherness into your shadow box

you know you'll feel a kind hand
somewhere in the middle of your back
it's not that you want to be relieved
of your burdens
it's what you're here for
to feel the problems before you
like a filing cabinet

but there's someone in the prairie grass
his face so full of light
he's milk-eyed

you think maybe this's the Savior you nailed
he seems to understand

you let his ideas roll over you
you even forget the bitterness you learned
all your life
though you know there's a loveliness
in suffering
but you let go of it a little

you assume the air
walk over what'wz supposed to be your grave

you even feel it's the way it's supposed to be

this Savior who sucks you into himself
this man with his eyes in backwards.

CHARLES O. HARTMAN

The Clearing

> All paths lead to darkness.
> —Frank Herbert

This one leads north
along the east boundary.

It dips
and rises, veers to skirt a tree
closely or cut the grade of a hill, returning
straight as it can to north.
             For a dozen years
on the land I never found this path.
They brought me every summer
from where we lived,
from Texas, from Missouri, Michigan, New York,
years before the freeways.
The land my mother's mother had given her
for a dollar, for a wedding gift,
called my parents: mountains,
woods, the lake
whose best beach belongs
to a thin-mouthed club you have to be
born into, my mother's
own daunting mother.
             Two turns
down the hill, my grandmother's first
house, Waterbrooks—
old as the Revolution, lit by kerosene,
its dark compact as a cannon—

welcomed my fear at night,
going up with a candle. One evening
my mother asked her cousin
the minister for a prayer for me to say;
embarrassed as my father, he declined.
Why was the barn there but to be
motionless, fragile around my feet,
full of the smell of long-gone hay and horses?
The lawn was boulders and sling chairs, a view
over stone wall, long field, trees,
straight to the Presidential Range. The way curved right
around the house to the brook's
still pool and leaning over it
granite like a house the glacier left.
I read *The Yearling*, built
a water wheel a hand-span wide
of whittled sticks and bark
to turn in the green-gold shallows, climbed
the rock I never thought of as an old man's head
and looked down the brow into the pool,
shivering. Sunlight
treasured the warm stone,
the pockets of brown needles,
the crowding boughs.
                              One summer birthday
they gave me a hunting knife
like one my father found and fixed the handle on
to carve a walking stick from a slim moose maple.
I cut bark
from a wide birch beside the winding drive
for sheaths and toy canoes. My mother was
a sudden fury—
never a living tree—I should have known—
and took the knife away, for good.
I stand tear-blind beside her
where with a tiny hammer and small tacks
she strives to give my bark
back to her mother's hurt tree.

Later she moved
half a mile the other way, up
to Miss Ethel's House,
built on another hill a century before.
Miss Ethel Who, I couldn't keep in mind.
The place was names everybody knew—
Parker and Potter, Nesbitt, Jordan, Thorne,
Greenhalge and Greeley, the General, Doctor Shed—
some matched with faces
visiting at evening, some
only with houses, side roads, tracts,
the dead and living inextricable
from stories hinted, never told
since everybody knew them.

At the top of the hill, light,
a stove we didn't feed, water not pumped by hand,
didn't remove the house
much more from woods. They filled
the attic window where I slept
across the enormous chimney wall
from where my parents looked out past the road,
the field, more trees, to Washington
and Madison, Adams and Jefferson.
Out back, my way,
was target range for .22s. My father and I
destroyed tin cans all afternoon. One day I stayed
with twenty rounds to knock a sapling down.
I dug bright slugs
out of the ragged stump
and kept them like metal tears in a small box
in Michigan, Missouri, home.
                              But here,
between, there never was a house
to hold the woods at bay. Two cellar holes
half gone beside the road,
no one ever put a story to.
In the middle, out of sight of the road,
past the drive that used to loop where now

a car backs out the way it came,
the clearing, half an acre when I was ten,
the year my father and I worked down the slope
to clear the view,
the Presidents again, the glint of lake,
mile after mile of pine and maple,
broods on all the time I've known.
We got obstruction down
to one tree, worked our way
down the hill to find it, found it
too huge for two axes. That year the plan
was to build a cabin, but we couldn't find
enough straight timber in the second growth
and lacked the skill, the time, the hands.
On a low mound, with sticks and chips
I laid out paths and precincts,
my Institute of Stars and Distances.
Overhead my parents drifted
back and forth before the view.
Instead they bought a shed (Bill Someone's shed)
to move, like Miss Ethel's House.
The dirt road up this hill twists steep as fire.
I see the lanterns late at night,
a dozen men wandering around a flatbed
talking softly over the splintered wreckage
fallen to one side.
                    Here was no house
and isn't now. My mother's
mother's houses, up and down
the hill, belong to people I don't know.
I stay here, when I come here, in a tent,
never for long. There's water
in someone else's stream across the road
or from town in bottles. Nights chill
even in August. The clearing's half its size.
I can tell the trees, back in the woods,
that were the edge. The slope
is thicker than when we started.
                    For years

I never saw the place.
Then visited—I stayed in an inn in town—
then missed more years, then moved
back within a day's drive
once or twice a year.
The woods feel all implacable. They want
me gone. I feel it in the night
and the short north afternoons.
I hear them say Go home.

But here's a path I never knew.
Sraight from the road, into the woods,
it runs north half a mile and meets
a new road, an old one
opened up again for logging,
that peters out in swamp among pink flowers
and hordes of bees. Though it isn't mine, none of it
mine, this northbound path gives back
something or holds out something
promised me.
        I've drawn it
on the Survey map I keep
meaning to frame and hang, and pack each time
I change apartments. My mother's will
at last clears probate. Every year my father,
house-bound a continent away, receives
polite letters asking for a price.
Far from the ski slopes, miles from a paved road,
ten many-thousand-dollar poles from power,
waterless, houseless, halfway down the north
face of a northern hill, it waits
for me to come back once a year
and tell the trees
they're not for sale.
           Way up in the night
they whisper frostily together
down into the hollow dark.
Beyond the road water chatters on.
Something gnaws, and the patient scrape

echoes among trunks. Straight overhead
a reef of clouds is taking shape so fast
you see them firming in thin air.
In the other half of the sky
stars crowd every space among leaves.
Shivering, beside me the fire dies.

Midway

> . . . He asked him, "Do you see anything?" And he looked up and said,
> "I see men; but they look like trees, walking." Then again he laid
> hands upon his eyes; and he looked intently, and was restored,
> and saw everything clearly.
>
> Mark 8:23–25

January.
The hours after midday are coming
back, there is time
to climb from home
to height of land for the broader vision:
north and east,
Mount Moosilauke,
its four rivers of snow conjoining;
directly west,
the little town
on the highway, all its citizens
without a doubt
preoccupied
with matters they find as grave as any;
and all around,

the traffic of beasts,
invisible now, great and tiny.
A pregnant jumble,
near and far,
then and now, in a time of year
stormy and frigid,
but I have sweated,

stripped to the waist, it has been so clear.
The dead have been dead
it seems so long,
and yet their ghosts are perched on every
branch above me,
cloaking themselves
in the rising vapors from my body,
the day's sole clouds.

Deep in the Sunday
village, forlorn, the sound of swings
in the empty schoolyard
clinking against
their cold steel standards, like diminished
steeple bells:
ten o'clock's
sparse service was over hours
ago. My father
lays hands on my sight
up here, and friends, and my furious brother,
who at last seems calm.
The night is losing
its sovereignty, it will not be
overlong

before it loses
its winter boast, "Come out with me,
come out and stay,
and you'll be a corpse."
The crickets, partridge, frogs will all
come back to drum
their victory;
the whippoorwills will make their hum
and click as they mate,
the freshets will loosen;
the children, done for the year with lessons,
will elect to throng
the grassy playground. . . .

The past will turn itself over, shaking
out my brother,

friends, and father,
and they will be as before, but better,
as I will be,
unless—as so often—
I'm dreaming here; unless what I sense
is just another
misty version
of lifelong longing. It's hard to say. . . .
A moment ago,
I flushed a crowd
of flying squirrels, who in their soaring
out of their holes
looked so like angels
I rubbed my eyes. And what do I see?
On the far horizon

appears to be
a line of men, there in procession . . .
as darkness deepens, they look like trees.

Over Brogno

> If from behind the stars
> the perilous archangel came down,
> our thunderous heartbeats would kill us
> —Rilke

After the ten or twenty
        quiet minutes
                within the empty
church at San Giovanni,
                The lisping wavelets of the Como arm
                of the lake even less audible
                than the little implosions of dove-flight
                in the tower above like the shuffle
                of cards in a deck—

After my bourgeois
        reverie and rote prayers
                for the absent ones,
wife, children, friends,
                the lungs and torso at length light
                as wings as thought was transformed
                by consciousness of the cosmos below,
                the thronged dead, their buoyant
                deep dust
beneath soft stone
        on which I sat
                all weightless now in the pew—
the bells of noon
        had the *ploosh* sound of iron anchors

cast over into water.
I stepped out onto the dazzled piazza,
near blind to the chic *ragazza*
who smiled a greeting

as she passed
to the wharf's corner
where she'd eat and read her glossy review.
Her womanhood weighted me too,
and thus I made my sudden decision
to turn, rise, go
south to the snowy mountain
along the ancient mule paths,
avoiding the heavy

trucks, clutched
lovers, cars
so close I could almost touch them
on the wire-thin limestone
roads banked high with rock, where escape
seemed all but hopeless.
I wanted to rise above all, withdraw
from millennia's mulched refuse
underneath me,

innocent as it was,
innocent as the Virgin
whose icons at every
bridge across the *torrente*
where littered with candle, flower, coin—
earthy leavings and spillings
of quick and dead alike, moving
back and forth and back
along these tracks

like the bent
illiterate *contadino*
of whom I asked directions,
who courtly and gravely gestured:

"At every fork, choose a way that climbs,
if you must." To him there clung
sweet dung, dirt, dust,
as to others I passed, whom passing,
I commended to God,

Addio. At which
      they would bow in respect,
           it seemed, but seemed bemused,
as if the expression I used
           signalled not greeting but intention.
           Did I think I was climbing *à Dio?*
           Did they smile because it was odd to encounter
           someone like me over Brogno?
           Or at the superstition

that the higher powers
      are something one has
           to seek in a higher order?
But they returned to their labors.
           Enough had passed on these mountain paths
           that another oddness could pass.
           Somewhere within my heart I thanked them,
           for only a troubled abstraction
           could have been my answer

if they had asked me
      where I was going.
           And what was this humming, far past the final
boulder-built hovel?
           There on the summit, in the absence of wind,
           the tall tower, the unfleshed
           skull and bones on the chilling sign
           —*Pericolo di morte!*
           And something seen

or seeming seen,
      an immanence, an aura.
           I thought beyond

to our time's angelic throngs:
What deadly secrets? What secret soarings?
What particles abroad?
What specters of light that is more than light?
Brogno far below,
its inn and bar,
and I up there,
and what radio waves winging by
and bearing what lethal
abstraction from what capital,
what lecture hall, what briefing room?
Clamorous heartbeat, its clap
within like thunder. Without, the Angel.
I felt the heart must burst
or draw me down

to cottage and shack,
to human traffic,
where souls move close to ground.

God Attack

The girl floats down the country road— oh how the
glorious cows and pretty horses roam and graze. The girl
wanders past, daydreaming in the pastoral setting, the
icing on the cake she's eating every day. She's thinking
about the nature of god, but the message traveling
through the air converts, and lo dogs come instead, to
eat her. On the horizon they gather and growl and run
to set upon the girl and wrestle her to the ground
leaving blood, embedded gravel, nightmares, and later
scars. All thoughts of nature being god go by the way.
All nature gods turn ugly to her sight, and surely are
not god, not the one she had in mind when the dogs came
out of the blue, charging through goldenrod, which, if
she considers her allergies, should have been a sign.
She realizes with embarrassment that she wants to limit
god in this small way (and that others want to limit god
in other ways) and that to limit god at all is just the
opposite of what she had in mind when she was wandering
down the road, expanding. All in all she's glad that she
was only set upon by dogs. And thanks be to whatever.

Dancers at the Edge

I've grown used to the ones
who wander close, brave
with velvet antlers, who sneak up
when I'm raking leaves,
reading, or planting bulbs.
We eye each other, theirs
darker, larger, more reflective
than mine. These creatures,
wild and new to this world,
do not flinch at human
scent. I will teach them
distance, prepare them for
November guns. I clap
my hands, bang plastic pots
and wait for them to run.

Two dancers entwine tawny necks,
bow to taste wild mushrooms.
The poison is all in my head.

Modifies

What modifies your seeing?
You tell yourself you see the long strand
of the beach, the one man standing
against the sea, wearing a red hat,
wearing a hat blurred red but vibrant
like a burning cigarette. In the sea air
burning more sharply for the haze,
blue-grays, gray-yellows, while the sea falls
and birds cry out of the haze (you do not see them).
The morning light's defused yet almost shrill,
at least insistent. It makes a burden of itself
this scene for some unaccountable reason, like a sorrow
with no known object, seeking a subject.

Mondrian's Forest

in memory of Greg Levey, d. February 18, 1991

1. FEBRUARY 19, 1991

Every car drones a radio,
every shop keeps the TV on.

The smart bombs are thinking their way
into Baghdad, on video grids, in primary colors,

and yesterday in the middle of Amherst, a man
drenched himself in gasoline and lit a match.

Next to the blackened meat on the Commons,
Peace on a sheet of cardboard, and his

driver's license, safe, and the old oaks
safe, only the grass charred.

Already the papers have found
neighbors willing to say that he'd *seemed depressed*,

someone to call him *isolated*.
Nine Cambodian Buddhists come

down from Leverett in their saffron robes
to pray. Two Veterans of Foreign Wars

heckle over the chants and the slow
gong, a circle of voices on the block of lawn.

2. *TREES ON THE GEIN, WITH RISING MOON (1908)*

When Mondrian began
his world held rivers and trees, but not

the water's compliance and not
the ash's stillness, for he was in them.

He stood five trees against a red sky;
floated five more

in the mirror of the red river,
all ten wringing their black trunks

into green.
The trees on the water are breaking up,

breaking up, and still remain
trees in the center of their dissolution.

The trees on the bank flame up inside
their heavy outlines:

imagine a death in a man that pushes
first here then there at the lively

pilable skin. The limbs
distend, too full of ripening.

Thick oils eddy and ripple, a slick
on the turbulence of things.

3. BODHI

Today on the woods trail by Amethyst Brook,
I prayed, *Kuan Yin*. Kuan Yin, enthroned

in the Asian Museum, enormous in limestone.
She who hears the cries of the world,

her spine sheer as a bluff, and both hands open.
I couldn't say if the polished eyes

were open or lidded. *In the new represenation,*
reason takes first place, wrote Mondrian,

his labor then to rescue the trees
from the wind, to save his strict clean sight

from the eyes in his head,
that saw only through blood.

Ice breaking up, the meltwater surge
of the brook gouged her name from my throat,

the way it gouges the bank out from under the trees
and digs bare the root-weave. Not *she*

who answers the cries, Kuan Yin. Not *she who consoles.*
Her body is still, is stone: *She who will not kindle*

and blaze when she hears
a man burn.

Seven

for luck, and for the seven heavens, transparently stacked
like an archaeological dig into glassworks; we say broad

daylight, but it's also deep. I want to find the stratum where
virtue is pure description: the virtue of mercury

is speed. The virtue of the soul is joy. Break a thermometer
and mercury, so rapid and silver it seems to ride on light,

shatters into mirrors of itself: identical beads, all whole,
all fleeing. The mind's virtue is difference; the heart's,

sameness—deeper than before, this resonance, this ocean
diastole and pulse. The body, in its obstinate formality,

plain under the blue vault endlessly lifting, heavy on the
warming sand—the body's virtue is renewal. Cell after cell

it loses all that it has, and still goes on,
faithful amnesiac lover of the sun,

the sun that says *I have not left,*
that says *I have returned.*

DENISE LEVERTOV

It Should Be Visible

If from Space not only sapphire continents,
swirling oceans, were visible, but the wars—
like bonfires, wildfires, forest conflagrations,
flame and smoky smoulder—the Earth would seem
a bitter pomander ball bristling with poison cloves.
And each war fuelled with weapons: it should be visible
that great sums of money have been exchanged,
great profits made, workers gainfully employed
to construct destruction, national economies distorted
so that these fires, these wars, may burn
and consume the joy of this one planet
which, seen from outside its transparent tender shell,
is so serene, so fortunate, with its water, air
and myriad forms of 'life that wants to live.'
It should be visible that this bluegreen globe
suffers a canker which is devouring it.

What One Receives from Living Close to a Lake

That it is wide, wide
and still—yet subtly
stirring; wide and
level, reflecting the intangible sky's
vaster breadth in its own
fresh, cold, serene
surface we can
touch, enter, taste.
That it is wide
and uninterrupted save by
here a sail, there
a constellation of waterfowl—
a meadow of water
you could say,
a clearing amid the entangled
forest of forms and voices,
anxious intentions, urgent
memories: a deep, clear
breath to fill
the soul, an internal
gesture, arms
flung wide to echo
that mute
generous outstretching
we call *lake.*

In the Woods

Everything is threatened, but meanwhile
everything presents itself:
the trees, that day and night
steadily stand there, amassing
lifetimes and moss, the bushes
eager with buds sharp as green
pencil points. Bark of cedar,
brown braids, bark of fir, deep-creviced,
winter sunlight favoring
here a sapling, there an ancient snag,
ferns, lichen. And the lake
always ready to change its skin
to match the sky's least inflection.
Everything answers the roll call,
and even, as is the custom,
speaks for those that are gone
—clearly, beyond sound:
that revolutionary *'Presente!'*

KATHARINE COLES

Poem for the Last Decade

Easter, 1993
for Maureen, and for Fiona

1. AFTER THE PARTY ENDED

We all came in from the streets,
left our confetti and bruised
rose petals for the sweeps.
They hauled away the rubble
to dumps, nostalgia shops
where chunks of wall, graffiti,
and the splinters of shop windows
nestle down next to knucklebones
relinquished by martyrs and saints
of other centuries.
All of them forgeries.
No matter to faith.
We still had another decade
to weather. Nothing would end.

But let's start at the beginning—
or rather *in medias res:*
what in retrospect we call
the *Dark Ages,* because
science was out of fashion:
no physics but metaphysics,
the alchemies of the soul.
All the flowers were wild,
and the castles chilly,

their windows designed
not for panorama
but for catapults
or household items dropped
with hot-oil soup
onto uninvited guests.
The unstudied middle classes
lived in hovels trampled with mud,
warmed themselves over
the blazes of invasions

whose dates we memorized
as our century's late middle
wound down to another beginning.
Children, we were kept
in forts like theirs—
no windows tempting dreams,
on afternoons like this one,
of tulips burning down
before the storm's first wind.
And the women—pale,
with bad complexions (ages
before dermatology saved
our adolescent skins),
each knelt before her lover,
or before God, for whom
when she opened, she really meant it.
I've read of the brides of kings,
but those brides of Christ were something—
flayed, impaled, beheaded,
their wounds ornaments
of transfiguring belief,
for which we might feel the nostalgia
we muster now, watching
atrocities edited
to fit the standard screen.
Surely, we could do something?
The wall falls, and then

off camera, just out of earshot,
a child begins to scream.

2. OLD HOUSES

But that was long ago.
We're sentimental
about things closer to home—
the view of the desert from
picture windows facing south
to capture spring's violent skies;
our buffed floors and woodwork
stripped of layers of paint;
the dust of past lives
whose tedium we fail to account
because the present drops
its veil over them
so only the luminous moments
shine through. We're enraptured
by these mute doorknobs
we scavenged one fall afternoon
in that dust-hazed Paris shop:
elaborated with swans
and stylized, feral boars.

From the desert to our deck—
where this afternoon
the cat, from the window's wrong side,
stalks a tarantula
stretching spiny legs
under a sun that's called her to rise,
though it is too early,
and in the sky clouds churn—
the distance is not so great.
Nor from countries across the ocean,
to satellites, in orbit,
to the antenna on the roof:
distress reduced to digits
we measure and transmit.

A matter of seconds, from
the driver's seat to the curb.
Consider your brother, lost

in this country's urban outdoors,
to the sky's most brutal whims.
In his brain opens
a dark flower, a hole
into which every particle
of light vanishes.
Finally, his very name
will cross that threshhold—
eventful, verging on blackness—
though we will keep seeing it,

long after it's lost to him.
We watch the cat bat the glass
as if desire could melt it.
At least, you say, it's spring.
Though your brother would never return
to a city dulled like this one
with dust, the easy tricks
righteousness plays on the heart,
you scan the faces of men
posed at freeway exits
and market parking lots.
What will they do for food?
You're looking for a sign,
looking less for him
than for any one familiar.

3. THE CHARM

In the cat's dream
desire becomes a bridge
that finally holds his weight.
He curls his paw and growls.
Dusk brushes the windows
with rain and leaves, its blackness

crowding the panes, like a wood
worthy of any dark age,
any morality tale
in which the way back is lost.
At the piano, our voices
spiral a throaty staircase,
mount step-by-step a tower
that narrows until it opens
into shrill wind, a view
where heaven holds, still,
old charms, however tarnished.

Ordained by history
to doubt, to wait at the edge
of a desert scoured clean by weather,
we love its vaulted sky
for what science tells us it is—
static, dust and water—
in heavy books
only the faithful may translate.
Believe: there's nothing behind it
but more dust, light's refractions,
stars flying away
or collapsing into themselves.
In the first thousand years
Anno Domini, faith
knotted gentle ropes
around our necks, and led us.

Now, our fingers
rework the knots. Why not?
The theoretical strings of matter,
of heaven and earth, bind us
just as invisibly
as mythic resurrection,
and even more strangely,
to a cosmos too vast
to allow for intimate knowledge
of its divine spaces,

of particles so charmed,
so hypothetical we build
vast machines to speed them,
just so we can see

their traces, implications.
We've all the time in the world.
We knew we were impulsive:
the lightbulb flickers on
just like in cartoons.
But despite these magazine photos—
computers illuminating
a hemisphere at a time
the weather inside our skulls—
we're too easily bowled over
by conceptions of sky, of sun.
We raise ennui to an art
we work to make look effortless.
Outside the darkened window
this desert's electrical storm,
however passionate,

is only the beginning.
We watch our fingers, reversed
in the steam-glazed bathroom mirror,
typing on the traditional
fin-de-siecle lace,
our hands soft as flowers
elaborating wrist and throat.
Bathed and perfumed, we engage
in immaculate courtships,
ignoring the violent flush,
the convulsions of our hearts,
though in the aftermath
we twitch and murmur, dreaming
out the code in our cells:
the cloud of the explosion,
the flower of heat rising
from the jugular. Blood on the tongue.

The Golden Years of the
Fourth Dimension

for Elaine Smith, November 4, 1934–July 14, 1994

> For uncounted centuries, clergymen had skillfully dodged such perennial
> questions as, Where are heaven and hell? and Where do angels live? Now they
> found a convenient resting place for those heavenly bodies.
> Michio Kaku, *Hyperspace*

1. I confess, I am like them—fabulists, theosophists,
readers of the moon, of tabloid science, fin-de-siecle
purveyors of raps and voices making matter

of the thinnest air. Oh, the drapes and flashing lights,
the glittering fissures.
                         Elaine would have loved it—to imagine
they *are* tiny, those angels, enough

to make a world of a pinhead, a ballroom
vast enough for the cosmic dance, the space

they inhabit smaller than an atom.
A simple one, say hydrogen. The lightest thing
we're made of, or so we thought. Though now

I imagine angels crawling my blood, heavenly
metastasis, working from the inside
out, and why not? What difference

can they make to us, those dimensions, higher
but so miniscule we contain them? Until,
say, the atom splits. Tears

open into our space: a rent
so bright we can't look into it, can see
only fallout, aftertraces of dust

decaying into poison. Not the moment
angels glance out at us, surprised

at the rupture, as if
by a camera's candid flash projected

into cubist life. Though still
invisible, to the human gaze. Dropping nail files.
Rubbing sleepy eyes. You don't believe

they spend their time singing, thinking of God?
How could we know, then, what we'd unleashed?

2. But this was long ago. And before that, the century's
extravagant turn, its desperate theologies—

what to save in the face of Darwin? Of Einstein?
Of Lenin?—who said the fourth dimension

was no place for revolution. Oh, yeah?
my dead friend may be saying, sallying forth

to see what needs her fixing. Others
proved him wrong—and they kept coming,
didn't they?
        So, matter mutates

into energy after all—not only radium, fixed
in Madame Curie's gaze. But our simpler flesh,
compressing under time. Or so I hope, today,

listening to eulogies full of sweetness, weighted
with what seems unspeakable—which is relative,
after all—and remains

unsaid. How Elaine's image decays
before her body, weakened inside-out. Life

into half life. In the end, we take
what we can get: love, say, which serves

itself. Mine, too. I admit: I loved her
wired tight and angry. "Shit,"
she'd say, "tell it like it is." A quality

her sister-in-law, smiling, pronounces
as if it were an epithet. Elaine left her

helpless.
          But what right do I have? Elaine
scrubbed my stove, or leaned against it,

waving the sponge at me. Scrubbed
my mother's kitchen floor, and later mine,

on her hands and knees, backing up,
talking, into afternoon. Loved

what never earned her love,
and she knew it. Ran, one day,

over her lawn to greet us, right into traffic,
waving her hands. Every car swerved,

missed. She had a month to live.
          That physicist,
leaning, a century ago, over radium

decaying—she breathed its dust, inhaled
the last century's air, blew it out into this one,

where, for example, the Czar is overthrown
in solid three dimensions; where Elaine

is mourned in a suburban chapel. Who am I
to criticize their grief? I touched her hand

one last time, though it was cold and still,
at least to my inadequate eyes,
and the mortician had sewed her mouth

into its dourest frown. Someone said
how beautiful she looked, and at peace.

3.   I never saw

the Czar, except in photos, a figure
made of light.
                    And there is no difference,

after all, between time and space, between
loving her from week to week
as she was, sponge in hand, and loving her

now, maybe across unspeakable dimensions,
translated into spirit by desire. Is there?

Except to the human heart. It's all
the spiritualists wanted, evidence

of their own persistence, somewhere to go
when they're finished here. If she's anywhere,

she's energy, not matter. Beyond
our reach.
                    Consider that moon,
for so long so distant

it might as well have been, well,
a *heavenly* body. And now, as of this month

twenty-five years ago, men have walked
its surface, have seen the earth rising

into a moony, blue and white romance.
Twenty-five years is nothing, except to us.
Only six more: another millennium, a turn

of events she wouldn't have wanted to miss.
And so many scientists want to tell us

this is no mere metaphor. Yes. But
even the scientists talk of light as if
it were a lucid ocean beating our shores;

even they, knowing *so much,* know
only the approximate, the magic change.
Light, some say, may be

vibration from another dimension.
                              Or not. The scientists,
too, are fabulists, in love with their own
whimsy and invention. In such a universe,

what good are pure numbers, but to the mind?
And the rest of us, who have believed

in what is beyond us, have always thought
it must be, after all,
too large, not too small, for us to witness.

Spiritual Fallout

It has happened a few times. Enough times, actually, so that he worries about it. Sometimes during the prayer of the day or the reading of the lesson. Often during the sermon. Usually when the congregation is seated. Always when it's fairly quiet.

When it happens, he digs his fingers into the cushioned pew or the green cover of the hymnal, pushes a fingernail into the gold outline of the cross on the cover, deep enough to leave an indentation, a rut, then follows the line around and around, digging deeper into the crease of the cross, until the urge is gone.

But he knows it will return. And he is never sure when. He's not sure that next Sunday he might not do it. Next Sunday, as the preacher stands before the congregation and front pews filled with confirmands in white robes and red carnations. As he rattles through a sermon about the Holy Spirit, trying to explain how the Holy Spirit is just like the radioactive fallout from Chernobyl. Unseen, powerful.

The preacher is quite serious, but he doesn't realize what he is saying. The congregation doesn't realize. The confirmands are quietly peeling the wrapping paper from the gifts they were given earlier in the service and one by one are finding small commemorative dinner plates left over from the fifieth anniversary of the church celebrated five years earlier. They don't know that, in English, Chernobyl means "wormwood." The plant of bitterness, the blazing star from heaven that poisoned a third of all the earth's water. The Holy Spirit.

The Holy Spirit that rose from Reactor Number Four in a cloud three miles high. The Holy Spirit of plutonium still inside the cracking tomb of Reactor Number Four. The Holy Spirit of exposure. The Holy Spirit of radioactive milk. The Holy Spirit of leukemia and tumor. The Holy Spirit of Beylorussian children.

He squirms and squeezes the front edge of the cushioned pew. He might do it now. Jump to his feet. And yell something, like "Hogwash!" or something really stupid, like "Everybody duck!" Or break into the first verse of that Hank Williams' song:

"Hear the lonesome whippoorwill."

before two deacons and the church custodian spring onto him faster than anyone dared to spring a few weeks earlier when the man in the pew that the sun hits hard stiffened during the sermon.

"It sounds too blue to fly."

And while they try to quiet him, the preacher covers the microphone with his right hand to keep the outburst muffled from the radio audience, from those who stare beyond the kitchen window to the muddy ruts in the driveway, from those who listen at an open window for the cry of a lone eagle.

The Soul May Be Compared to a Figure Walking

In the forms' bare spaces they ask my occupation.
I'm tempted to tell the truth for once,
tempted to write,
"I am one who finds similitudes for soul."
Yeats reports that some moralist or mythological poet
compares the solitary soul to a swan.
Heaney suggests, "the soul may be compared
unto a spoonbait that a child discovers
beneath the sliding lid of a pencil case,
glimpsed once and imagined for a lifetime."
Yes. I write these out for confirmation.

The soul may be compared to a figure walking
Bent Creek Road southward from the Parkway.
Two miles down a dirt road, barred, leaps to the right.
He climbs the barricade. Takes the offshoot,
hoping it is forbidden.
A blunt wood closes in, trees compact, ingathered
as if to counsel reticence in that rage of space and air.
One tall tree guards the road's end, in Park Service red
warning no vehicles, no camping.
The figure neither drives nor camps.
Beyond the cherub tree a high meadow opens,
gold under the sky, grass beaten gold by wind.
A meadow with its golden carpet tilts
toward the mountains lying many-figured:

Crag, Fang, Wall, the sleeping Dinosaur,
great Pisgah in the distance like a blue bride

veiled and terrible.
Above, the bowl of air is perfect quiet.
Yet something roars amid the trees.
He looks for a lake of falling water,
finds but wind enraged from valley floor upward,
finds but wind harrying the contours
of his coiled-serpent hill, bursting forth
wherever it finds obstacles to turn to song.
Lie down the voice says. *Lie amid gold and sleep.*
The figure listens and obeys.
The soul may be compared to a sleeper
on the burnished slope. Wind finds me sleeping
in the gold rucked grass. It hymns
the names of my lost ones, stirs the deeps of memory
grown by now to seem the story of the world,
breathes *David David* expecting me to join the song.

I tell it I am part of a different story.
I tell it I've come a pilgrim and will be going
when I've had my fill of dying amid space and light.
I tell it sing what it wants and go its way.
I hear my voice in the high field,
like a stranger's, or a bird who, catching breath,
boils triumph in the hawk's receding shadow.
I think I'm saved because I danced free
from the dream that came with manhood,
that Gobi littered with crowns and bones.
I think I'm saved by the gods of this mountain
who find it in themselves to forgive everything.
I wait for the angel who sundered
to make whole again, tears upon him like a crystal shirt.
Fearless I lie down, a weight plunging through the worlds.

Child, the flame stream of the west wind says.
Child, say the huddle of out-gloried stars.
I answer, "I am here, just as I was." I wait for them
to answer recantation. Forgiveness. To answer sleep.

The soul may be compared to a sleeper on a golden hill
who even in dreams takes someone, lovelily, to task.

O father who has not loved me. Lord who has not loved me.
I sing back into the wind. It listens and pours on.
I think it was not meant this way.
I left the road. Stumbled on another.
Found it mounts among the mountains sole and beautiful,
a grace unguessed, given to the proud and small.
The wind and the braced light know.

They bend to my lips as if they expected
me to tell a secret kept from them in splendor,
as if like men of elder times
I lay down amid my ruin all the while contriving
to pump back from the sprayed oak flowers
and be carried in the hands of rain.
As if they expected me to breathe out—
nectared and mysterious—
the air of other worlds than this.

Watch, sky says as I rub my eyes in spilled light.
Listen, wind whispers to the shaken gold,
as if some god were answering in his sleep.

Pearyland

I APOLOGIZE FOR NOT being able to tell you the whole of this story. It begins at the airport at Søndre Strømfjord in Greenland and it happened to a man named Edward Bowman. He'd just come down from Pearyland, by way of Qânâq and Upernavik, then Nûk. About a hundred of us were waiting around for planes, his out to Copenhagen, with Søndre Strømfjord socked in. He'd been at the airport for six days; I'd been there just a few, with four Inuit friends from Clyde Inlet, on Baffin Island. In those days—1972, just out of law school—I was working with Canadian Eskimos, helping to solidify a political confederation with Eskimos in Greenland.

We were all standing by, long hours at the airport. Some people went into town; but the notion that the weather might suddenly clear for just a few minutes and a plane take off kept most of us around, sleeping in the lounges, eating at the restaurant, using the phones.

Bowman was at work on a master's degree in wildlife biology at Iowa State, though by that time he may have already abandoned the program. His thesis, I remember well, had to do with something very new then—taphonomy. He was looking, specifically, at the way whitetail deer are taken apart by other animals after they die, how they're funneled back into the ecological community—how bone mineral, for example, goes back into the soil. How big animals disappear. Expanding the study a little brought him to Pearyland. He wanted to pursue in northern Greenland some threads of what happens when large animals die.

I should say here that Bowman wasn't eager to talk, that he didn't

223

feel compelled to tell this story. He didn't avoid my questions, but he didn't volunteer much beyond his simple answers. His disinclination to talk was invariably polite, not unlike my Inuit friends', whose patience I must have tried all those years ago with my carefully framed questions and youthful confidence.

Did he go up there just to look at dead animals? I asked him. In a cold place where carcasses decay very slowly? Partly, he said. But when he'd read what little had been written about the place, he said, his interests became more complicated. Pearyland is an arctic oasis, a place where many animals live despite the high latitude—caribou, wolves, arctic hares, weasels, small animals like voles and lemmings, and many birds, including snowy owls. Bowman said he'd tried to get grants to support a summer of study. Of course, he was very curious about the saprophytic food web, the tiny creatures that break down organic matter; but, also, no one understood much about Pearyland. It was remote, with a harsh climate and very difficult and expensive to get to.

No funder was enthusiastic about Bowman's study, or his curiosity. (He told me at one point that part of his trouble in applying for grants was that, after working with the deer carcasses in Iowa, he just had an instinct to go, but no clear, scientific purpose, no definite project, which finally presented the larger institutions with insurmountable problems.) Eventually, he was able to cobble together several small grants and to enlist the support of a foundation in Denmark, which enabled him to buy food and a good tent. For his travel north to Qânâq he was going to depend on hitching rides on available aircraft. With the last of his funds he'd charter a flight out of Qânâq for Brønlund Fjord in early July and then arrange for a pickup in mid-September. All of which he did.

When we met, the only cash he had was his return ticket to Copenhagen, but he was not worried. Somehow, he said, everything would work out.

Now, here is where it gets difficult for me. I've said Bowman, unlike most white men, seemed to have no strong need or urge to tell his story. And I couldn't force myself to probe very deeply, for reasons you'll see. So there could be—probably are—crucial elements here that were never revealed to me. It's strange to think about with a story like this, but you'll be just as I was—on your own. I can't help it.

What Bowman found at Brønlund Fjord in Pearyland was the land of the dead. The land of dead animals.

When he arrived, Bowman made a camp and started taking long walks, six- or seven-mile loops, east and west along the fjord and north into the flat hills, into the willow draws. The fjord stood to the south—open water at 82° North in July, which surprised him; but that is the nature of arctic oases. Summer comes earlier there than it does farther south, and it lingers a bit longer. In winter it's relatively warmer. Some days, Bowman said, he wore only a T-shirt.

Bowman's treks brought him within sight of many animals in the first few days, but he wasn't able to get near them. And, a little to his wonder, not once on these long walks did he come upon an animal carcass, not even a piece of weathered bone.

The only thing he worried about, he told me, was polar bears. He saw seals regularly in the fjord, so he expected bears would turn up; but he saw no tracks or scat, not even old sign. He wasn't afraid of being attacked so much as of having a bear break into his food. He had no radio, so he ran the risk of starving before the plane came back. For this reason alone, he said, he had agreed to take a gun, which the Danish government insisted he carry. How he learned where he was, that he'd camped in the land of the dead, was that one morning he went for the rifle and it wasn't there.

Of course, no one was around, so its loss made no sense to him. He looked underneath everything in his camp, thinking, absent-minded, he might have left it at his defecation pit, or taken it down to the shore of the fjord. Or that in his sleep he'd gotten up and taken the gun somewhere and thrown it away. He said he entertained this last possibility because he was never comfortable with the idea of having the gun; and who could know, he said to me, what the dreaming mind really wanted done?

The day after he missed the gun he saw a few caribou close by, less than a half mile away. He was eating breakfast, sitting on an equipment crate, watching the wind ripple the surface of the fjord and tracing with his eye a pattern in the purple flowers of a clump of saxifrage. The animals' hard stare caused him to turn around. He gazed back at them. Four animals, all motionless. It struck him then that in that first week or so he hadn't seen any caribou or muskoxen grazing or browsing.

He reached for his binoculars, but in that same moment the caribou dropped off behind a hill. He saw no other animals the rest of the day, but the following morning the caribou were back in the same place. This time, he sat very still for a long while. Eventually the caribou walked down to where he was, only about twenty yards away.

"Where is your place?"

Bowman said when he heard these words he thought it was the animals that had made them, but when he turned around he saw, far off near the edge of the water, a man, an Inuk.

"What place are you from?"

It was hard for Bowman to understand that this man's voice was coming to him clearly even though he was standing far away. He didn't know what to answer. He didn't think the man would know about Indiana, so he said he was from very, very far away, to the west and south.

"What do you want here?"

Bowman told me he wished to answer this question in such a way that he would not offend the man because he had a strong feeling he might be hindered in his study here (which, he pointed out again, was nearly aimless). Or possibly harmed.

"I want to listen," he said finally.

"Do you hear the wind? Meltwater trickling down to the fjord? The arctic poppies turning on their stalks in the summer sunshine?"

"Yes. I listen to all this."

"Do you hear the songs of my brothers and sisters?" asked the man by the fjord.

"I'm not sure," answered Bowman. "I don't think I've heard any singing. Perhaps if I listened better."

At that moment, Bowman turned quickly to look at the caribou. They'd come much closer. Swinging still further around, he caught sight of two wolverine, that odd lope of theirs, as they came bounding toward him from the west. Then the Inuk was right next to him, sitting on another crate, looking out over the waters of the fjord. Bowman couldn't make out his face from the side.

"I'm the caretaker here," the man said. Bowman could see now that he was about forty, fifty. "What do you want? What is 'Indiana'?" he asked.

Bowman, startled, described where Indiana was. Then he tried to explain what he did as a biologist, and that he was specifically interested in what happened to animals after they died. After that, he told me, he shouldn't have said anything more, but he went on until he ran out of things to say.

"The dead come here," the man said when Bowman was finished talking. He stood up. Bowman saw he was short, only five feet four inches or so, his short-fingered hands massive, the veins prominent, his forehead receding into a line of close-cropped, raven black hair. "You've come to the right place," he said. Then he walked away. Although he walked slowly, soon he was very far away.

The caribou were gone. The wolverine were still there, watching him, but after a while they, too, disappeared.

Bowman did not see the man again for four or five days, and then he just saw him at a great distance, walking along the low edge of the sky.

One morning Bowman crawled out of his tent and saw an arctic fox resting on its haunches, looking at seals in the fjord. When he made a sound—his sock scraping on tundra gravel—the fox turned around quickly, surprised, and ran away. As he sprinted off, Bowman saw he had no shadow.

Bowman tried to arrange each day according to the same schedule. When he awoke, he took his binoculars and studied the tundra in every direction, writing down whatever he saw—arctic hare, muskoxen, snow geese. He ate, then took a lunch and his pack and went for a long walk. He made lists of all the flowers, the tracks he came upon, the animals he saw; and he fought against a feeling that he was not accomplishing anything. Every day he wrote down the temperature and he estimated the speed and direction of the wind and he made notes about the kind of clouds he saw in the sky. Altostratus. Cumulonimbus.

One day the man came back. "Why aren't you trying to hunt?" he asked. "How come you don't try?"

"When I was a young man I hunted with my father in Indiana. I don't do that now." Bowman told me he wanted to be very careful what he said. "I don't hunt here, in this place, because I brought food with me. Besides, I don't know these animals. I have no relations with them. I wouldn't know how to hunt them."

"No hunting here, anyway."

"I know this is your country," Bowman said cautiously, "but why are you here?"

"Caretaker. Until these animal spirits get bodies and are ready to go back, a human being must be here, to make sure they aren't hungry. If the animals want something—if they want to hear a song, I learn it. I sing it. Whatever they want, I do that. That's my work."

"Have you been here a long time?"

"Yes. Long time. Soon, someone else will come. A long time ago, before Indiana, there was more work. Many caretakers. Now, fewer."

"What do these animals eat?"

"Eating—it's not necessary." After a moment he said, "They are feeding on the sunlight."

"When they are ready, where do they go?"

"All everywhere. They go home. They go back where they're from. But too many, now, they don't come here. They are just killed, you know. No prayer." He made a motion with his fist toward the ground as though he were swinging a hammer. "They can't get back there then. Not that way."

"Which ones come back?"

The man regarded Bowman for a long moment. "Only when that gift is completed. Only when the hunter prays. That's the only way for the animal's spirit to get back here."

"Do they come here to rest?"

The man looked at Bowman strangely, as if Bowman were mocking him with ignorant questions. "They get their bodies here."

"But only if they are able to give their lives away in a certain manner, and if the hunter then says a prayer?"

"Yes."

After a while the man said, "Many religions have no animals. Harder for animals now. They're still trying."

Bowman did not know what to say.

"Very difficult, now," said the man.

"What do you hear in this place?" the Inuk asked abruptly. "Do you hear their songs? Do you hear them crying out?"

"In my sleep," Bowman ventured. "Or perhaps when I am awake but believe I'm sleeping. I hear a sound like a river going over a wall, or wind blowing hard in the crown of a forest. Sometimes I hear heartbeats, many heartbeats overlapping, like caribou hooves."

"The souls of the animals calling out for bodies, bodies calling out for their souls."

"The bodies and the souls, searching."

"Yes. They come together, falling in love again like that. They go back, have children. Then one day someone is hungry, someone who loves his family, who behaves that way. Wolf, human being—the same. That's how everything works."

"Is there another place," asked Bowman, "where the animal souls go if they are just killed?"

The Inuk looked at Bowman as if he weren't there and got up and walked away.

He didn't come back and Bowman didn't see him again.

The animals around Bowman's camp grew less shy. They began to move past him as though he were growing in the ground or part of the sky. The caribou all walked in the same, floating way, some pairs of eyes gleaming, some opaque, looking at the plants and lichens, at the clouds, and staring at rivulets of water moving across the tundra.

Bowman saw his gun one morning, leaning against a crate.

During his last days, he said, he tried to sketch the land. I saw the drawings—all pastels, watercolors, with some small, brilliant patches of red, purple, and yellow: flowers, dwarf willow, bearberry. The land was immense. It seemed to run up against the horizon like a wave. And yet it appeared weightless, as if it could have been canted sideways by air soft as birds breathing.

The pilot came and took him out to Qânâq, nearly five hundred miles. Two days later he began traveling south. Now, with the rest of us, he was waiting for the weather to clear.

Bowman told me this story over three days. He said it only a little at a time, as though he were not certain of it or me. I kept trying to get him to come back to it, but I wasn't insistent, not rude. I had many questions. Did the animals make sounds when their feet touched the ground? Did he see airplanes flying over? Was he afraid ever? What was the Inuk wearing?

The hardest question, for I had no other reason than my own inquisitiveness to pursue him, was asking whether he had an address where I might reach him. He gave me an address in Ames, where the university is, but by the time I wrote he'd moved away; and like so many young people—he was twenty-three, twenty-four—he did not leave a forwarding address.

Sometimes when I am in a library I look up his name. But as far as I know he never wrote anything about this, or anything else.

The last day of September the fog lifted suddenly, as though it had to go elsewhere. Bowman's plane, which had been there on the ground for eight days, left for Copenhagen and an hour later I flew with my friends back to Frobisher Bay, on Baffin Island.

SYDNEY LEA

Presences

*B*ECAUSE THE FISH must have weighed five pounds; because she'd been game beyond words; because she was a brown trout; because each little spot on her flanks wore its own pale halo; because of her shape's sleekness as I held her in the riffle till she recovered and swam back into deeper, unbroken water; because this was the fish I'd traveled for—I lay down in the Wyoming sun to nap. September-cool: not a cloud, not a biting bug.

The cottonwood deadfall on the gravel bar had composted, so that the trunk, once rough, now made a fine pillow. I put down my head, all full of the recent perfection. Because the moment had been the stuff of dreams, only dream could be adequate to it.

And I was tired: from the hike to the river; from the minutes in its water, which scarcely looked to be moving, but which was imperious when you stood in it; from the concentration that such a fish demands. I stretched out, convinced that some spiritual benchmark in my life had established itself, and that whatever might afterward befall me, I'd have it as an abiding reference.

What you see in today's dream, it's often said, relates directly to something in today's not-dream. Joey and I had roamed this country for a week, dawn till dark, without encountering so much as fresh sign of bear; but as I reclined, the sunlight just warm enough on my face, the sand smoother than any bed, the cottonwood pillow almost itself a part of slumber, the grizzly came.

We'd imagined him for days, and that was apparently enough, was a *way* of seeing him.

I don't mean that the animal was visible, nor that my sleep was really sleep so much as that half-wakefulness in which sensory detail seems both ordinary and eloquent of a different, a visionary realm.

I knew of the bear's presence because of the wind, which had doubtless been there all along—there as I approached the pool where the big fish and some smaller others were sipping those blue-wings; there as I laid down the cast and my fly drifted over the brown trout's lie and she shot up to have at it.

But in the midst of the stalk and the battle, my mind didn't register the sound, huge air forcing its way through high gaps. Though the air didn't move on the beach where I lay, the passes above were full of somber glissandi, like the musical theme in a frightening film that portends The Awe-Inspiring Thing. And what out here would that thing be besides *ursus horribilis?*

Even now I believed I could hear the scuff of his pads on the sand-beach, the faint cough of surprise at my scent. He needn't charge but simply and casually walk, all mammoth head and shoulders, to where I lay; then he'd paw me from under the deadfall like a grub.

No sense for me to bolt—this is an animal that can outsprint a bloodhorse—especially in my heavy, ridiculous waders. You're supposed to climb, because a grizzly doesn't choose to do the same. But the only tree within fifty yards was the fallen one under which I huddled now, almost awake. This was still mostly a dream, I could pray, and so maybe in slumber I looked dead. Because that's the last recourse when the grizzly addresses you: play dead. Joey and I had joked about this. Sure: play dead while eight hundred pounds of mammal thunders over the earth, the froth from his maw trailing in the breeze, glinting in the last of sun you'll ever see.

All nonsense, of course. I woke to a water ouzel, disappearing now and then under the surface to fossick for bugs; to an eagle's high screams, faint in the windy clamor; to the purr of the river where it swung through an elbow.

Yet there had been a presence. I am sure of it even now. Perhaps it was facile to associate it with Bear, but there'd been something.

I once thought to make a cartoon of myself. Its first panel would show me in woods or moving water, grasping a gun or rod; in the thought balloon over my head I'd be sitting before a typewriter. In the second panel, you'd see me before that same type-writer, but the thought balloon would show me standing with gun or rod in woods or moving water. For I am a man, by turns, in the outdoors with his head full of books and words, and a man in books and words with his head full of the outdoors. Yet I hope that at mo-ments these men are merged, even if such moments exist in my poems alone.

One day—about eight weeks after the wind-driven vision of that Wyoming grizzly—I sat for hours, writing at something without much success. In my frustration I began to meditate on what now and then seems the paucity of milestones in my life. Such self-pity is a loathsome defect of my character: what better monument after all might I leave than my children, the second of whom, a daughter, ten years old at the time, had chosen this day for a house party? I'd stayed at home as token chaperone: Erika's guests were all female schoolmates, well behaved, completely capable of amusing them-selves as young girls do—with chat, inventive games, humor.

After the first hour of the party, I saw my irrelevance to it, and perhaps my intrusion. So I advised the kids that I'd be in my office if they needed me, as of course they would not.

Perhaps I needed *them*. In the absence of their patter and shuffle—or the presence of my typewriter's mocking silence—I in-wardly moaned that this was a day neither fish nor fowl. I might have gotten an angle on that piece of poetry and been by now some way towards its final draft; but no. I might have abandoned the proj-ect and taken myself outdoors; but not that either.

And now I recognized that this fall I'd spent less time than usual outdoors, fewer hours pursuing the grouse among draw, covert, side-hill. The wild provender in my freezer was not what it's normally been. The end of shotgun season loomed; I'd have to count on a deer. The bare shelves downstairs became, in this mood, an ungainly metaphor.

But surely all this just signalled slow blood. I simply needed some action, and if it could not come in verbal form, I'd go perspire. I find sweat an almost totally reliable curative. Having checked to see that he was at home, I wrote down the number of a neighbor the told my daughter and her friends I'd be back soon. They nodded distractedly, then turned again to the play they were rehearsing. I made to complain about how they'd dragged their props—cookware and clothing and bedcovers—into the living room, but thought better.

When I unlocked the kennel doors, the dogs nearly bowled me over. The younger and quicker of the pointers threw gravel at the end of our driveway, leaning into the corner down the woods road. I tooted her halfway back on the whistle, not wanting her out of earshot. The retriever, as usual, made a short dash, lifted a leg, then rushed back to be patted, and the older pointer, grown more meditative than her kennelmate with the hardworking years, pottered and nipped, in that inexplicable doggy way, at a few remaining stalks of grass.

I jogged, carefully, the dogs dashing back and forth by my legs. It had sleeted the night before, then lightly frozen. There were patches of ice along the twitch road, which runs downhill from home a few hundred yards. Where it peters out, there's something like a northward trail—made by game, by me and my dogs in our rambles—to the top of Stonehouse Mountain. It climbs eighteen hundred feet in less than a mile, over slippery, lichen-covered granite. The soil here pushed settlers out almost as they arrived, their labor fragmentarily evident in stone fences that show all through the woods; occasional boulder-banked cellar holes; barn foundations; a rusted bolt or the spirit of a sugar vat or a hinge.

I made my way at a pace just properly taxing, so that the blood coursed in my ears and my breath came in rhythmic heaves. To make them shed their ice and straighten out of my way, I knocked at the bent saplings before me with a staff.

The therapy was working. I dropped my outer shirt by the side of the trail. I'd make a loop then fetch it on the way home. My undershirt went wet with the forest moisture, but also with my own, which was what I'd been wanting. I thought how the poem left in my typewriter might write itself out here, if I made sure not to think about it.

I'd had certain things happen, or not, for years.

My legs felt strong and my wind full. I was a long way from dead.

High air when I dreamed the bear, and more air to come. I gulped it that morning of my daughter's party. But just now

I'm back in a different season from the same climb. Uphill, the woods are between the trillium—which have collapsed into their own cadaverous rankness—and the wild ladyslippers, little smug burghers that salute the birth of true summer.

But never mind such poetical cant for a moment, for I am also recently back from burying Larry, whose lungs had finally been borne down by the cancer in them, and in everything else, it seems, but his brain, which stayed clear to the end.

I first knew Larry when we both were three. He grew into a freckled, blocky Irishboy, tough and volatile. At length the toughness and volatility got mixed up with much too much booze, and he turned into a mean young man—then a middle-aged bum, flimflam, mess. Five years ago, he phoned me, drunk enough to call at 3:00 A.M., lucid enough to scream that he was in trouble: he'd awakened the morning before on an interstate highway, unsure whether this was Florida or Georgia or Mississippi, whether the car was bought or stolen or borrowed.

What could he do?

I told him he could opt to die or not to.

For two years, I took other such phone calls, always in the middle of the night, the words slurring through long distance static. When I got the last of these rescue signals, I summoned up what little hardness I had: "Larry, I don't want to hear from you again unless you haven't had a drink for twenty-four hours." The phone clicked, and I lay awake, wondering if he was as suicidal as he claimed.

A year went by, and I heard from him again. I listened with my best ear as he got through the small talk. His voice had a crispness greater, even, than when he'd been a healthy, hell-raising kid, back in our school days.

"You haven't had a drink," I said.

"Not since the last time I talked to you." I could picture the old smile that made his freckles swim.

We stayed in touch, by mail and phone, through the short years after. The poor man couldn't get a break, yet he was sticking it out.

He was a grocery clerk when he was diagnosed.

Larry had felt sick since midwinter, but he'd needed to work long enough to get company medical insurance before he could afford to see a doctor. By then it was too late, though it would probably have been in any case.

"*Where* is the cancer?" I breathed into the telephone, horrified.

"Where *isn't* it?" he answered. "Liver, lung, bone. . . ."

"It makes me lonely all over."

"It'll be all right."

"But it's sad."

"Sure. But there could have been something sadder."

"What?"

"I could have died the way I was."

I didn't see him again; he was gone before I could get to the city where he lay. And in fact, before he died I came to think of his cancer for some reason as a city itself, slum infested, beyond any law. I pictured the breeze-blown detritus: plastic wrappers, cinders, tabloid pages. I envisioned the morass of grime from which winked broken wine bottles, shards of ruined windshield, those little sharp poptop keys. The disease was an inner urban sprawl, dark figures in every aperture and alley.

Yet an angel came to that city. An angel and one other.

Before we buried Larry on that cloudless May afternoon a few days ago—all his friends from school years gathered at the plot—his brother told me a strange thing or two. He reminded me first, however, that although his pain was overwhelming, Larry turned down morphine, insisting that his head remain clear.

At 6:45 he told his brother that their mother—dead long since from cancer herself—stood in the room. She was not visible, he explained, but she was there, and she bore a message of assurance.

Just a few minute later, the mother left and Jesus arrived. Or so Larry claimed; then he turned to that Presence, whatever it was, and said "I love you."

At seven in the evening exactly, Larry died.

At the same hour, Larry's sister was stabbed seven times by an assailant in her bookshop. She survived; indeed, she was standing among us at the burial ground. And after the funeral, another friend of ours told me how a light had followed him as he walked from his office to his car at seven o'clock. Yet another told how he'd had an appointment that day in Pittsburgh, how he'd misread directions, how he'd pulled over to roadside at the scheduled hour—seven—and concluded that he was lost, forever, beyond recall. Then I remembered the sudden exhaustion that came over me at the identical hour, when my wife and I always read to our three-year-old before putting him to bed. I slept a sleep like death till nine the next morning.

I make no elaborate case here. I seek neither to persuade anyone of anything, nor even to assert that my life has changed—for it likely hasn't: it seems, yes, that they arrive, those spiritual benchmarks in a life; one pledges to attend to them; and at length one goes right on as ever.

Though many of us survivors had drifted out of touch with one another, as with Larry, over the decades, we quickly fell into the old closeness—no, it was a greater closeness, the posturing of male adolescence corrected not only by our ageing but also by the dead man's final heroism and serenity. *His* was the Presence of that day, its genius.

I do not climb for the view alone, since I've got it by heart. Indeed I almost prefer to climb into fog, the kind that cloaked the mountaintop in the forenoon of my daughter's houseparty. I felt as though I'd stepped into another element altogether, as though I were underwater but able to breathe. Such a thought lifted me back to the Wyoming streamside, to the moment when the brown trout— having taken my little dun, having fought with the courage of wild things against me—quivered for a minute or two in my hand. A moment before I let her go back to her pool. Before the bear arrived.

I can *will* such details into memory if I choose; but I prefer them to recur by means of some unexpected, unwilled association as they did on Stonehouse Mountain, the day's wetness suddenly transporting me. The spots on the fish's belly and loins reappeared in mind, each brighter than new-minted coin, each distinct, and—a thousand and more miles away—the air I breathed became freighted with the scent of western rapids and hot stones and fly repellent and bison dung, as well as with the glorious odors of the White Mountains where I lived. And they and the Wyoming mountains I'd visited rolled together and life seemed all it could ever be.

Coming out of my reverie, I noticed a dainty doe's track through the frost that lingered above two thousand feet. She had crossed the trail on tiptoes; just then I preferred that print to a heel-heavy buck's for a sign. Coarse and heavy myself—bearded, two hundred pounds, sweaty, my boots all mire—I was in the domain of delicacy.

I did not worry for my dogs; they'd long since been deer-broken. They champed and thrashed in the understorey to either side as I stooped and read the doe's track, fresh enough to fill with fogwater as I beheld it. I closed my eyes, and the fish swam through that water, and the stream out west flowed into it, and it reflected that overhead glory of an early Teton fall, so deep it's something other than blue.

But I was an ignorant man, and I still am.

Uphill forty more yards, two granite slabs leaned together, making a cave. There was no evidence yet of traffic in and out. Come winter, it would shelter a fox or perhaps a second year cub. Just now, I fancied it underwater too, and my fish peering from it, suspicious.

At home, the schoolgirls were play-acting. I imagined them as mermaids, or water sprites. Why not? Uninvited to their free-form drama, I could go on surmising that their visions, like mine, were aquatic today, even though at this time of year I'd normally be preoccupied—in imagination and action alike—with earth and air. It was still legally hunting season for birds, crouching on the woodsfloor, leaping into low sky before my pointers. But water it was, even though there'd be a long, hard winter before the runoff, the spate, the ebb, the occasion to look for a trout nearby.

Perhaps my thoughts ran as they did because I couldn't have hunted in any case. Not only did I have to be roughly within summoning distance, nine girls in my house and my wife and our other children away for the day, but also the going would have been too hard for me and my dogs. It's one thing to take an hour or so and follow a trail, however sketchy, to the top of a mountain; it's quite another to break through sodden, icy brush all day.

I'll let the shotgun season die in peace, I concluded, and—that resolve turning me melancholy again—I forged on. The sweat had started to cool, and I was breathing too shallowly. My fish had swum into her cave again, and when I willed her out, she looked different, like an exhibit in some tawdry sporting museum. I let her swim back in.

My younger pointer bitch shot across the trail ahead of me, leaping her slower brace-mate, who trotted the other way. Each cast an eye toward me, checking in. "All right!" I called, and they hurried on. Yet I thought suddenly how I'd missed the retriever for a few minutes. He wouldn't have gone far; he never does. But having once lost a dog on such a hike—he got out of hearing, he never came back—I'm more cautious even than I need to be.

I gave four short, quick blasts on the whistle, and waited. Two more minutes went by, and I was mildly unnerved. He is the most reliable, the most companionable, the least rangy of my three. I blasted again, and again I waited. Two *more* minutes, and no retriever.

This went on. I had last seen him fifty or sixty yards back down the trail. I dropped my plan to get to height-of-land; that peak would abide forever, but a dog is mortal, and now suddenly I wanted him more than anything on earth.

My soul ached for a dog . . . who showed himself in the next instant, by the side of the trail, near where I'd left him a few minutes ago. I scowled and bellowed his name and shrilled at the whistle. He lifted his muzzle momentarily, then, hunching his shoulders and grinning in that manner of a dog embarrassed, he disobeyed me, lowering his head again to whatever it was he sniffed there by the mossy, overturned basswood.

I lifted my stick as if to threaten a beating, but he kept busy with something—something no doubt extraordinary, because he is the most biddable of dogs and never resists me. I stood stock-still for a moment, perplexed: this is a duck dog, a retriever, but he might for all the world have been pointing just then, at whatever it was, flattened to blend with the umbers and beiges of the late-fall carpet.

Suddenly I heard that mid-range howl of wind I recalled from the day the dream-bear approached. It must have been blowing between the tops of Stonehouse and Mousley right along, but my crunching bootsoles and my heavy breathing and my water-fantasies must have deafened me to it, even if the trees and the brush were all sideways now in the gale. Since there is scarcely a thing in the New England woods besides the woods themselves to hurt you, I can't say what I felt, hearing that music again: maybe only the vestige of a fear felt in another place.

I walked the few steps to my dog. He had something, all right, though he had not taken it up in his mouth. I squatted and saw that it was the severed tail of a red fox, which, despite the dull gray of a cloudy autumn, glinted brightly, its ice-beads like pearls.

The sleetstorm of the preceding night had buried whatever sign might have surrounded this foxtail, and there was no trace of the rest of the corpse. Does the animal trot somewhere even now, ridiculous without his fine brush? Or is he dead and devoured almost entire, nothing left but this muff of hair over frail bone, splendid, bejewelled? And what might have killed him? A fisher, a lucky bear or coyote, a rover dog?

The sound of the wind in the pass was louder and louder, or was it my thoughts that made the crescendo?

It was beautiful, that unbloodied remnant, full with the imminence of white winter, a deep scarlet with undertones of silver. I thought of my daughter Erika, and how I must bring this bolt of fur back to her and her Thespian troupe. I imagined their widened eyes. Perhaps Erika would want to hang it in her room. If not, I thought, I would nail it to the shed wall between the two kennel doors. It would look good there.

But as I reached to take the foxtail up, the wind's roar moved to a still louder pitch, and I could not lift what I meant to lift. I contemplated it, rather—long and sleek, like the body of that trout I'd released. The wind still bore an uncertain burden. I straightened, my eye yet fixed on the dazzling fur before me; but in my lateral vision, there was something I could almost see. I could certainly feel it.

I remain an ignorant man, far too much so to say I was touched then by any spirit from the natural world, the human world, or any imaginable other.

But something was there.

DAVID HOPES

Eve

*E*VENINGS EARLY IN summer I hike the old logging roads that rise from Bent Creek. I go at evening because that's the time to see box turtles. The turtles dig themselves to the shell rim into the loose dirt of the roads, to have its heat around them as deep into night as possible. I can count on seeing three or four, probably the same ones each time. I pat their shells as I pass, saying, "Blessings, ancient one." This is a ritual I insist is necessary though I am aware I made it up. The turtles' aspect is at once feminine and changeless. That some of them bear the bright shells of males is insignificant. It is difficult to get them out of my mind afterwards. They are goddesses, of course, presiding spirits of patience and eternity. The world balances on their great grandmother's back.

Anything powerful enough to shock me earns subsequently a period of deep reflection.

The design of the shield of Achilleus in *The Iliad* shocks me for daring and vision notable even in the labor of a god. Dante's discovery that mortal love is a type and roadmap of divine love shocks me, that a thing should be at once so beautiful and so lucky. Keats's assertion in the "Bright Star" sonnet that it is one's right to insist on eternality and carnality in a single ecstatic moment shocks me. The adagio of Beethoven's A minor quartet shocks me, that human creation can be at once transcendent and, in the ordinary sense of the

241

word, meaningless. That the elements in my body have come from the throes of variously expiring stars shocks me speechless.

What shocked me recently was the "Eve Hypothesis." The Eve Hypothesis suggests that human mitochondrial DNA can be traced back to a single individual African woman alive a quarter of a million years ago. Mitochondria are tiny power packs within each cell: retorts, as it were, of the chemistry of the life process. Some scientists think the mitochondria may itself be an internal stranger, originally a separate organism housed in us by a symbiotic arrangement as old as multicellular life. Every cell of every body has them, and their DNA, their genetic code, is a donation exclusively from our mothers. The fire within the fire is feminine.

Divert yourself sometime by imagining the ancients possessed of modern scientific technology: Ptolemy with a two-hundred-inch reflector telescope, Aristotle with an electron microscope. Had the female heritage of mitochondrial DNA been known to Aquinas he might have declared them to be the vessels of Original Sin, little bullets of despair passed eternally down from Eve. He'd have the physical operation basically right, though the metaphysical assumptions remain untestable. Milton might have thought them the encoded voice of the fallen archangel, crumpled, hidden, repetitious, a letter memorized because it is too terrible to read.

The fact of this legacy from our mothers is astonishing enough; that it all should have passed through the genetic matrix of a single historical woman is almost too much to contemplate. It is science imitating myth, or rather the long delayed admission on science's part that it has always been a mythology, and that the great and true stories tend to run over and over on the same paths. We have known Eve in our blood forever; confirmation by science is at once welcome and presumptuous.

This single woman was not, of course, utterly alone in a human population that even then must have equaled that of a Midwestern county seat. It's just that all humans now alive trace their cellular genealogy directly to her. It was a tough time. There were many casualties. Some women bore only sons. She bore at least one daughter, and through her the world.

Whatever the circumstances, she is the Chosen Progenitrix. The Vessel, The Mother of the World. The Beloved.

Eve.

Whether she was paired with a single Father Adam is presently unknowable, and irrelevant.

Given the power to recede in time and lay eyes on any person, I'd chose this Eve. I'd crouch on the savannah, watching, trying to find myself in her gestures, in the ruffles of her voice, in the widening of her eyes when she peers toward the rising moon. I'd plumb her for my ten billion brothers, my ten billion sisters who learned their marrow and their blood from her, the Yin and the Lotus.

I'd try to tell her of her children. "All will be well," I'd say, thinking as I said it that it may turn out to be the truth.

She'd answer, "I know," and go on her way beneath the moonlight.

It's deep summer. A deer holds up one hoof, peers over her shoulder to look. She calculates the energy needed to run, and decides to stand still. She's safe. It's just me, running Bent Creek in the milky light of summer. Rains have been good this year. The creek and the river it feeds are swollen, the yellow and purple flowers riotous, the mosquitos abundant. Yet somehow the dust is immortal even after rain. Dust coats the road while the woods gleam with moisture. Dust gilds the leaves and weathered trunks. Dust flies from the wheels of passing pick-ups. Dust eddies in a backwash of Bent Creek like handfuls of scattered gold. Birds in the dusty branches taunt me, knowing I leave my glasses in the car when I run and cannot see them. The creek runs below like a companion who cannot quite keep up, yet who will be there, singing, to meet me at the end. Lovers cling together down in the thickets, their radios blaring, the oily sweetness of their campfires joining the smell of dust and forest on the hill path. Their heads swivel as I pass, swivel back to the matter at hand.

At the roadside I find the shattered shell of a box turtle. The sheath sloughs as I touch it, exposing the white bone below, four molded panels joined by jagged seams like stitches in an ivory cloth. I know what turtle this was, and that she must have been killed deliberately, and by men. No animal around here is capable of shattering a turtle shell. I pick up the fourfold shield, stuff it in my pocket for remembrance, for luck, maybe, if I don't consider of what kind. I run on.

Half a mile later I stop, bend over with my hands against my belly, burst into tears.

Something has unbalanced me. *O, mother,* I hear my bones cry into the dust, *forgive.*

REG SANER

The Real Surreal
Horseshoe Canyon

*F*OR YEARS I'VE BEEN hoping one day to lay eyes on certain ancient, blood-red silhouettes that even in bad photos look ghostly. Or look, as a friend had put it, "real surreal." Years intending someday to go see for myself, no idea why.

As to that, for how much of our lives have we known what we were doing? Truly *known*? Mostly, I've never. Though I've lived a long time in Colorado, I was born in the state of bemusement. At birth, no silver spoon; only a question mark. Example: why drive nearly four hundred miles (the last thirty, red dirt) just to see pictographs? All I know is, I have.

Seated this Utah evening on the rim, and I do mean the very leg-dangling *edge*, of Horseshoe Canyon I wonder other things too; such as, "Didn't sundown come kind of early?" But then a last roseate flood of direct rays breaks through cloud, and the wind-sculpted sandstone forms blush crimson. Gorgeous. About that I've no doubt whatever.

About the pictographs themselves I'm less sure. A man I like had said, "Oh, yeah, Horseshoe Canyon." Y' gotta see 'em." But why trust his judgment four hundred miles worth? Because I love Utah canyons? Because I rather enjoy never quite knowing?

I drink beer, munch pistachios, watch scarlet cloudlight wane across hill-huge, sugarloaf domes eight hundred feet below me. Their sandstone hunks and hills and pinnacles are so sensually rounded as to make wind seem a voluptuary. Yet I'm grateful that the hot August wind of this afternoon has lulled to a breeze. And aside from the inevitable Southwestern gnats, no insects.

"Who needs pictographs," I think, perhaps as a hedge against disappointment. "Summer evening, this canyon—they alone would be worth it." In case the rock art isn't? I grow dimly aware of an incongruity. On the doorsill of the twenty-first century, and a U.S. population poised for reveling in cyberspace, here I sit taking prehistoric relics for granted. By now, awake to that fact, sunset long gone, I find I'm sitting with a half moon in my lap.

Exhilarated by the good light of morning, I head downtrail into the canyon knowing memory hasn't deceived me: my passion for southeastern Utah is keen as ever. Knowing too that the rimrock trail I'm descending leads eventually to *big* pictographs, not mere doll-size, canyon-wall daubs. Along the so-called "Great Gallery" some virtually tower, I'm told: high as eight feet tall.

Fascinated by ancient things, I know those pictographs certainly qualify; they date back to somewhere between 500 B.C. and 500 A.D. True, that thousand year "margin" of error seems enormous. But because radiocarbon dating won't work on rock art, a lot of it can't be dated at all. Even splitting the difference between the earliest and the latest dates tells me I'm homing on painted creatures whose lives began two thousand years ago!

Considering wind, weather, and bipeds, what's "surreal" is the fact they've survived. Done in paint hardly more than colored mud patted or spattered onto bare rock, they owe their long lives to the arid Southwestern climate. And to the overhang of some cliff. And, equally vital, to human respect.

At the ruckus my boots make, yet another dust-colored whiptail scoots into its ankle-high bower of rabbit brush. Since both plant and lizard are ancient life-forms, if sheer antiquity triggers my affection, I should love them too, shouldn't I? Fact is, I do. Whiptails have been for years my old reliables, my desert trail companions. "How ya doin'?" I say to this one. "Eating plenty of gnats for me? Attaboy. Keep up the good work."

Dipping into canyons you become a time-diver who swims the geological past. If you begin under Utah's August-blue sky you also dip into heat, the more the deeper. And if you're me, descend further into the interrogative mood: "Are two quarts of water enough?"

For a mere seven miles they should be. I plan to check out the rock art then return, no dawdling. But even at 7:45 A.M. salty droplets keep smudging my sunglasses. My hat band rides on a film of sweat. My blue chambray shirt is soggy at the armpits, and under my light daypack its cotton is sopping.

"What if," I ask myself, "I get there and find those pictographs half-canceled by the over-scratching of vandals? Or greatly over-rated? Or both?" Despite the hype by its devotees, very little rock art I've seen is "art." A lot of it is "Kilroy was here" stuff—at least to my eye. Plus, a shamefully large portion has indeed been vandal-struck.

So," my quizzical side asks, "why bother?"

Maybe I just like the deep time of deserts. Back in Boulder I drive past shopping complexes that weren't there a week ago. I pass sub-urbs that haven't yet lived long enough for a house cat to have died within them. But Southwestern canyons—especially those ungrazed by cattle—remain as they have been for thousands of years. Hal-lowed, almost, by time's weather? For me, yes. The high walls of this one with its sun-drenched sheerness, its cougar-hued strata, and with its higher strata of fox-brown sandstone, and higher yet its glossy "varnish" of manganese oxide made indigo blue by the reflecting sky—all evoke the word "cathedral." Derisive skepticism even lets it stay there a full half-moment. Impressive, this canyon.

Also hotter than hell.

The "High Gallery' would have been easy to miss. Not only are its pictographs, oh, maybe sixteen feet above the foot of their jagged eastward escarpment; they're in full shade—which is welcome— but take some squinting to make out. "Like clothespins!" I think.

Prosaic but true. The main figure especially, which seems barely a yard long. His knobby head and round shoulders, the slim and arm-less torso of his red silhouette—if it is a he—are just like an old-fashioned, round clothespin. Except for *much* shorter legs, if that's what they are, and for the very unwooden way each painted shape seems to flow or hover: a whole array of such figures whose tapered silhouettes broaden toward the shoulders like souls of red smoke, some twenty-seven or so.

But it's hard to say how many. Even the best preserved are a faded cranberry, while the faintest . . . well, they may not quite *be* there. Could be mere weather streaks. Nonetheless, a good two dozen—of what? Some sort of deities? Earth spirits? Sky spirits? Why so many, and why here? Because this place had been in some way sacred? Nobody knows. All the same, it is. I know that much, or know it till my skeptical side asks why. And asks, "Sacred? What's that supposed to mean?"

Out of squawbush to my left a dove flies up. Makes a whispering, half-whistling sound as it climbs.

From three dinky pools of rank water rises the mingled smell of black leaves and wet sand. By midsummer a few random pools are what's left of the stream. Which, when in spate, had wrapped great swatches of flotsam around cottonwood trunks near the streambed; grasses and twigs and dead branches half-woven together like the beginning of basketry. Over plump cobbles thirty feet away shuffles a badger looking stodgy and comic. While paying me no mind whatever.

Those who painted such enigmatic figures saw the very things I'm seeing this minute. They relished this shade, breathed this morning air. Heard the stream speak in tongues when it flowed. Whoever painted them climbed down, hands reddened by hematite ground fine and mixed to a paste. He stood here looking up to appraise his work. As I'm doing now at stone wall become interface. Fellow earth. Across two thousand years that divide and unite us.

"The Alcove," so called, is a typical cavelike niche at the foot of the canyon's west side. It yields surprise and dismay: lots more pictographs—cruder, mostly, yet easier to study by being shoulder high on their now fully sunlit wall—and greatly varied in design. But lightly marred, scratched over, alas, by among others, "Wick Read / 1928."

What brainless vanity! Even if he's still alive, and even if I owned a gun, and could find him, I guess he'd be too old to deface. Have he and his ilk also slashed at the pictographs I most want to see?

That thought nudges my worry gland. I descend from "The Alcove" to continue down canyon, weaving among hundreds of cottonwood and willow wands slender as arrows feathered with leaves—as if shot into the streambed's moist sand. Though in a scrub oak grove east of my route several mule deer browse on Indian rice grass, Easterners must otherwise puzzle: "What would possess Indians to live in a canyon?" Yet it's obvious that's where the water was, and is, when there is any. And shade. Up above you have a high, dry, mainly treeless plateau, compared to which down here you find oasis conditions.

Fond of the passionate red put forth by claret cup cactus, I bend low to examine one with blooms fully opened—anthers all pollen-flecked and expectant. It sums up the desert. Cacti may open their chests to show, like the heart of their mystery, a stunning red blossom; but every such disclosure is terribly well defended.

Always, Southwestern desert gives you little enough of one thing, more than enough of another. Mere pinches of soil; barren, seven-league stretches of hardpan. Few and far between the cool shadows, sun everywhere blazing off blond or honey-colored walls and the waxy leaves of sparse cottonwoods. If those prehistoric peoples here before us looked squarely at this desert world and each other, yet loved them as this light so mercilessly shows things to be, they—by doing so—must've lived on the far side of some threshold we've long since crossed and forgotten.

Passing the clumped, sulphur-yellow abundance of chest-high rabbit brush in full bloom, I toss my head back for the final few droplets of one canteen, and I get noon sun square in the eyes. Apart from the occasional box elder or cottonwood, shade during the next many hours will be the size of my hat.

Arrival at the "Great Gallery" takes a while, even after I reach it. Its long smooth wall of spectral images, some pale as death, some intense as freshly dried blood, are unmistakable. Disappointing? Impressive? Actually, neither—at first anyhow. Just very strange, and surprisingly *there*. "But are they worth it?" my querulous side asks. "Worth the sweat and the miles?" Beneath a cottonwood's merciful shade I flop down to study them, see what I think.

Before I'm quite settled, though, the spontaneous part of me says, "Worth it? What a question!" And my doubt-ridden side acquiesces: "Indubitably."

Either for painting or for viewing, no site could have been better. Not only does it afford a fifty-meter span of cliff wall, much of the rock surface looks unusually smooth. At the base of that span, cliff-stone has fractured so as to leave a fairly level terrace or pediment. That makes it easy to stroll the entire figural array close up. First, though, I want the overall view. While some figures are small as a hand, most are unusually tall, and simple as a mummy's silhouette. Their lack of head-detail creates an ominous effect; except that some have been painted with eyes, which in a corpse seems especially weird. So maybe that's who they are, the venerable dead, open-eyed and wrapped for travel; legs bound together, arms tightly bound at their sides. But as if standing upright.

"Floating" might be a better term. Their earthen red presences seem to levitate somewhere between the cliff surface and within its depths, making stone transparent. Several "mummies"—for that's indeed what they seem—show "internal" colors of mysterious design: faint green, white, pallid blue.

Even by sun dazzle they loom; specters that hover and say . . . something. Something other-worldly. Are they our oldest fears, archaic terrors alive in us still; panic-deep but made tolerable by projection as spirits? With the advantage of at least being placable by rite or sacrifice? So I guess but don't know. The experts call shapes like these by a big word, "anthromorphs," but as to who left them here, specialists can only surmise and infer. They tell us that the painters lived before the Anasazi, thus were hunter-gatherers; ones called the "Barrier Canyon" people. So we know little more than these phantoms staring out from lost times choose to reveal.

As a lone hiker in just such canyons for many a year, I've been struck by the fact that solely as geological deposits the canyon escarpments seem awesome enough. Our geological sense, however, is barely two centuries old, whereas our primitive senses are ancient as blood coursing out of the mammalian past all the way here from the reptilian. Even in my eyes, erosional fractures and hulks often appear to be "other": now some sort of giant, now a kind of ogre. Once seen that way, reason doesn't quite dispel them—not entirely. Though reason forces those grotesquely animate features back to being just stone, an afterimage of the creature that seemed to glower or forebode continues in dim persistence. Naturally the mind smiles at its own childish apprehensions. Then smiles again, more humbly, realizing how much more natural fear is than reason. The aspect of mind called "blood" is several million years older.

Well, I think, if one's "enlightened" psyche can still feel naked sandstone coming somewhat alive, how much more intensely, irresistibly, prehistoric minds must've felt the same. In drawing our present line between living things and those we think of as not having life, we humans were fearfully slow. To do it took millenia beyond knowing, and I've a hunch we haven't drawn it right even yet.

Along the sandier, more open reaches, shadows of sagebrush and shadscale bushes begin growing longer. Dimples in trodden sand take on an indigo tint. Up out of sight and out of hearing along the rim, piñon jays will soon chatter and gather like static, scolding rivals away from favorite boughs. I hadn't supposed I'd stay much more than half an hour, and here I've spent the whole afternoon, fascinated. And spent all but a last one or two swallows in my second canteen.

Meanwhile, a hitherto dismissive opinion of rock art as "art" has softened. The more I look, the more my curiosity tinges with respect. If we judge "art" by its emotional power, these eerie creatures have plenty of that. A power I for once don't care to analyze, only receive. Sometimes, instead of my gazing at them they turn the tables on me: I'm the one looked at. So steadily, so ominously, they partly translate me to whatever, whoever they are. As if I'd been summoned.

Had I come across them in Greece or Italy I'd say they stood waiting for Charon, the ferryman of the dead. But no, they've already crossed the river Styx. They stand waiting for me to come, cross over to them. So after years of intending to look upon these very forms, and after four hundred miles of road, my arrival becomes a vague departure. Toward a sodality of red shadows. How the last, long breath of an entire people might appear in a dream.

Exactly that. Momentarily, they're in the same dream I am, imagining myself already in theirs. Here in remote desert that most city dwellers would scorn as "the middle of nowhere," a stone panel reveals to me some forty ghosts who summarize all of us, the living and the dead; past and to come. Earlier I had thought, "red smoke." This setting makes that phrase terribly apt. Straight up, straight up above the Barrier Canyon people, therefore above us too, impends one massively brute and beautiful crush, stratum stacked atop stratum. A highest ledge jutting out exactly above "the people" is battleship thick. When it falls, as it must, . . .

Mongo hunks and overhangs aren't "the truth," exactly. Stone tons are just facts. Truth can only be human. When set off by pathos as painted by our cousins, the Barrier Canyon ones, however, those stone facts become—if not "the truth"—implacably true. But the painters of such grave, rouge-tinted figures couldn't have had any glimmer of that, could they? Couldn't have known the score in *that* way? Mere primitives?

In any case, I'm one of their number. Sharing an August sun they too had to tighten their eyes against, when its glare picked out every dint or bit of nubble on this tawny smoothness of wall. So for as long as Indian eyes and eyes like mine have been coming here, the sky has been both Utah-blue, and dark as a rock's insides. Has been sunfire, and daylight petrified.

Certainly these forms prove museums woefully artificial. If with a pavement saw you detached even the tallest, most ornate of them as slabs to be tastefully floated two inches, say, off some gallery wall—well, no amount of subdued Hopi flute music backgrounding that display would allow them to be seen as themselves: archaic, profound, apparitional.

Here, only here, in their natal canyon can they be what they are, far taller than I am; but—given the cliff's towering vertically—they're thin, miniscule, powerless. Yet profound, too, as all the daybreaks and moonrises, all the summer rains and winter snows they've been presiding over for two thousand years. Because isn't that what they've been doing down through those lonely centuries—being true to themselves? And true to us.

Turns out, I'm not alone in feeling so.

From a steno pad that the National Park Service has placed on site, I leaf through penciled reactions, pages of them, set down by others who've experienced this pictographic display. Many entries comment on the canyon's beauty. Too, many angrily denounce vandals of rock art. Many praise the Park Service for helping keep that to a minimum. "Worth the trip from Rochester to see this panel," says one. But others have come from as far as Australia, not to mention Canton, Ohio, and Berne, Switzerland, and Belgium, Japan, South Africa. From all over.

Most entries dated "July" mention heat. In a child's block printing, Marie Talkington of Spokane says, "Had a great hike, spotted 4 deer, 10 lizards, 0 snakes. The hottest day of my life. Very pretty, lots of bees and bugs, but nice for taking pitchers. I would grade it way cool."

Another kid, a week later, grumps dissent: "We are from Brooklyn and all seven of us are sitting here in the heat and I am 10 years and I am very very very hot. My mom told us to go here and I am dying here my mom forced me and I wish I had ice cream and I wish I had a very cold water and I wish I was at Brooklyn."

For some the hike was strenuous, for others a cakewalk. One entry gripes there aren't enough trail cairns, which the following entry pooh poohs: "You couldn't miss your way unless you had your eyes closed." Baron and Crista from Klamath Falls, Oregon, advise against making things easy: "Keep the road unimproved, keep limiting the access, otherwise it'll be another Mesa Verde."

The thirst motif recurs when a kid signing just "Nicholas" speaks his need by drawing a man and a woman, each holding *large* bottles marked WATER—then adds, "I like this place a lot." Then in a P.S., "The mule deer try to hide, but I can see them."

Other signees use few words. "Wonder full," and "Unbelievably amazing and beautiful!" and "So spiritual!" and "A religious experience," and "No words, just wonder." That word "spiritual" strikes a note sounded more often than any other, as when Susan Ward of Walnut Creek, CT, says, "Moving ghosts gave off a scary, unknowing feeling. What does this really mean?" Clint Nathrop of Idalia, Illinois, echoes that: "This spot leaves me with a feeling of mystical awe! What a privilege!"

These reactions occur to Liz Sammartino of Canton, Ohio, who begins similarly by rising tiptoe: "Amazing! To have lived at this time, the enjoyment and the freedom they must have had," she goes on; then redeems sentimentality with "and I'm sure much sorrow."

Yes, surely much of that. Especially in desert, hunter-gatherers live and die by a single season of rain, not to mention sickness, reptiles, vermin, broken bones.

Yet no amount of reverence can replace fluid that Utah's radiance sweats out of us. "Good to be here," says an unsigned entry, "but I wish I was back at the truck for a beer." Left with only a swallow or so of water for my hike out, I'd rather not think about beer. As his early-morning sign-in on July 20th, however, a ranger had written, "Today's going to be another roaster," making thirsty thoughts hard to avoid. Next day must've been torrid also, because on July 21st Heidi from Wiesbaden, Germany, had made her entry a penciled sigh: "Water would be nice."

Nothing plaintive, though, about the surprise announcement by Jill Klexner and her new spouse: "Today is day 3 of our married life. Honeymoon in Horseshoe Canyon." Its spell has evidently acted on others that way, as attested by P. Wilson & Frank Cooley, who write, "We met here 3 years ago & were married a year later. Someone 10,000 years back decided we needed a special place to start. We'll return."

"Return?" Pondering that, I find myself nodding, "Me too."

"But you've been here, done this," says my logical side. "You've just spent *hours* gazing. Why come again?"

"Oh, I gazed all right," comes my answer. "And maybe also spoke with them too. Or at least listened."

Spoke with them or with something. With the spirit of place, possibly. Meaning their spirits? The Barrier Canyon people? Meaning my spirit in theirs? As usual, I don't really know. Oh, I *know*. The dead have only the voices we lend them. Nor could pictographs, however ancient, have put me in touch with dwellers of a canyon called "the other world." I know—or think I do—that such a world is reachable only in this one. Terrain of the real surreal: where something not a "thing" or even myself seems part of the talking.

Early as next summer, perhaps, or surely the one after, my inner critic may agree that's reason enough to come back. For the conversation.

Having taken longer than planned, I've a thirsty trail ahead of me, up to the rim, but enjoy the sun's longer shadows. And blue-green swallows beginning their daredevil evening feed. I become half-entranced watching my boot toes scatter sand, each stride kicking ahead a delicate, parabolic spray. Sand not yet stone; though it has been, and will be again.

At a blossoming stalk I'm delayed a longish while by wondering what it is. Nothing I've seen, not even in field guides. The whole plant is encrusted coral-thick with blossoms small as a shirt-button. It stands slightly above knee-high, with tree-like structure; but instead of green stalk, each thin branch is prodigiously bloom-clustered in florets like micro-hollyhocks or tiny roses of Sharon. From each minute petal's outer tissue, eggshell white, lines finer than eyelash lead down into a calyx of rose-hip red. Every stalk is aburst with enthusiasm bespeaking Nature's careful and lavish sides at once. Never have I seen anything either more beautiful or astonishing, because *where* it flowers is part of what it is. Yet in all that extravagant expense of petals on a single plant, nothing Nature spends is spent.

Continuing uptrail I'm bemused. Why should a single blossoming plant simply ravish me? I mean, why, beyond its obvious beauty should I continue being haunted by it? The exuberance of its blooms? Their profusion? My knowing nothing about it—thus ignorance made mystery? Those were factors, but hardly explained the depth of my reaction. Surely I had sensed that the plant's beauty and exuberance were more than just related to place *where*. As if those profuse florets and the canyon were somehow part of each other.

With that awareness came a hint as to why I'd long wanted to visit those pictographs. A hint that my habitual scorn of sentimentality hadn't admitted. The appeal of the Barrier Canyon rock art surely had had *some*thing to do with oneness, the oneness of an ancient people and place. I had wanted to touch that wholeness, that integrity, of a people whose fates had given them a harsh, arid, merciless land to make do with; and who had found it beautiful; and who, whatever their shortcomings, had loved it with all their hearts.

Citizen of a nation where for all too many of us no lake, plain, plateau, river, or forest is more precious than what can be done to them, or made out of them; born into a culture where all too often the only sacrament is money, I had come to this canyon—in part, anyhow—to visit a people among whom the earth was never for sale. A sort of kinship? To go that far . . . well, "sentimental" would be the kindest thing you could say about it.

Nonetheless—and perhaps naturally—I'm by now seeing late afternoon in the canyon as they, "the people," would have seen it. Trying to. On whimsical impulse I begin "recognizing" this or that lizard along the trail as one of the Barrier Canyon people in cunning disguise. I try catching a whiptail, knowing I can't. It's just that I'm amused by how quickly they dart and scoot. And how tantalizingly close they allow my hand to come. Then gone, skedaddled! Even the youngest—barely three inches, tail and all, thus presumably less wily than their elders—easily elude me. With a sudden flick, each leaves my fingers snatching at tawny dust exactly matching their skin.

The trail rises, switchback on switchback, the canyon floor recedes further into blue shadow. Much of its way now ascends over bare stone littered with shale bits brown as coffee beans that make a grinding crunch under bootsoles.

In mountains, eight hundred feet of ascent isn't worth talking about, and I'm used to mountains; perhaps it's thirst slowing my stride to a daydreamy trudge. Entries from that steno pad keep coming to mind, almost as voices. For frankness, of course, my favorite had to be the Brooklyn kid, just as for hardihood I must admire any girl who finds the hottest day of her life "nice for taking pitchers." For humane insight, though I savor Liz Sammartino's phrase, ". . . and I'm sure much sorrow." Which in turn recalls the apprehensive note of her closing words: "I hope people remember this is spiritual ground and not to ruin it."

Though wishfulness isn't my style, on reading that hope sounding like a prayer I had felt something in me say, "Amen," as I do now, remembering. Even my rationalist side sees the logic. If you believe there's such a thing as desecration, you believe in the sacred.

Out on the Wild Fringe

I DREAMED OF GRIZZLY PEAK last night. I dreamed of the ferns and the creek and the burned area where the giant Ponderosa pines are. I dreamed of the hawks and eagles. I dreamed of moose.

Sometimes when I hike into the Grizzly Peak country, I see bears; other times, coyotes. I've seen mountain lions in Grizzly Peak's woods.

There's one log I like to sit on, in a high, hanging, grassy valley near Grizzly Peak's center. I like to eat lunch there, near Flattail Creek, and watch the trout pass beneath my feet. I like to hike in through the Grizzly Peak country, up the steep ravines, through the forest, and then sit in that lonely valley and eat my lunch: a handful of raisins, a sandwich. I sit facing west and know that as big as the trees are out here, they get even bigger farther west.

In the late summer, there's one larch tree on the ridge that turns gold a week before any other tree in the forest, and in the late afternoon you can see it glowing up there on that ridge with the sun behind it, lighting it like a candle in the dark forest of green, and though you will never reach it before dark, you can aim for it, navigate by it, until the sun goes down.

I'm at the edge of something up here, the electrified, galvanized seam where two landscapes crash into each other: a Pacific Northwest rainforest and the northern Rockies' cliffs and mountains. It's among the last low-elevation rainforests in Montana, at the very outer fringe of the Pacific Northwest.

257

Every atom in this valley is special, is sacred, has a ringing to it, is different from any other place on this green earth. Once salmon ran near here, a hell of a long way from the ocean. The Yaak River drains this country, empties into the Koorenai River, empties into the once-magnificent Columbia River; salmon used to be able to get a long way up this system. There are still a handful of sturgeon in the Kootenai; there are thought to be maybe twenty of them left up here. And a few bull trout, about ten miles from Grizzly Peak's center, cruising up and down the creeks beneath the big cool cedars and larch.

Nearly every species in and around Grizzly Peak country seems to be down to populations of single, or at best double, digits. Nine or ten known grizzlies. Maybe five or six wolves.

It is a magic zone, a seam, this fringe, combining the two worlds—the Pacific Northwest and the northern Rockies—and it is at this perimeter where the wildest of the wild things meet: those species that have been driven from the Northwest and those that are still hiding out in the Rockies.

Wolf, wolverine, grizzly, raven, badger, weasel, marten, mink. Moose, deer, elk, even woodland caribou. Great gray owls standing three feet tall. Golden eagles, with a six-foot wingspan. Bald eagles, their snowy head brilliant like an angel's as they wheel in the blue sky of winter.

I'm making it sound like a big place. It's not. The Yaak Valley itself is only 371,000 acres. Grizzly Peak and the uncut woods around it comprise only 6,000 of those. But if you've got a heavy pack, it can take three days to cross it, dawn till dusk in the summertime. It's *jungle*. And steep.

This isn't good country for people. It's too cold in the winter, too rainy in the summer, and there aren't many jobs up here. No infrastructure, other than the jungle itself. But the relatively low elevations in the valley, and the heavy rains, produce big trees—or used to, before the virgin forests were cut down—and because of this, more timber has come out of the Yaak Valley than any other valley in Montana. Year after year after year.

For reasons of inaccessibility, no roads have yet been built through the three-day wilderness of Grizzly Peak. The top half of the mountain is a bare mesa, with no trees, just grass; and the timber below is wind-stunted, pissant, trunk-split lodgepole. But grizzlies live in there. And other things. It's *thick*.

If every standing tree in Grizzly Peak's core were cut, there would probably be enough sellable timber to last the local mill about two weeks. The mill's clearly hurting, having been jerked around by management; it could use some wood. But to trade a whole mountain for two weeks?

Still, it seems that's what may happen.

There are no designated wilderness areas in the Yaak; out of 371,000 acres, not a single one is protected as wilderness. In federal legislation now pending in Congress, the Montana Wilderness Bill, 20,000 acres of bare-topped Roderick Mountain, near Grizzly Peak country, is being proposed for wilderness designation, but not little Grizzly Peak itself.

Six thousand acres! It would be the smallest federal wilderness area in Montana. What kind of a country can't afford to add 6,000 acres to its wilderness system, when grizzlies live there?

For a long time, the timber industry up in the northwestern part of the state has been feasting on the federal wildlands in this valley, sawing more than a thousand miles of roads into this forest and cutting the big trees, clear-cutting entire mountainsides. And now the hills are washing away and the Yaak River is silting up and there aren't as many trout.

Out of one hundred mountains in this valley, there are only two small roadless cores—the Mount Henry–Pink Mountain country and the Grizzly Peak–Roderick Mountain area, which still is uncut on all sides, top to bottom.

You don't need to visit the jungle to write a letter to Congress on its behalf. All you need to do is respond to the poetry, the diversity of the words describing what is still left there on that three-day mountain, the last untouched mountain in the valley.

Peregrine falcon. Boreal owl. Townsend's big-eared bat. Harlequin duck. Woodland caribou. Lynx. Flammulated owl. Common loon. Bald eagle. Golden eagle. Hooded merganser. Black-backed woodpecker. Pileated woodpecker.

Wavy moonwort. Mingan Island moonwort. Small lady's slipper. Round-leaved orchid. Sparrow's-egg lady's slipper. Kidney-leaved violet. Maidenhair spleenwort. Bog birch. Crested shieldfern. Green-keeled cottongrass. Spalding's catchfly. Linear-leaved sundew. Northern golden-carpet.

You can look at the words without ever having to see the place and know that even if you are not a letter writer, this is a time when you must be, before we slide over into the twenty-first century and Grizzly Peak is lost.

Maybe this year, after a hundred years of white folks living in this valley, maybe with outside help, we can get Grizzly Peak—and the other last wilderness cores—protected.

Grizzly Peak is what keeps coming into my dreams. But if you are going to get there on foot, in real life, and you are a wild thing—a grizzly, a wolf, a caribou—you have to come in from either the northwest, via Canada, or the northeast, via Mount Henry. I favor the northeast approach, out of the Mount Henry country.

The wildest thing I've come across in the Mount Henry country— wilder than the black bear with cubs that chased me up a tree, wilder than the mountain lion that stalked me by ducking down in the grass and flipping its tail back and forth, up and down, like a question mark—is a beautiful, elegant, spirited woman named Jeannette McIntire, the actress, who fifty-plus years ago was Jeannette Nolan, the radio actress.

She married John McIntire, the actor, when they were both so young, and straightaway they left New York City and bought up a bunch of land in this foolish wild valley, which fifty years ago, people say, was just like Alaska.

They had a son, Tim, and a daughter, Holly, and for a long time lived happily ever after. Tim's gone now, in the beautiful night stars above the valley and in the woodcock's haunting spring calls over the marshes, and tough old Mr. McIntire is gone. (He played the wagon master on the TV series *Wagon Train*.) Holly, a photographer, married the poet Charles Wright, and they have a son and live in Virginia. But Mrs. McIntire is still living up north in the valley, on the northernmost piece of private property, fifteen miles from the nearest neighbor, which is us.

In the forever light of long summer evenings, we'll go up there and drink gin and tonics with Mrs. McIntire. She'll fix an elk or venison roast for an early supper. We'll watch the green meadows, the virgin grasses head high, and Mrs. McIntire will tell us about radio days, about her and Mr. McIntire's being young and in New

York City. They did the radio show *The March of Time* with Orson Welles. They had fans all across the country, all over the world.

But every chance they got, they came back up here, not just to hide, the way I do, but to live a life. To embrace their meadow. And they did. They saw a million stars on ten thousand nights. Saw mountain lions, wolves, and bears. Saw swans flying over the valley, saw ducks and geese migrating south fifty-plus times; saw them come back, too, fifty-plus times.

Her cabin smells of rawhide, of sweet leather, of wood smoke and deerskin. There is another woman here in the valley, Nancy, who tans hides, and Mrs. McIntire—Jeannette—likes to wear Nancy's makings.

Art—music, plays, books, movies—has always meant a lot to Mrs. McIntire. When she and Mr. McIntire first homesteaded the meadow below Mount Henry, they came across an old cabin at the back of the property: more of a root cellar than a real cabin, but where a trapper had evidently spent a winter or two, because there was an old stove and some rusting-out canned goods left behind.

In the trapper's cabin, says Mrs. McIntire, there was a pit—a great hole—where everything had been shoved and then buried. A kind of earthen basement. Mrs. McIntire said that one day she and Mr. McIntire began to unearth all the stuff that was down in that hole. An old desk. A handmade chair. And stacks of papers. Reams and reams.

"He was writing *plays*," she says. "And they were beautiful. We sat there and thought about him being up here in those hard winters, all alone, writing these gorgeous plays all winter long, at the turn of the century, and then *burying* them, and, well, with us being actors, we just broke down and wept."

Mount Henry is the tallest mountain in this valley. Sometimes it gets snow on its top even in the summer, and that's a beautiful thing to see. The top of it is sheer rock, bare like a volcano, but there are forests below, and right at treeline there are two little lakes, deep and cold.

There's an old fire lookout tower up on top of Mount Henry. It's been abandoned in favor of satellite surveillance that produces digital and color displays of thermal variations—fires. But back in the not-so-old days there was an old guy who'd sit high up in that tower at the top of the world and watch for smoke. He'd pack in with his mule string and stay up there a month or more at a time. Grizzlies would come claw and bite at the lookout tower's stout legs, trying to topple it. At first it was only ten feet off the ground, but because of the grizzlies, the lookout guy extended the tower to twenty feet off the ground. He'd come riding through McIntires' meadow on his way up to the lookout each summer—the snows lingering even into July—and he'd eat dinner with them and listen to hand-cranked Victrola music and stay the night before going on up into the real wilderness—the one that's still there, though smaller, like a memory.

And all through the summer, year after year, it became a tradition for the McIntires to go out onto their porch at night, with their children, Holly and Tim, at the edge of that meadow, and say good night to the man in the lookout tower, so far above them, at the top of that lonely, windy mountain.

They'd see his lantern burning—one tiny light at the top of the mountain—and would imagine that he was reading, or writing letters.

The McIntire children would light their own lantern, hold it up for him to see, and then extinguish it. And they'd watch as up on the mountain that light dimmed, then flickered, then disappeared, only to come back on again: once, twice, good night.

In the spring, the river would run fast again as the woods woke once more and the singing birds returned. The meadow would burst out as green as limes, shimmering with life—blackbirds cackling in the reeds, beavers building backwater trout pools, and always, the big creatures coming out of the wilderness to bear their June young in that meadow at the edge of the woods: the deer, the elk, the moose.

Smoke rising straight and clean from the single chimney, Mrs. McIntire cooking on the wood stove, or out for a walk. Mr. McIntire working in the barn on some equipment, or out riding in the woods. Etching it all into his mind, as if to take it with him when he left for the stars, so many years later. And the two of them sharing it— sharing all of it.

In the spring, to make the meadow more lush and pleasant for the elk, and to grow a cutting or two of hay, they would go into the meadow with their two draft horses and an iron sled, a stoneboat, and would lift each round stone by hand, each glacial boulder, and load the stoneboat until it was full, and in that manner, load by load, pull all the moraine from the meadow and dump it at the meadow's edge.

The meadow grew purer and greener, and became more and more of a line, an edge, at the border of the wilderness: a comfortable transition, a fringe, between what was wild and what was not— though you would certainly have to say that the McIntires' love for each other was wild, in the best sense of the word, alive and well— and so perhaps that green meadow there below Mount Henry was a line between the wild and the wilderness.

And perhaps that is why the McIntires were able to live there so comfortably and for so long: because they also belonged to what was just across the line.

Northern bog lemming. Wolverine. Moose. Pine marten. Fisher. Elk. Black bear. White-tailed deer. Mink. Mule deer. Muskrat. Bobcat. Weasel. Beaver. Ruffed grouse. Blue grouse. Spruce grouse. Gray wolf. Coeur d'Alene salamander. Torrent sculpin. Inland (redband) rainbow trout. Short-head sculpin. Westslope cutthroat trout. Bull trout. White sturgeon.

In the 1970s, wars ranged throughout northwest Montana over which federal lands would be protected as wilderness and which lands would be released to private industry, to the hounds of corporate (and often subsidized) overlogging.

The McIntires fought valiantly to have the Mount Henry wilderness protected. They stood up in the face of the local timber mill and asked that just that one mountain—just one core out of one hundred—be spared. The McIntires went back and forth to Washington, testifying to Congress about the wild nature of the valley and asking that Mount Henry be designated as wilderness. But in the end the local politicians won, and the animosity over Mount Henry— what's left of it—still lingers.

Lingers, hell; it's emblazoned in the earth. As if to set an example against those who would try to protect any forest in this valley, the

U.S. Forest Service permitted timber sales with boundaries that appear to spell, when clear-cut into the mountain across from the McIntires' meadow, the word *HACK*. (A rallying cry for saving wilderness had been "Don't hack the Yaak.")

But they hacked it. They scalped every mountain within view of the McIntires' meadow, except for the crown of Mount Henry. They haven't gotten there yet, but they're coming. The letters now stand several hundred feet tall: the *H* and then the *A* and then the *C*. (They ran out of mountain, clear-cut the letters too huge to add the *K*.)

One of the McIntires' favorites, Caribou Mountain (no caribou now), was carved away almost entirely. That was twenty-five years ago, and still very little is growing up there, just the bare scarred faces of entire mountainsides. The soil washed away after all the trees were cut, and the beautiful centuries-old forest soil was stripped away by Pacific storms and spring runoff in only one year, leaving behind a lunar, gray, runny kind of pus-looking bareness, a forever bareness. They left only enough spindly lodgepoles to surround and frame those empty letters, those last-laugh letters: *H-A-C*. . . .

The McIntires had a beautiful love, and during a large part of it, a beautiful life. They tried to protect one mountain, a thing of beauty and wildness, for those who would come afterward—one mountain out of one hundred—but they came away with zero, in this, the wildest place.

I don't want their work to have been in vain. Their lives weren't in vain. They lived all their life among beauty, and so that was not wasted. But their own basement is full of boxes and boxes of letters, of articles and documents, the paper struggle to protect a real place, a place at the fringe of everything; a place easy to forget, easy to give up on.

I know it's not noble or artistic of me to ask for letters in an essay. It's not nicely thought of in literary circles. But I don't have time for any of that crap. Maybe in the next century. Maybe, if the last of this valley's three-day wildernesses are protected—Grizzly Peak, and part of the Mount Henry country—maybe then I can cedar-thrash my way into the woods and sit on that log up above the creek, the one I keep dreaming about, and write a pretty poem or two. But not now. Right now there isn't time for any of that fairy-dust crap. Right now there are letters that need writing.

I'll tell you flat out that the way to stop the destruction is to write

Congress, write the Representatives (U.S. House of Representatives, Washington, D.C. 20515) and the Senators (U.S. Senate, Washington, D.C. 20510) and tell them to protect Grizzly Peak and the other roadless areas in the Yaak. Write Montana's Max Baucus in the Senate, and Montana's Pat Williams in the House, and Minnesota's Bruce Vento, who chairs the House Subcommittee on National Parks, Forests, and Public Lands.

The words on this page, or any page, are just stick figures, abstract etchings in dust. But letters to Congress—reams of them—this is the musculature, a pure and reckoning force of which even the grizzly would be proud. This is what is needed—not poems.

This is what I am asking for. Surely we can save six thousand acres.

Don't turn away. Do not turn away.

War Story

*T*HIS WAS THE STORY he gave his wife once he'd married after the war, and the story he gave his children, the story he gave his children's children.

It was no hero's story, he knew, but only a story of what he'd done, how he'd served with the blessing of his hands at a time when he'd been needed. Only a story of how he'd helped.

And they listened every time he told them the story as though this were the first time they'd heard it. It was in the way he told it, the way he held his head, the angle of his jaw, the cut of his eyes as he chose the words, words not meant to impress them with the feats of the man before them, but words meant to share the shard of the war he'd witnessed.

They listened, and knew him because of the story. They all owned a piece of him, carried the story in them like shards of their own lives, his story their own story, they believed, for the way he told it made them feel as though they had been there.

They listened.

The told them the story of himself, a young man who worked aboard the *Yorktown* as ship's cook third class, a boy, really, who'd somehow solved a mystery that involved the making of donuts, a boy who'd become famous for the way he fried them up, made them so that they seemed a part of heaven, light and sweet and true. There were, of course, other foods he helped cook aboard: Boiled Spiced Beef and Macaroni & Cheese and Ham & Pineapple and Baked Stuffed Meat Loaf; Griddle Cakes and Oatmeal and Scrambled Eggs and Bacon; Rice and Boiled Carrots and Turnips and Beets and Stewed Tomatoes; Iced Caramel Cakes and Coconut Layer Cakes and Hot Raisin Rolls.

But the donuts were his. He made donuts for them all, for machinist's mates and radiomen, petty officers and ensigns, the barber, the dentist, the signalman, the captain. And because they respected this ship's cook third class for the donuts he made, they all knew his name, gave him no nickname, as everyoone else in the galley had: B.O. was one, Cleaver was another, and Flour Boy and Greezy and Turnip Truck and Potato Head. But they never called him even Cookie, that nickname that was no name at all. They never called him Donut, as he'd expected they would. Even the flyboys, the kings of the ship, never called him anything but his name: Dorsett.

He told his family how he'd come on board a year before the Midway, was there at the Coral Sea when everyone had all but given up on the ship; was there when she'd washed into Pearl, a trail of oil on the water behind her like a thick shawl swallowed by the sea; was there on board when they got the call back to sea three days later, most all hands in town and sleeping off drunks or still tanking up, nobody—least of all the Japs—believed she'd be ready for action for at least another month.

Then they were at sea, steaming and steaming, the boilers doing their work to take them somewhere they did not know for duty they could not say.

And then they were at the Midway, and there were swarms of airplanes, Japs and American alike, the ship's cook third class now an ammo passer inside a turret, any idea of donuts long gone with the heat and fire and blast and heat and fire and blast. He knew only the ache in the muscles, an ache he could not tend and that meant nothing inside this heat and fire and blast that turned the barrel of the 40mm he worked red-hot at the muzzle. Still they shot off round after round after round, this donut king only an ammo passer here abovedecks and sweating and aching, and the ship's cook third class told them, too, of seeing nothing from his turret but planes above and smoke and fire from the muzzle, that steel red-hot.

Then had come the direct hits, the hit and hit and hit that shook them from the turret, then the listing to port of the ship, the listing so full and heavy he knew there was no hope for her. Next had come the call—a siren sounded, men shouted—to abandon ship, and the ship's cook third class had been no hero, had done as everyone else did and acted only to save his life. He'd felt himself a coward, felt somehow he ought to stay on board and do what he could for these men and this place that had always known him by his name. But he'd been ordered to abandon ship, and he followed orders, stood at the lip of the ship's port side, the ship still listing as though she meant to tip them all off, a dump truck letting loose a load full of sailors, and he jumped, jumped what seemed a mile down off the deck into blue water, others falling down around him, and then had come the feel of cold water swallowing him, and the depth to which he slipped once swallowed. He told them of how he could see light glittering above him, all wind knocked from him with the cold and the impact, and how he saw beside him and above him quick slashes into the water like knife blades, like terrible white blossoms of air as man after man plunged into the water around him, and he'd thought then, for the first time—he'd not even thought this inside the heat and fire and blast of the turret, not even with the shock of direct hits—that he would die, here and now, a sailor drowned by another sailor slicing into him from far above as he tried to swim for air, swim for air, tried to reach that glittering light above him, reached for it, around him crashing slices into water, slicing around him, cutting and cutting.

Then he was above the glitter, his eyes bitter with salt as he filled his lungs with air, gasped for it, though even that seemed too gentle a word to describe what he felt. He wanted to breathe in all the air there ever was, wanted his lungs filled with it, wanted his entire body to explode with it, and he turned, saw men bobbing up all around him while still there fell more men, fell more men and more men, everyone bobbing up in only a moment's time.

He told them of how there was a man beside him, a sailor he'd never seen before, a man not three feet away from him, and how the two of them looked at each other, mouths open, taking in air. Then they smiled, both began to laugh at the same moment for whatever triumph this had been: they'd jumped from the flight deck to open sea, and had lived. These two men had lived.

The other sailor blinked, wrinkled his forehead. *Ain't you Dorsett?* he said, and still grabbed for air. The ship's cook third class nodded, still smiling, his lungs not yet full enough to let him utter even the simple word *Yes.*

Damn, the sailor said. *Sure glad the Japs didn't get you. You just keep making them donuts and I'll keep eating 'em,* that sailor said, and they both laughed again, laughter that came as they still tried to gain air, and they swam through the falling men toward the destroyer that'd pulled up to fish men out, the *Balch.*

He told his family of climbing a rope ladder up the side of the destroyer to a deck swarming with men shadowed in smoke, all of them wet and shivering and as much like ghosts as he knew he would ever see. No real ghost would ever rival these, he knew, would ever make his heart twist and tear, make his still-empty lungs pinch and burn the way these figures in smoke made him feel, all of them with sooty faces, wet and trembling bodies, coughing and yelling and coughing.

Then the smoke seemed to part a moment, and the ship's cook third class glimpsed the side of the *Yorktown* itself, the huge gray of it, men still jumping from its side and slicing down into the cold blue water, men still swarming up before him and onto the deck, men and men and men. From where he stood aboard the *Balch,* and with the way the *Yorktown* listed toward them, he could see the flight deck, could see the turret in which he had passed ammo, could see the bridge and the signal light and the broad white line down the middle of the deck, the stripe with which those flyboys aligned themselves, and then he looked to the sky, saw that the planes had all gone, the Japs disappeared in the belief they had taken care of business, had sunk the *Yorktown* itself, cv5 left to history and the depth of the ocean here at the Midway. They had sunk her.

But she didn't sink, merely listed to port a few degrees more, then stayed put, and they all watched from the *Balch* for the rest of that day and on into the night, stars above them like a million cutting angels in the black, watching over the *Yorktown,* making sure she didn't sink.

He told them of the way dawn came the next morning, the way the wind picked at the ship's cook third class's thin blanket as he lay on deck, tried to take whatever sleep he might out here beneath all the stars, stars fading fast now, whispering out and leaving no trace of themselves as gray light took over, then pale lavender, then orange, then yellow, until finally there surfaced above them all a blue so perfect and blue the ship's cook third class thought maybe he'd dreamed the life of those stars, thought maybe he'd slept after all, and the stars, those cutting angels that'd stood guard over their ship and over these sailors, all these raggedy sailors aboard somebody else's ship—well, maybe those stars'd only been a piece of his dreams.

But then had come strange word, passed man to man on deck, a whisper itself as quiet and hushed as the way those stars had disappeared, that men were going back aboard the *Yorktown*, a detail that would try to save the ship.

And he remembered his name then, remembered the way everyone aboard had called his name, remembered this was the way the ship had known him: Dorsett. He was only a cookie, only made donuts for men whose lives were much more important, from the flyboys on down to the machinist's mate on the fifth deck, two decks below the galley. He was only a cookie, but it was what he could do, had done, what he did with his hands.

So, out of no shine of courage or glint of bravery or glistening heroics, he stood from where he knew, finally, he had not slept at all, had in fact seen those stars like angels, had seen them whisper their way into nothing, had seen that sky move through its colors to this blue; and now he moved among other men, all of them whispering, some of them standing, like himself, and moving until they were a clutch of men, a detail for a detail, all of them moving along the passageways in search of a co to whom they could volunteer to head back aboard, do whatever it was that needed doing.

It was a salvage detail, of course; they'd astounded the Japs with the *Yorktown*'s being right back in action here at the Midway, and now they would scare the living shit out of them with repairs made while at sea, making ready to use her again. A ghost ship, the Japs would believe, risen from the dead.

So they moved down the rope ladders they had climbed only a day before, leaped into boats that ferried them from the *Balch* to the *Yorktown*, where they climbed rope ladders back aboard.

There were 141 of them, and 29 officers, and their job was to salvage what was salvageable, to make the list less pronounced so that planes could land and leave again, to make this vessel marlin-spike again, if they could.

They all knew they could. They would cut loose whatever they could to port, lessen the weight in order to right her. And they would repair the deck, make it landable again, and they would stay on board and do this work until they were finished. They would be the first ones here when everyone else came back on, and they would be the boys lining the flight deck to welcome that first flyboy, their king, back to the *Yorktown*.

It was this ship's cook third class's detail to feed them all, all 141 sailors and 29 officers, to keep them in food that would give them the energy to do the work that needed doing, and he was glad for it, glad for the hands he'd been blessed with, glad for the duty he'd pulled, glad to be back here. They knew his name. They knew he would feed them.

There was no power on board, so that he'd had to go belowdecks, all the way to third, with only a flashlight. He could only know what he saw in the beam from the light, and what he was as he descended the first of the ladders was a world at odds with gravity: the whole of it was bent to port, and for a moment as he stood on the first deck he'd felt a stab of vertigo, felt as if he were about to fall down for the way the doors, all dogged down tight, were tilted to the left, the starboard walls too near as he stood, the port walls too far away, his whole body leaned to starboard, one foot higher on the floor than the other. But he shook this feeling away, held the flashlight on the first dogged door a few moments, focused there and set his mind to the task at hand: he had to feed the men, had to make his way deep into the vessel and come back up into daylight with whatever food he could find. This was his job.

He opened the door, found in the beam of light the next hatch, this too dogged down tight, and opened it. He went down this ladder, tried to stand strong on the narrow steps, and imagined carrying up boxes—would he find boxes?—of food at this angle, and in this dark. But this was his job, and he knew he would do it. He did not know how, did not know if, in fact, he could. But he knew he *would* do it. There was no choice.

Then came the first terrible metal groan of the ship, its first tremble, and he lost the light, saw it bounce at his feet, roll down the passageway away from him, the walls echoing the groan of the ship. He stood in the darkness, the flashlight finally stopping a good ten yards away and pointing down the empty passageway. He held a hand to either wall, pushed hard against the steel to hold himself steady. And still the groan echoed through the ship, through the walls, through his hands and into his bones. It was a dark sound, a sound like deep, slow thunder, the kind of thunder he heard in the middle of the night when he was a kid in Pennsylvania, the kind of thunder that seeped into his sleep, cast tremendous shadows over his dreams, until he woke up to the idea of the sound and the sound itself there with him, lightning long gone, only the dark and the sound, and suddenly he knew he was still only that kid. That kid in a farmhouse in Pennsylvania was huddled here inside him, and he knew that kid would never leave him, not for the rest of his life, not until he died. He would always be that kid, waking into thunder and darkness, just like here, now.

The sound edged away, finally, left him in a still darkness that seemed even darker for the lack of sound, and he made his way along the passageway to the flashlight, picked it up, felt the weight of it in his hands. He would not drop it again.

He opened the hatch, went down the next ladder, finally made it to the third deck, his deck, the deck he owned, and now he had begun to get used to the pitch, the weird purchase his shoes made on the floor at this angle.

He shone the flashlight from side to side, saw spewed everywhere what he'd thought had been stowed: in the passageway outside the galley were dozens of empty loaf pans, and somehow silverware was out, too, and spatulas and metal trays, all of it mounded up along the port side wall like heaps of steel trash. He reached the long steel tubes of the tray trough, the place where men stood on line and pushed along their trays, cookies inside the galley itself standing opposite them and ladling out heaps of food. He reached for the tray trough, held tight to one of the tubes, and shone the flashlight inside, to the galley.

The long row of steel vats in there glistened in the light, and the griddles to the left seemed perfect, intact and clean and shining. The deep-fat fryers inside still stood upright, waiting, he knew, for when the men on deck would file along here accompanied by the rest of the crew, all hands lining up for the first true meal back, and for a moment he let himself imagine the celebration feast: Baked Spiced Ham and Sweet Potato Pie and Roast Tom Turkey and Mashed Potatoes and Garden Salad with Cardinal Dressing and Fresh Apple Pie.

And his donuts. Donuts for them all, for all the men back aboard the *Yorktown*.

He saw all this in a moment, saw it all in the tilted world, even smelled the feast in the dark, and then came the next groan, this one smaller, he believed, though he could not be certain. Still the sound seeped into him, still his legs shook with the movement, still the air itself seemed to groan. But he did not lose the light. He held on, and the sound left.

He climbed up into the galley, moved past the empty vats and griddles, made his way to the reefer room, where he pulled upon the steel doors to find the heavy air of spoiled food, the power gone for all these hours. He could only give them what they had in cans, he knew then, and left the reefers, headed for Central Stores, and the rows and rows of food he knew would be in heaps on the floor.

He found the door, dogged down as per orders, and opened it. Central Stores was on the starboard side, across from the galley and the far passageway, a room large enough to bunk fifty men, and when he opened the door, cans rolled toward him, slammed into his shins as he tried to stop them all from falling out of the room and toward him. But he could not stop the cans from rolling out, and stood aside, let gravity take over and settle the cans where it would.

Here was the food: canned hams and canned peaches and canned asparagus and canned beets and more canned hams. He would make them sandwiches, he knew, ham sandwiches for all, and he then left the cans, weaved his way back along the deck to the bakery, where he knew the tall steel cupboards held bread. It was day-old at best, he knew, but still it was bread, and when he shone the light into the bakery and saw the tall cupboards had tumbled to their sides, saw that the doors stood open, dozens of loaves of bread on the floor, he knew he could do the job. He knew it.

He slammed open canned hams on the table in the galley, tore through them with the huge can opener fixed to the edge of the table, spun its black wooden handle faster than he'd ever done on duty. He cut bread with a knife he'd found under a vat, then opened the cans of peaches. He made sandwiches, his hands sticky with the sugar gel from the canned hams, made dozens of them, all with only the light from the flashlight, and he wondered how long the batteries would last before burning out. Still he made the sandwiches, and opened the cans, cut more bread.

He found, too, a cardboard box from deep inside Central Stores, a box that'd held twelve canned hams, loaded into the box sandwiches and open cans of peaches, the lids still attached and pressed down, figuring he could let the men grab up a sandwich, dip their hands into the cans. This was a war, and this was a ship they were trying to keep from sinking: no plates, no utensils. Only hands.

He carried the box above his left shoulder like a waiter with a tray, the flashlight in the other hand. Twice as he made his way up ladders and through hatches the ship groaned, and twice he believed he might fall, let loose all this food, all this work. But he stood fast both times, and finally, what seemed hours later, he emerged on the hangar deck, that deck just below the flight deck, and into smoke and heat and shine of light coming in the open hangar bays at port and starboard. When he found men, he knelt to them, handed them sandwiches, pulled out the cans of peaches.

They were men with welding torches and men with sledgehammers and men with shirts and no shirts. They were men cutting loose entire turrets, even the one he'd worked himself, and letting them fall into the sea, and they were men hammering plywood planks to the flight deck, covering up the holes where they'd taken hits. They were men who were all of them sweating and working, just as he himself, ship's cook third class, was working, and they all turned to him when he arrived, and they spoke to him.

Dorsett! they said, and *Goddamn, it's Dorsett!*

They said, *Where the hell's the donuts, Dorsett?* and *Dorsett, where's my Delmonico?*

They said, *Thanks, Dorsett. Thanks tons, Dorsett.*

They said, *Glad you're here, Dorsett.*

He fed the men, and the more trips he made below the more confident he grew, stepped where he ought, held fast when he needed, balanced the box when the groanings came. Deep inside the ship became his own kingdom, his domain rich in darkness and the smell of good food and spoiled food, rich in groanings he saw as perhaps hell itself, him settled down inside the blessing of this ship's hull and meting out food to the sailors working to save her from that hell.

He told his family how he worked for hours feeding the men, each trip only piecemeal, a dozen or so men fed out of a box. He followed the same passageways down and up each time, the same passageways he'd followed his first dive in. And on each successive trip up from the black it seemed the sun pierced him even more deeply, his eyes surrendering to the darkness of his kingdom, him squinting and squinting into the light, and still he worked, still they called his name, still the groanings came.

He slept for a while, and he ate a few sandwiches himself, and when he ran out of peaches, or at least could find no more in the heaps of cans inside Central Stores, he opened a can of yams, dipped a finger into it, tasted it: sweet and thick and orange—he could even taste the color of it down here in the dark!—and good enough for his men, who drew out fingers full of the yams, brought them to their lips, lapped them up. *Ham and sweet-potato pie*, one welder said, the blue tip of the torch he held hissing in the late afternoon sunlight. *Might as well be Christmas Day, Dorsett*, he said, and the ship's cook third class had smiled, nodded, gone on to the next man.

And slowly, slowly, the ship started righting, the list less evident, he could feel it in his feet, the longer these men worked, until it seemed almost too easy for him to walk the passageways, and it seemed the earth itself had somehow twisted on its axis, moved back into place, and he imagined again the feast down here in the galley, the heaps of steaming food, the men all laughing, calling out the nicknames of the cookies as they ladled food onto their trays: *Greezy, give me another slice off that turkey*, they would call, and *B.O., hustle your ass with that sweet potato pie*, and *Flour Boy, how about a couple-three more rolls?*

When evening came, and the blue that had broken above him early that morning had given up to orange and lavender and gray and, finally, a black riddled with those same stars, he moved through the hangar deck, the open bays to port and starboard letting in the miniscule light from those stars, toward the bunks at the fantail, bunks stacked four high and nearly filled with men already sleeping, snoring, wheezing in the black. But before he mounted the last ladder up to the bunkroom, he'd stood there on the fantail, looked out to sea:

there were those stars, spread as thick as he'd ever seen them, and below them lay the Pacific, a perfect black, unforgiving and relentless as a dream soaked in thunder, and he swallowed, thought he might cry at the beauty and terror of these both: stars and the sea.

But he did not cry, because he was too tired for it, too aching after feeding the men all day long. He turned, left the stars and that sea behind him, and climbed the ladder, moved into the bunks, found one. Some of the men were still working belowdecks, but most were here or in other bunks, all work on deck shut down for the blackout, the *Balch* and *Gwin* and *Monaghan* somewhere not far away, all of them blacked out just in case the Japs were headed back, and he fell asleep in a listing bunk with the good knowledge in his head that those ships were out there, and stood guard over him and his men, because they were, yes, *his* men. They were his, and this was his ship, and this was what he could do with his hands. And they knew his name, even this ship knew his name: Dorsett.

He told them of how he woke up when the sky was still dark, though some of the stars had whispered out, just as yesterday morning, and how the routine began again. He went below, shone the flashlight across Central Stores, started in. This was breakfast, though, and now he found cans of jam, opened them, slathered bread—bread going old, he could feel, bread gone hard—and still he slathered, stacked, carried it all up the ladders and through the hatches.

And he told his family of his last trip down, and how he could not know this was the last trip, but had somehow felt it, felt that all of this would soon be ending, felt it with the way his hand touched the cold steel walls when there came another magnificent groan, its sister tremble; felt it in the staleness of the bread in his hands; felt it in the way the light from the flashlight cut into his world down here, that light his only guide, his only way to find the landmarks needed to gain his way along the same passageways he'd traveled for over a day now. He felt somehow that this would not last much longer, any of it, and that he would be returned to light and food and normal duty—Donuts, he thought, donuts!—sooner than he could say.

Which was when, he told them, there seemed to trickle down

through the darkness, the powerful and infinite darkness the flash-light only pretended to penetrate, some kind of commotion, a sound that seemed the sound of voices, and he thought that perhaps the ghosts of the stars above had descended, had gathered in the hull of this ship—he'd been working over thirty hours now, had been wandering a path through a ship dead in the water, had been working his hands and working his hands all this while, so that his mind down here on the third deck had begun to give itself up to its own wanderings, its own depth of fear and blackness, and ghosts of stars seemed the next logical sound he might hear—and now those ghosts were wandering the passageways, guarding him, guarding him and all the others with their beneficent light.

They were the voices of ghosts he heard, nameless voices, and as he slathered jam on a slice of stale bread, he heard a strange and quiet and careful whine from somewhere around him, and he knew, suddenly and fully, that this was a torpedo, and that they were about to be hit.

The torpedo slammed home, and the sound he heard was suddenly nothing at all like the thunder he'd heard when he was a sleeping child in a farmhouse in Pennsylvania. This was thunder up close, this was lightning striking here, right here, this was power and force and violence all in a moment, and now he was on the floor among spilled cans of jam and among loaves of old bread and among knives and vats and deep-fat fryers, all of it illuminated with only the jagged tumble of the flashlight as it bounded off the floor, rolled and bounced, all of it in a moment, a moment that included the ghost voices, and the careful whine, and the explosion. The death of the world, he'd thought down there, all in a moment.

He lay there on the deck floor, the flashlight somewhere off to his left and under something, and he tried to stand, tried to pull himself up by the edge of the table. But he could not move, the table edge a mile away, the darkness slicing him in half.

Still there came the voices, and he knew them now not to be ghosts, but men, all these men he had fed now screaming abovedecks, the sound somehow filtering down to him, and he knew now the goddamn Japs were here, and here he was, flat on his back.

He told his family how he closed his eyes then, let the black sur-round him totally, not even the small light from the flashlight in him now, and suddenly he took that blackness, took the dark, and made it work for his good, made it become a piece of himself that would take him from this place. He swallowed, kept his eyes closed, and he sat up, saw in his mind's eye the edge of the table, and now felt it with his hand, and he pulled on the table, felt himself rising in the dark, felt himself standing, and now in his mind the entire ship was lit up, power restored, the picture of his domain as rich in detail and clear of purpose as the black of no flashlight had been empty of all things. The white walls were clean and glistening, and all the bread pans and silverware and metal trays were stacked and stowed; loaves of fresh bread were stored neatly in the tall metal cupboards—he could smell the rich yeast smell of them, even warm butter—and Central Stores was an immaculate room, each shelf inside filled with perfect rows of canned goods.

He saw all this, saw it as clearly as if it had been the day before the Coral Sea, even the day, perhaps, this old boat was christened by Eleanor Roosevelt herself all the way back in 1936, back when he, ship's cook third class, was still a kid in a farmhouse in Pennsylvania.

He saw the *Yorktown* unblemished, clean, marlinspike. He saw it.

Then came the next careful whine, and the next terrible blow, this one larger, closer than the last, and the floor rippled beneath his feet, threw him up into the white light of these glistening walls, threw him up into the polished shine of griddles and vats and metal trays, threw him up and up and up, the groans of the last day, that sleeping thunder, only a simple whisper next to the sound that stabbed into him now.

He did not know how long he was out, only knew when he opened his eyes to the old black that the ship was listing more than it had ever listed. This was all he knew.

He felt himself begin to slip down the floor, felt himself falling as the ship listed, a steady movement, and he sat up, grabbed hold of something his hand found, something sturdy and attached to the floor. He saw the small glow of the flashlight a few feet away, wedged back beneath something—a fryer?—on the high side of the room, and he stood, walked toward it as though he were climbing stairs. The ship was listing to port again, the passageways he'd worked all this time down there on the low side, and he stopped, lay flat on the floor and reached for the flashlight, took hold of it, its weight in his hand welcome, an old friend.

But then there came a different sound, the one he'd hoped never to hear, the one every sailor hoped never to hear: from the low side, down to port and inside the decks beneath him, there came a gentle wash of sound, like a distant river, an easy and calming sound.

She was taking on water.

Still the list grew, degree by degree, and still his feet fought to keep him standing. The passageway was below him, across the galley on the port side. But he would not go that way. He could not say for certain which hatches below were dogged, nor which doors; he could not say where either the first or second torpedo had struck. He only knew she was taking on water, and she was listing more deeply each moment.

She was sinking, and he was three decks down with only a flash-light.

He turned to starboard, made it out the opposite side of the galley and into the passageway there, a passageway that paralleled the old one he'd traveled. This passageway was littered with debris, too, just as the port had been. But it was a different place, the positions of metal trays and huge cooking pans and all else on the floor down here not the same, and he told his family of how he'd had to navigate a new course to find a new way out at the giant angle of descent the floor was making and in the midst of all this debris inside the ship he loved and was losing at that very moment.

He leaned against the starboard wall for balance, shone the flash-light in quick sweeps across the floor, saw old loaves of bread that had somehow made it this far from the galley, saw a wadded-up sailor's cap, saw steam trays everywhere.

And he told them how he'd seen on the floor a cookie's apron, draped out on the port side of this passageway like some ghost, just lying there, and he told them of the name stenciled across the front of it: *Flour Boy*, and how he'd paused over the apron a moment, for some reason moved to pick it up, bring it back to the kid—Kaminski was his name, Butch Kaminski, a kid even younger than himself— but then the ship lurched to port yet again, and the wash of water beneath him grew louder, no longer a smooth and calming sound but the sea itself, the sea coming up after him, the hull of this ship no longer the protective blessing he'd believed it, but a blessing lost, pierced through with torpedoes, events out of his hands bearing down on him hard and wanting him, he knew, dead.

So he left behind the apron, made for the ladder up, where he found the hatch to the second deck dogged down tight. He put the flashlight in his back pocket, hoped still it would not burn out—he had two more decks to go—and wheeled the hatch open, climbed up and made for the next dogged door, the next ladder, the next hatch up. All of this while the ship fell to port, all of this along new passageways, all of this with the sea swimming up beneath him and behind him, a black sea, he knew, that would swallow him, above him no glittering light like there'd been two days ago when the same sea had swallowed him once he'd jumped. There would be no light here, that water black and moving fast, ready to bear him away to his death inside this ship he loved.

Finally he made it to the hangar deck, saw men making for the low side, the port bay, and as he moved down the deck face, he saw these same men he'd fed all these hours abandoning ship, saw them silhouetted against the light, then saw them disappear. And out past them was a ship pulled in close, the *Balch* still out there, and he saw men scrambling up the rope ladders just as they had two days before, and he wondered at this fact, the fact he'd have to abandon the same ship twice in less than two days.

Now he was on the lip again, below him the same sea that would swallow him in its blackness were he three decks below, there in his kingdom. But here it was a kind and perfect blue, and he only paused a moment before he jumped yet again, fell down and down and down toward the men he'd kept fed while they tried to save the dying ship behind him. He was swallowed again, and this time it seemed he sank even deeper, fell even farther from that glittering light above him. Only then did he realize he still held the flashlight, that it was still on, made in the water its own vague stab at illumination, and then he let it go, watched for an instant the flashlight sink, watched its beam twist and whisper into the cobalt beneath him. Then he looked up, saw the glittering light above him again, and he reached for it again, reached for it while other terrible white blossoms of air cut through the water beside him—he was not the last man off—and then the sea itself buoyed him up, let him break free, and he swam for the *Balch*, swam for safety.

He watched from the deck the *Yorktown* sink only a few minutes later, saw her go under, saw her disappear forever from the face of this earth. The kind and perfect blue sea fashioned itself around her,

and took her down while men around him wept, and while he himself, ship's cook third class, wept, too, wept openly and without
shame for this loss, this life, the job she had done.

He wept, and turned, crossed the deck, his back to where she'd
disappeared, and he told them how he'd simply sat down on the deck
and looked out at the sea.

Then someone was standing beside him. He felt a boot nudge his
leg, and he looked up.

The man had been crying, he could see, his eyes red and shining.
But he was smiling. He had his hands on his hips, and he looked at
this ship's cook third class.

He said, *You never brought me my Delmonico, Dorsett*, and he
shook his head, still smiling.

There was his name.

Dorsett.

And he saw the picture in his mind of the white glistening walls,
of the exact order inside the galley of a ship now settling into its life
past its old life, this new life in the black at the bottom of the sea. He
saw the loaves of bread—still smelled them!—and saw the silverware
in its bins, saw metal food trays stacked and shining. He saw it all,
and knew this would never leave him, and knew, too, that he owned
this story, a story of darkness and light and water and groans and
thunder and a child in Pennsylvania, and he saw all of this was like
the ship's own gift to him: a story, and his own name. The truth.

He looked up at the man, saw the soot on his face, saw the torn
dungarees black with machine oil.

And he told them of how Dorsett said nothing, only felt himself
smile up at the man, Dorsett smiling while he still wept.

He told them this story.

And they listened, believed they knew him because of the story,
believed they owned a piece of him, a shard of history. They believed
they knew him.

But he hadn't told them all of the story.

There was a piece of truth he never told his wife once he'd married
after the war, never told his children, or his children's children. There

was a piece of the story he never told anyone, kept only to himself. His family owned a piece of him, he knew, with each telling of the story. But there remained a piece of the story that owned him, that held him to its own truth, that part he never told but knew all the more intimately for the fact he never chose the words to speak it.

It wasn't Flour Boy's apron he saw in the sweep of white from the flashlight as he made his way along the passageway out, behind and beneath him the quiet rush of black water. It wasn't the apron he saw, but the boy himself, Butch Kaminski, ship's cook third class, a boy younger than himself, and it had been the stenciled words *Flour Boy* he'd seen across the back of the boy's shirt, him lying in the pitched angle of the passageway, face down.

It was a nickname, Flour Boy, and for a moment in the darkness splintered by the beam from the flashlight he tried to recall how Kaminski had come to this name, what he'd done to have been thus christened by the men on board this ship. But he could think of nothing, no reason for those words, Flour Boy, a nickname now dead, dead as the body before him, and he saw his own hand now reaching down to the boy, reaching and reaching, finally taking hold of the boy's shoulder, rolling him over amidst the clutter of old bread and steamer trays, to reveal to him a face blue and black with death, his arms blue, his hands blue, the body here these two days.

He did not tell his family any of this, nor did he tell them how he'd tried then to lift the dead boy over his shoulder there in the passageway, tried to carry him because, he believed, there might have been a family somewhere who would want this boy brought back, just as for himself there were a father and mother on a farm in Pennsylvania who certainly would want him back, and a woman out there somewhere, a woman he did not yet know but who would be his wife, and there were his children she would bear, and there were his children's children, all of them waiting for his return, waiting for this man, this Dorsett, this nicknameless cookie, to come back from this war. There was a family, he believed, who would want Flour Boy back, and so, the flashlight tight in his one hand, he lifted the boy, staggered beneath the weight of a man whose nickname, however reasonless, seemed enough of a reason to bear him back.

Nor did he tell them how, once he'd made it the twenty yards to the next ladder up, then made it up the first three steps, the weight of this man, the cumbersome burden of him, became too much, the purchase of his own feet more and more uncertain with each degree of list until, only those three steps up, he finally had to move back down, finally had to ease the boy gently to the deck floor. He did not tell them how the boy's body had seemed to seat itself, then slip onto its back, all of it as simple and slow as if Flour Boy had only allowed himself to fall asleep sitting up, then let himself onto his back, black lids closed, blue arms beside him. He watched all this in the shine from the flashlight, only watched.

Then he saw in the light the glint of the boy's dog tags, the silver trace of chain at his neck, and he knew what he'd been taught in basic training, knew the purpose of dog tags.

He did not tell them how he saw his hand reach yet again, reach to the blue neck of the boy, then pull, pull hard, until the chain gave up, and how he held the thin metal plates up to the light from the flashlight, and read the name there: KAMINSKI BUTCH, and the numbers beneath it.

He did not tell them how he slowly slipped one of the tags from that chain, held the single plate in his hand, then knelt to Flour Boy. He did not tell them how he pried open the boy's mouth, the lips black in this light, nor did he tell them of the touch of the boy's teeth, the cold of them. He did not tell them how he placed the metal plate vertically in the boy's mouth, wedged it between the upper and lower front teeth.

He did not tell them how he'd stood then, and raised his foot to the throat of the dead boy, his boot tip just touching the jaw, all around them both now the sound of water, a distant river rising.

And he kept secret from those he loved the hard kick he'd given then straight to the boy's chin, a kick which drove the tag deep into the boy's jaw and skull so that this body, this Flour Boy, if ever he were to be recovered, would be known: the dead body would carry a name.

And he did not tell how this part of the story ended, the chain and remaining tag surrendered to the first co he could find aboard the *Balch*, but only after he'd seated himself on the deck and watched his ship die, had seen the kind and perfect blue sea fashion itself around the *Yorktown* and all those left aboard, had watched the sea draw the ship down and away from him forever, inside it the ghosts of names lost to war, a whispering black sea inside that hull like the truth of death now inside him, the true story no words could save.

This was the story he did not tell, a story buried in him like the deep, slow thunder he'd heard in the middle of the night when he was a kid in Pennsylvania, a story as sharp in him as the need to breathe in all the air there ever was, a story as cold in him as the swift kick of a boot into the jaw of a dead sailor younger than himself. This was his story, the shard of true history he'd been given.

And because this was the story he would not give them, they knew him not at all, neither the wife he had found after the war, nor his children, nor his children's children.

His family owned a piece of him, he knew, with each telling of the story. But there remained a piece of the story that owned him, that held him to its own truth, a war story with no end.

Dorsett, they'd called him.

No one he knew.

CAROL BLY

In the Maternity Wing, Madison, Minnesota

THE SIMPLER THE ANIMAL the stronger its sense of place. In all their lives, miniature monkeys do not venture beyond the few trees of their babyhood. No matter how diligently the Department of Natural Resources live-catches and relocates them, tough old mama beavers devote themselves—successfully, too—to getting back to the familiar lodge.

You need not be intelligent to love a place. Love of place is a natural emotion. It comes free to us all. What's more, love of place is an extrovert's emotion: for one thing, it is nothing if not particular and its point of concentration is something visible—these stars, for example, not the Southern Cross, this prairie of stiff grasses, not the Andes' feral relief, or these trees or this building at a particular north latitude and degree of west longitude.

Love of place is no part of "the whole armor of God"—that invisible kit that St. Paul advised people to put on. Love of place is not what liberal-arts education is about. Love of place is nearly, not quite, irrelevant to the two most marvellous qualities of our species: first, our idea that mercy is a good thing, even when it is practiced towards people whom it is not profitable to be merciful to; and second, being just to people is a good thing, even when it doesn't do us any benefit. Justice, in fact, is all the more to the purpose when it is exercised for those who cannot slug it out for themselves to get what's fair. That group includes newborn babies and men less heavily armed than other men, small governments situated at the edge of large governments, women who choose not to arm themselves heavily, most children, most old people and *everybody*, even the bullies, of future generations who can't stand up to us about the poisoned or denuded earth we leave for them.

Mercy and justice are reasons to love our species, however poorly we practise them. At least we have the idea, which is more than you can say for snakes or even lions. I love us for that. I don't love our species because we have fond feelings for particular places—a back yard near the forty-seventh parallel or some road an aunt walked on, or in my case just now, the maternity wing of the Madison, Minnesota, hospital. In fact, being crazy about some remembered place is a dumb emotion.

Dumb emotion or not, I have it. I love a number of particular places. Right now I want to think about one of them, the maternity wing of a small town's hospital. But this essay is also about how some people get liberal-arts educations and some people don't. I have had that kind of education called the liberal arts. Its major principle is you practise turning mere *things* into *thought*. That's the idea of it!—to get things into their basic crystalline form—to feel their structure inside yourself, to lay down any sword you happen to be carrying since you have already memorized the idea of swords and internalized the good of swords if there is some good to them. Liberal-arts educated people prefer essence to surface every time. They boast nearly constantly, too. Socrates and Epictetus started the Western World boasting about contemplation, boasting about making assays of things, boasting about reflecting on them. Like extroverted hobbyists Socrates and Epictetus commended their kind of thinking to others. Good thing for them, just as it is for people who push other people into learning crochet, that our species is dead keen on getting advice. I am continually surprised by how carefully we listen to wild counsel from one another. Still, there are limits. Most of us feel disdainful of St. Paul's contumely and his over-confident way of telling us what to do—I can barely imagine going up to friends and saying, "I suggest you put on the whole armor of God."

This much has to be said for place-lovers: they do not boast so much as theory lovers. E.B. White's "Once Again to the Lake" is annoying because he goes on and on and on about a place where only the very rich could ever go, but at least he doesn't boast of it or counsel us to get portfolios of $1,500,000 so that we, too, might go there. I have never heard people boast about love of place. They don't say, "Listen, I love my field with its organic loam more profoundly than you love your cottonwood's shadow in the moonlight." But we pro-thought types do boast—for two reasons: first, we want attention since we tend to be low on money, and second, we do deeply feel that memorizing life as it floats by makes for happiness. We want everyone in on that happiness.

Memorizing life as it goes by is the peculiar habit of a liberal-arts education. This habit says, in a rough parallel, "Get everything into documents and folders! Back-up everything on disk. Carry many uninitialized disks in your pockets." We memorizers tend to memorize not only *good* places like the Madison, Minnesota, hospital but lesser experiences as well—enemies' remarks and scrappy comparisons between one person's idea of God and another's—a truly stupid quarrel, as Whitman said outright. Memorizers pick up and memorize lesser stuff than any original hypotheses they make. Because they deliberately cultivate the habit of "internalizing," as psychologists say, they internalize unearned admiration of themselves and they internalize old emotional responses and worst of all, they internalize cultural junk—such as the class system. I mean the psychological class system, the habit of seeing some people up, other people lesser. I want to tell about my internalizing of some cultural junk and how it affected me in the nice hospital where I gave birth to four children.

The Madison hospital was and no doubt still is a small, unbelievably friendly small-town hospital. The town is some 20 miles from the South Dakota border, about 165 miles due west of Minneapolis. I liked having babies. I used to wake several times each night, once or twice to breast feed the baby, once or twice to take fruit juice from the nursing staff. They were up and about all night anyhow, making themselves toast somewhere far down the hall, checking on critically ill people, letting me hold my baby longer than usual policy. I told myself, again and again, "Memorize this wonderful place and this wonderful time of life so it will be *inside* you and you will not feel bereft when the baby is grown and you are old, even all-the-way old, doing the inescapable, solitary work of dying."

At night a stroke victim gave his rhythmic cries for hours. I called softly to the licensed practical nurse. She came squeaking along on her rubber-soled shoes. I asked whether they couldn't give something to whoever was in pain. I had such gall: how could I make a suggestion unless I took myself for more sensitive, more humane, than she? Ridiculous. Still, the thrum of that fellow's cries got into me the way vibration gets into any tinny object.

"He's not in pain," she explained. "He is trying to die." I decided to memorize that, too: two brand new human beings lay in bassinets or in their mothers' arms, while someone else was trying and trying to do that part of life we call the death.

"You will not always be in the maternity wing," I told myself a little fiercely because I was afraid of death, "cossetted by the staff, preferred, even, to other mothers because you are breast-feeding not bottle-feeding, your child: some day you must gear up to do as chipper and considerate job of dying as you can." I memorized that to myself, and then went off the subject, since a little character-building thinking went a long way. At that time I liked the psychologically slack business of self-congratulation over having had a baby.

The Madison hospital has huge picture windows. At night on the prairie, of course, but even in the town, which was so small it didn't spoil the night with its lights, the scarf of stars slowly pulled across the sky. My first child was born in January, so the sky looked profoundly cold and more than ever unconnected to human beings. All those tons of fire—the stars—do not love *our* gravity field at all; they do not care about *our* place. They wordlessly obey their own bosses out there. They are programmed to race farther and farther apart from one another, cooling, collapsing, exploding and starting the whole lot again. It is nothing to them whether we name their births twelve thousand million light years away or not. I held my first baby for hours, trying to feel affectionate to those far spaces. It was no good. I only wanted to make a warm place for my baby with walls to keep out the cold stars and I wanted her not to die until she was so old she would want it. It was such a queer thing—feeling the hot new baby, feeling judgmental about the stars and the night because they were indifferent to me (there is nothing like indifference to wake up the judgmental instincts of a judgmental person anyhow) and commiserating with the stroke patient.

Late on my first full day, a powerful woman, just then the only other mother in the hospital, shuffled and scraped her way into my room. "You want visitors?" she asked. But she was already in. "They never leave my baby with me that long," she gave mine an unexpressive glance.

A nurse came in with a tray of wildly tinted drinks—cranberry cocktail—who knows what chemicals have been tucked into that stuff—orange juice of the canned kind, grapefruit juice. I take one of everything.

"How come she gets all them?" the other mother said.

The nurse raised her face in a canny mix of balefulness and dignity. "She," she said, with unmistakable emphasis, "Is a nursing mother."

There it was—good people and lesser people—the American two-class system, albeit a pastel version—merely breast-feeder vs bottle-giver. Behind breast-feeding versus bottle-feeding, however, lay another up/down paradigm: educated people vs uneducated people.

Someone has to be *down*, so the others can feel more *up*. I bring this up because I loved the Madison hospital, but the American class system was astir in it the way beetles and rats are astir in a ship's hold. Those of us who believe in the liberal-arts sort of education are always advising ourselves and others to *internalize* this or that: memorize this moment! memorize this place! We are the originators of that expression travellers use: taking it *in*. "Been to Paris?" "Yup, took in Paris, all right. Berlin, too. Utah Beachhead." We incidentally internalize the two-class way of thinking along with the other ideas. Taking for granted that someone is more, someone else less, is natural grit. It blows around in any culture. Up/down thinking sometimes floods in with the good ideas like mercy and justice the way a whale's mouthful of seawater takes in those fish the whale had in mind alongside a few thousands of other sour-tasting fellows, lower on the food chain, who slop right in, too.

In animals we call a two-class system "pecking order." In us we call it "primitive feelings of entitlement" and several other names. Whatever we call it, it is awfully low on the thought chain. Like whales, however, we toss it back and are mellow, the way we are about the few thousands of bacteria who live and have their being in our throats.

Like any woman, I was used to that particular psychological evil. In 1962, non-college-educated males looked down on women. A good many college-educated ones did, too. I knew what it was to be in the *down* group. I knew it was such a prevalent evil I couldn't expect even so kindly a place as the maternity wing of the Madison hospital to be free of it. Two-class thinking was, hey!—reality. I wouldn't even mention it except that I only recently identified a specific genus of two-class thinking that I had brought into the hospital inside myself.

Before discussing the corruption of two-class thinking, I would like to say that the Madison hospital was free of every other ordinary psychological ill. In the 1960s, a time when hospitals were abandoning their identity as loving institutions, the Madison hospital went on serving patients with extraordinary kindliness. In the 1960s, and more so now, TV offers us hospital administrators as ogres. Ours was not an ogre. He was nothing like the cool zombies who lick up new tricks from the Harvard Business School. Our administrator was half crow's-nest lookout and half convoy commander. Half of his job description was keeping a sharp watch against under-the-surface threats from the outside, like a sailor who has the watch. His enemies were certain, but not all federal legislation, certain, but not all pressures from insurance companies, the litigious nature of American society itself—and the new, frightening demographic changes. He kept the hospital's mission flexible the way a convoy commander has to be ready to change the zigzag. He managed ''by walking around'' as the authors of *In Search of Excellence* made so much of. He visited those of us in the maternity wing. He did not duck clear of the dying and their relatives. What's more, his hospital treated anyone ill or wounded. Thirty years later, a farmhand told me that she could not have a deteriorating knee looked after because she could not afford insurance. In the 1960s, and perhaps now, the poorest farm help or unemployed person in Lac qui Parle County got treatment in the hospital. The hospital was kind. At the gross level, the American class system scarcely showed there. One could miss it the way one might not notice an unlabeled bottle that stands motionless on a shelf alongside bottles of useful medicines.

I was in the *up* group of the maternity wing, not just because I breast-fed babies when the other new mothers didn't, but because my husband was educated and I was educated. Not only did my husband bring me roses and presents, but my two aunts and my father sent flowers and presents. The nurses praised my baby. They scarcely spoke to a rough-spoken mother whose new baby lay in the next bassinet to mine.

That other mother had a curious look about her. Her skin was opaque. It looked more like coarse-woven cloth than skin, giving off no light—like burlap. One of the nurses, often finding her standing at the foot of my bed, would brush by her and say "Excuse *me*" with the accent on *me*. (That pronunciation says, "It is you who need to apologize, not I.") The paternity of at least her first child had been a question that regaled coffee klatches some years earlier. She then married. She had a great many babies after that. More important, she was a poor person. When the rich people of our town had children conceived unconventionally, it was not forgotten, but the effect was a glint of glamor about the mother, not disgrace. This woman was ten or twelve thousand dollars a year too poor to qualify for that category. What's more, her husband "put her in the field," as we called it: that is, she helped with the farming as well as doing the household and childraising. Her heavy skin was the gift of wind and the rub of dirt. Her grammar was like most bad usage: a series of shy, courageous, unfocused approximations—snatches of phrases, sometimes a single word shot out like a stone from a slingshot. Sometimes her tone reminded me of the comic magazines of my childhood. Germans in enemy uniforms were forever shouting *Verboten!* at one another. (We who were kids in the 1940s had a working Nazi accent we could pull out for gags.) Some of this mother's exclamations were like those hoarse explosions.

Psychotherapists and clinical social workers have a reason for asking us to speak fully, *in whole sentences*. Only sentences contain exactitude, not guesswork. If we are lucky, someone taught us in school or in therapy to speak whole sentences. Conversely, psychologically or culturally *unlucky* people have a damnable time making a real sentence: they haven't the confidence for it. "Oh!" they cry. "Doctors! Show me a doctor and I'll show you. . . ." They have strong feelings—hatreds, admirations, memories—and would like to express them—but they also have a profound need *not* to express them because the listener might be scornful. What they are hurting from, and stymied by, is *cultural abuse*. Therefore, they say unclear halves of statements and then look at you opaquely, so that you will *not* see in: they are afraid you will locate something in there and shoot at it.

The other mother came into my hospital room a lot. She didn't particularly want to talk about labor, but she was willing to because I was obviously interested in it. She gradually told me that she didn't cotton to labor and delivery. She didn't cotton to breast-feeding, either. We had to dodge around, she and I, for topics to talk about. I was madly enthusiastic about my doctor but hers had disappointed her somehow. She did not cotton to him, she told me, but in bits. In fragments, gradually, she told me she did not cotton to the nurses too much either. "I don't know," she said. Then she said in an including and friendly way, "Well, you know! . . ."

I was not the conversationalist I am now. I have always been fond of filthy language, but I hadn't such a dirty tongue in my head back then. I hung clear away from her, all those things and people she didn't cotton to. *Now*, if I listened to that woman, as she prowled about the foot of my hospital bed, once shyly putting such work-hardened fingers to the roses that I bet she could not feel the instant when the petals touched her skin—*now*, I would respect her enough to ask her a question about the very subject she most wanted to talk about. I would ask her conversationally, "What do you think is the most jack shit thing in the world?"

For a split second people freeze at such a question, but then their faces break open like splendid shards of mica. "What do I think is the most jack shit thing in the world? What do I think is—! Do you want to really know what it is? It's—" and the room fills with clarity. You can practically watch the clarity and warmth filling the room. Of course such a question would empty the room of tricky pose and let it fill with clarity and warmth. The questioner has risked sounding both foolish and vulgar. In our up/down world, the listener gains confidence by comparison—and feels trusting, if not respectful. A parallel: let us say that we are campers who have taken shelter in a cave. Relaxed, indolent snakes lie around here and there, moving along in the cracks and behind our pile of rucksacks. Then there is an intervention. Word is, everything tricky and chill: get out. The snakes start easing along towards the cave entrance. There is a gratifying moment when the last two leave, making their tandem wriggles in their repulsive way. Now the cave fills up with large, nonaggressive, fur-bearing animals, mammals like us. They plunge in, ranging around, sniffing, yawning, some of them growling and deliberately barging into one another with their heads, so they lose balance and have to rebrace themselves on their huge feet. From a sojourner's point of view these mammals are not ideal but they are an improvement.

But I didn't think to ask the other mother anything. I was passive. I had my own responsibilities. They felt holy to me. After all, a new child lay on my breast. I had sung to her "Maxwelton's Braes Are Bonny" (Annie Laurie) and "Auld Lang Syne" and the Skye Boat Song because I am a Scottish American, and "Jeg Er Sa Glad Hver Juli Kvell" and "Ja, Vi Elsker Dette Landet" because her father is a Norwegian American. The baby's tiny ear wasn't two feet from my mouth. I knew enough not to inquire, right above a baby's ear, "What do you think is the most jack shit thing in the world?"

The other mother settled for gossip about the big shots in town. How she had been treated by them was her subject. But first she had to make certain I wasn't one of them. Any fool could tell I was educated—bad. On the other hand, everyone knew that my husband and I had neither television nor "water up to the house"—indoor plumbing. She and I felt our way from very-small talk to medium-small talk to actually-engaging talk. Eventually she made the observation which was and is a central bugbear to me: human beings will give up everything before they will give up their position in the pecking order.

From time to time one nurse or another would tell me that if I was tired I could call and they'd close my door so "people" didn't "just wander in." They meant the other mother—whom else? Several times they told me my baby was "just beautiful, just beautiful." In the late afternoon of my first day in the hospital I tottered down the hall to have a look at both babies. I noticed something fascinating: the other mother's baby was beautiful, too. It had fine features for someone only three days old. It had gorgeous curly hair, a lot of it. The next time a nurse brought me my baby and praised it, I told her that that other baby was utterly beautiful, too.

"All babies are cute," the nurse said, "But yours is a doll."

"That other one is beautiful," I repeated.

"You let me know if you want anything," the nurse replied. There it was.

This *it*, the up/down philosophy, had been in the delivery room at four-fifteen in the morning as well. It showed up just a few minutes after the baby came. My first child's birth was straightforward and comparatively easy. In 1962 mothers got a shot of demarol during labor, and when doing the final work of delivering the baby we got a whiff of gorgeous stuff called Trilene. In the delivery room were people dear to me—my sister-in-law, who was a licensed practical nurse, the family doctor, and two RNs who floated in and out of my notice partly because I was busy enough and partly because a patient in the main part of the hospital was in critical condition. When someone laid the baby, with its white and red splotches on my stomach, I got very high. Then one of the RNs, a new person there, leaned over me and said, "Now—isn't this the greatest experience of your life?"

I was boundlessly ecstatic, so I would agree with anything anyone said. I was just about to cry, "O yes! Yes! It is!" when I took note of an oddly intense expression in her face. The nurse was regarding me powerfully, not passively: her face hung right over mine. She was not *asking* me for my answer—she seemed to be *willing* me to say yes. I took warning. Something lay under the surface here—O yes, in the next second I thought I knew what it was: the nurse wanted me to sell out my life as an intellectual and thirty-one-year-old freethinker! She wanted me to say that giving birth to offspring—which anyone knows rats and rabbits do fifty-two times faster and four times more often than we—she wanted me to say that was *better* than all the alternately grave and merry and complicated doings of the mind and heart. I could hear it in her tone. She wanted me to sell human beings short.

Well, I would have to stand up for the mind. I felt myself trembling and self-satisfied, a latter-day Nathan Hale as fixed on my cause as he was on his.

"No," I crowed up at her, "It is lovely but it is not the greatest experience of life!"

The nurse's face changed. She squared away, straightened, then vanished. I was free now to enjoy the baby. I decided to do some outloud meditation, too. I asked the doctor his opinion on several abstruse issues: I knew he was busy over to my left, doing something with the placenta over a slop tray. His hands were still red with my blood. I was taken with that idea a little, but too high to stick to any subject. I told the other nurse some profound things, too. I thought I was a rare treat, intellectually.

Thirty-two years later the woman who had been the new baby told me that after delivery, a mother's body sends her some chemicals that are like pleasurable drugs—so all my springy Weltanschauung that night was just drugs. O well.

At last a nurse gave me a ride down the hall on a gurney. It was even more luxurious than the wagon rides of my childhood. I had been the baby of my family, with three older brothers. In return for trade of chores or promises not to tell on them or sometimes from the goodness of their hearts, one brother or another pulled me back uphill in the wagon. It was such swank to feel the cracks of the sidewalk sections thumping underneath and not to have to toil uphill myself. On this gurney ride now, I thought, raising a child will be serious work. This may be the last free ride. You had better memorize this feeling, I said to myself.

Then I lay awake happily. Outside in the January cold, the stars were, as always, indifferent. I felt so happy that I did not mind it that the stars love only themselves, not us, and that no guardian of ours walks their night-soaked paths around the galaxies. It is enough, I thought, to live at all—with luck, the whole three score years and ten.

The next day a blizzard blew its white flanks and empty banners all day, just outside my window. I heard, while choosing a glass of juice to drink, that the doctor had gone off into the country on someone's snowmobile in order to pronounce a death. The driver and he couldn't see to get through, and had to return. Inside our hospital everything was warm. There was less of the hiss of wings, the nurses' tennies, the hall was quiet now, because at last the stroke victim had died. The other mother came to visit when I awoke.

I woke remembering the nurse's odd question: "Now isn't this the best experience of your life?" Why should she want me to sell out the life of thinking? Socrates may have thought life without reflection wasn't worth living, but very likely some millions of people hate impractical thinking. They don't quite like people who do think, either. They don't cotton to them.

The other mother came in with her burlap face and heel-less slippers. Whenever my husband was there she would edge out, but give him a straight look before leaving. I had to guess at her feelings. Her face was like a gunny sack that waits all day on the farmhouse stoop: in the evening, *he* has promised, "when he has a chance to get to it," the head of the household will do that chore—but for now it waits. Only now and then you see the slightest, most subtle denting or bulging in the burlap—some tiny movement that tells you that the latest litter of kittens is in there waiting.

The other mother did not cotton to most of my conversation. On my third day in the hospital I decided I would lick down my baby. Now it may have gotten to be the in-thing in Marin County, California, or in the basement of the Museum of Modern Art to lick down your babies, but I hadn't heard of anyone's doing it in the Madison, Minnesota, hospital, and my feeling was, it might not catch on at first. When female guests came to visit, I moseyed around the subject to find out if anyone else had done it. I could get no sense of it. I certainly could not say to the other mother, the next time she shuffled in, "Would you share this—about all those babies you've had . . . did you—did you happen to lick any of them down?" I feel that she would not have cottoned to the idea. Vegetarianism has come in—shamanism has a little following among engineering students now—but I did not then and I still don't think that licking babies all over has caught fire much. I tried to imagine how it would go if I plainly, openly, brought it up. "Look," I rehearsed it to myself. I would have to make it sound practical, like a proposal about sun-drying diapers. I would tell her, "Well, of course reindeer do it—they do more, actually. They eat the whole placenta, which returns a lot of B vitamins and protein to them . . . so it's natural, you see!"

That mother's face would not have moved a millimeter.

I had one other subject to try with her. What did she think about the stroke victim dying in the hospital? She did not know that man. She had no feelings about his death.

"Well, look," I wanted to say, "Someone else's death . . . someone else's death is nothing but a kind of universal engine parked on the lay-by track ahead. So long as we are upright, our train goes smashing past on the main track. We note that engine stopped all right, but we go madly forward in our own lives. . . ."

Such remarks are an imposition. There is nothing the listener can say unless he or she has the same impression. I would not be surprised if someone listening to someone else likening death to an engine on a lay-by track simply leapt to his or her feet and swore, "You just shut up about trains! And death, too! Death, too."

I had taken the nurse for an enemy of intellectual life. I thought I was a more sensitive listener to the other mother than the nurses. I was sure I should fight for my right to *think*!

How slowly, how a thousand times slowly, a human being learns anything! My first child was born in 1962, thirty-two years ago. Yet only in 1992, by a fluke, did I discover what the nurse's expression meant, when she had leaned over me and said, "Now wasn't that the best experience of your life?"

I discovered the meaning of it because an associate of a Twin Cities organization called the Center for Arts Criticism wrote a letter in the Center's newsletter. Among her remarks she said that probably rural people should be encouraged to pursue "craftsmanship for its own sake," not real art—not passionate, universal literature. Rural people, then, should make quilts and bind books, while the rest of us, the *up* people, get to tackle the great subjects of our species. Rural people can spin and knit and carve while we others will try to figure out why it is fun for some human beings to discount the feelings of others, why it gives pleasure to some powerful males and females to torture and kill others, and how we must go about some long-range brainstorming to stop it. Rural people can cross-stitch while we others try to figure out why we human beings so much wish that the night, with its weight and fires, cared for us? Here is a joy that one doesn't learn through quilt-making: it is how to live happily, how to be conscious of death, but choose not to be terrified.

I saw a subtle will of our species: it is to divide us into those who will be encouraged to meditate and others who will be conditioned not to want to. Those others, the junk culture tells us, had better learn a craft. All her life, that nurse, who bent over me, had been told to be practical. When she decided on prenursing for the first two years of her four-year b.s. in Nursing, she did it to be practical. Her Sunday School teacher didn't quote to her Shakespeare's line about free choice: "Study, sir, what you most affect."

And like everyone else she knew, I had misread her face. I had been drinking mouthsful and stomachsful of the American class system without noticing the taste. Her face had not ordered me to sell out the intellectual life! Her face had said, "I do not want life to be only practical! I want life to be odd, and holy—as if we are all connected by invisible cloth."

The nurse's face meant to say, "We human beings feel our way along that cloth. We see the cloth because it lies in such spacious darkness, but we can memorize our ideas about it. First we can memorize the very idea that such cloth is there. I want to know that that is true."

That is what the nurse's face really said, but I mistook it.

Her face said, "In the American class system, some people are

never told to memorize an invisible idea." Her face said, "Please tell
me that that is horrible."

I did not see the slight movement behind her face which said that.
The whole thing made only a moment's dent in her ordinary expression.

All That Is Hidden

I REFUSE TO SIGN THE "hold harmless" agreement issued by the Barry M. Goldwater Air Force Range. We need this piece of paper before legally entering the Cabeza Prieta National Wildlife Refuge, which is within the range's boundaries. The document absolves the United States Government from "any claim of liability for death or injury arising out of . . . usage of, or presence upon, the said Range."

Those who sign are warned of four facts:

1. That there is "danger of injury or death due to falling objects, such as aircraft, live ammunition, or missiles."

2. That there is "danger of injury or death due to presence of not-yet-exploded live ordnance lying on or under ground."

3. That there is "danger of injury or death from the presence of old mine shafts and other openings or weaknesses in the earth, as well as other natural and/or man-made conditions which are too numerous to recite."

4. That the land "cannot be feasibly marked to warn the location and nature of each danger."

"It's a formality," my husband says. "Just sign it." He is irritated by my unwillingness to do what we have to do to get into beautiful country.

"It's not a formality for me," I answer. "I want my government to be accountable."

And so I enter the Cabeza Prieta unlawfully.

I am traveling with my husband, Brooke, and ethnobotanist Gary

Nabhan. We are here to count sheep: desert bighorn. Nothing official, simply for ourselves.

The night before, in Organ Pipe Cactus National Monument some fifty miles from the Cabeza, I dreamt of searching for a one-eyed ram. Brooke and Gary tease me at breakfast when I tell them of my night image.

"Sounds phallic to me," says Brooke.

Gary offers a retort in Spanish or Papago or both and does not translate.

In Celtic lore, the spiral horns of the ram are attributes of war gods. In Egyptian mythology, the ram is the personification of Amon-Ra, the Sun God: "Ra . . . thou ram, mightiest of created things." It is virility, the masculine generative force, the creative heat. In the Bible, it is the sacrificial animal.

Conversation shifts in base camp as we load our daypacks for a seven-mile walk to Sheep Mountain. I take two water bottles, sunblock, rain gear, a notebook and pencil, and a lunch of raisins, cream cheese, and crackers. I also slip in some lemon drops.

Gary hands Brooke and me each a black comb.

"A subtle grooming hint?" I ask.

"For cholla," he grins. "To pull the spines out of your legs when you bump into them."

We begin walking. It is early morning, deeply quiet. Each of us follows our own path in solitude, meandering through mesquite, paloverde, ocotillo, and cholla. The animated postures of the giant saguaros create a lyrical landscape, the secret narratives of desert country expressed through mime. Perhaps they will steer us toward bighorn.

Ovis canadensis. Bighorn walk on the tips of their toes. Their tracks are everywhere. In the vast silences of the Cabeza Prieta, these animals engage in panoramic pleasure; hidden on steep, rocky slopes, they miss nothing. Elusive, highly adaptive to climatic extremes, desert bighorn are graced with a biological patience when it comes to water. Research shows that bighorn here have gone without water for periods extending from July to December, maybe even longer. But most sheep find watering holes or small depressions in the rocks that hold moisture after a rain, enough to drink at least weekly.

Bones. White bones are scattered between the lava boulders. Given the terrain, tracks, and scat, it's a safe bet they're bighorn. There are ribs, vertebrae, and a pelvis that looks like a mask. Where the balls

of the femurs once fit is now empty space. I see eyes. I look around—
nothing stirs, with the exception of side-blotched lizards. Now you
see them, now you don't.

Brooke and Gary wait ahead of me. Before I catch up to them, I
see a saguaro that looks like the Reverend Mother, her arms gener-
ously calling me toward her. I come; at her feet is an offering of
gilded flicker feathers.

The men tell me the sheep tank is around the next bend; according
to the map, we are less than a mile away. Bighorn could be watering
there.

Gary has found a pack-rat midden made out of cholla and shrap-
nel. He tells us how enterprising these creatures are in building their
dens. "Quite simply, they use what's available," he says. The glare
from the silver metal blinds us. "We can trace the history of desert
vegetation in the arid Southwest through these middens," he continues, "sometimes as far back as forty thousand years. Food remains
become cemented with pack-rat urine. The fecal deposits represent
centuries of seed gathering."

Brooke accidentally brushes against the den as he turns to leave.
He winces. A cholla hangs from his calf, spines embedded in flesh.
Out comes the comb, out come the needles. The clouds are beginning
to gather and darken. Barrel cacti are blooming, blood red.

Bighorn are tracking my imagination. I recall the last one I saw, a
young ram with horns just beginning to curl. He was kneeling on
wet sand as he drank from the Colorado River. His large brown eyes
looked up, then down to the flowing water. In the Grand Canyon, we
were no threat.

Threat. Rams. Rivals. The bighorn was the mascot of my high
school. The football song comes back to me ("Oh, the big rams are
rambling, scrambling, rambling. . . .") As Pep Club president, I cut
ram tracks out of black construction paper and then taped them to
sidewalks leading to the front doors of athletes' homes. Where the
tracks ended, we placed Rice Krispies treats with a "go-fight-win"
letter wishing them luck. In the desolation of the Cabeza, I wonder
how I have found my way from the pom-pom culture of Salt Lake
City to this truly wild place.

No sheep tank in sight, although Sheep Mountain is. We decide to
climb the ridge and eat lunch. The view will orient us and perhaps
even inspire us to think like a ram.

Gary pulls out of his pack a small glass bottle filled with something resembling red beads. "Try a couple of these on your cream cheese and crackers," he says.

"What are they?" Brooke asks, taking a handful.

"Chiltepines. The Tarahumara believe they are the greatest protection against the evils of sorcery." We trust our friend and spread them on our crackers.

One bite—instant pain, red-hot and explosive. We grab water and gulp in waves, trying to douse the flames that are dancing in our throats. Gary, blue-eyed and blissful, adds more and more to his crackers. "I once at thirty-nine chiltepines in a competition," he says nonchalantly. "In fact, in all modesty, I am the Arizona state champion." I bypass lunch altogether and suck on lemon drops, praying for a healing.

It begins to rain, lightly. As far as we can see, the desert glistens. The Growlers, jagged black peaks, carry the eye range after range into Mexico; no national boundaries exist in the land's mind. The curvature of the earth bends the horizon in an arc of light. Virga: rain evaporating in midair, creating gray-blue streamers that wave back and forth, never touching the ground. Who is witness to this full-bodied beauty? Who can withstand the recondite wisdom and sonorous silence of wildness?

All at once, a high-pitched whining shatters us, flashes over our shoulders, threatens to blow us off the ridge. Two jets scream by. Within seconds, one, two, three bombs drop. The explosions are deafening; the desert is in flames.

The bombers veer left, straight black wings perpendicular to the land, vertical rudders on either side of their tails. The double engines behind the wings look like drums. The jets roll back to center, fly low, drop two more bombs. Flames explode on the desert and then columns of smoke slowly rise like black demons.

The dark aircraft bank. I have seen them before, seabirds, parasite jaegers that turn with the slightest dip of a wing. I am taken in by their beauty, their aerial finesse. And I imagine the pilots inside the cockpits seeing only sky from the clear plastic bubbles that float on top of the fuselage, jet jockets with their hair on fire following only a crossline on a screen.

We are now in a cloudburst, the land, the mountain, and the aircraft disappearing in a shroud of dense clouds. Rolling thunder masks the engines and the explosions. Everything is hidden.

"Basic ground warfare. Tank busters," Technical Sergeant Richard Smith tells me. He is the spokesman for the 58th Fighter Wing at Luke Air Force Base, twenty miles west of Phoenix. "What you witnessed were Warthogs at work."

"Excuse me?"

"Warthogs, known by civilians as the Fairchild A-10 Thunderbolt II. They are extremely maneuverable machines that can stay close to their target." He pauses. "Did you watch the war?"

"Yeah, I watched the war."

"Then you saw them in action. These babies carry sixteen thousand pounds of mixed ordnance: bombs, rockets, missiles, laser-guided bombs, and bullets. They are specifically designed to destroy enemy tanks, and they do. Twenty-three hundred Iraqi vehicles were knocked out during Desert Storm."

"And what we saw below Sheep Mountain?"

"Mock air-to-surface missile strikes. Some twenty to thirty aircraft use the South Tactical Range each day. This is a 'live fire' area where we train our pilots. It has been since the 1940s."

"Has any ordnance accidentally been dropped on the refuge?"

"Never."

"And how do the jets and noise affect the bighorn sheep?"

"They don't."

Not everyone would agree. Monte Dodson of the U.S. Fish and Wildlife Service maintains that "bighorn continually exposed to sonic booms, as on the Cabeza Prieta Wildlife Refuge in Arizona, may develop severe stress problems that inhibit normal daily living patterns, as well as reproduction."

What I know as a human being standing on the ridge of Sheep Mountain on the edge of the Cabeza Prieta National Wildlife Refuge is that primal fear shot though my bones. In that moment, I glimpsed war.

Instead of counting sheep, I am counting bombs. The A-10s that swept the sky at high noon are gone. F-16s have taken over. They are silver and sleek. I will learn from Sergeant Smith that these are one-person, single-engine aircraft designed for air-to-air attack, hence the nickname "Fighting Falcon." Like the peregrine, speed is their virtue. Five hundred miles per hour is a usual clip. The F-15E, also employed above the Cabeza, is a two-person, double-engine jet capable of defending itself air-to-air as well as air-to-ground. It is known to intimates as the "Strike Eagle." Lying on my back with binoculars pointed up, I realize that I am engaged in military ornithology.

Four jets screech above me, and every cell in my body contracts. I am reduced to an animal vulnerability. They can do with me what they wish: one button, I am dead. I am a random target with the cholla, ocotillo, lizards, and ants. In the company of orange-and-black beaded gila monsters, I am expendable. No, it's worse than that—we do not exist.

Over the ridge, bombs batter the desert. The ghosts of war walk across the bajada. I imagine their grief-stricken faces, gaunt, cheated. Bombs counted: 23. Sheep counted: 0.

We have dropped down from the pass. Gary and Brooke continue hiking up-canyon; I choose to sit near a windmill where there is a cistern of water, still hopeful for a look at desert bighorn.

More jets, more bombs: the machinery of freedom. I scan the hillside with my binoculars. The small black boulders are covered with petroglyphs; the etched images are pink. I walk across the wash for a closer look. Miniature rock murals are everywhere. Who were these artists, these scribes? When were they here? And what did they witness? Time has so little meaning in the center of the desert. The land holds a collective memory in the stillness of open spaces. Perhaps our only obligation is to listen and remember.

Bighorn. I walk toward him, stoop down, and run my fingers over the primitive outline of his stone body. Wavy lines run out from the hooves like electrical currents. This ram is very old, his horns spiral close to a circle like moons on either side of his head. And then I stand up, step back. This stone sheep has one eye.

Night in the Cabeza restores silence to the desert, that holy, intuitive silence. No more jets. No more bombs. Not even an owl or a coyote. Above me is an ocean of stars, and I wonder how it is that in the midst of wild serenity we as a species choose to shatter it again and again. Silence is our national security, our civil defense. By destroying silence, the legacy of our deserts, we leave no room for peace, the deep peace that elevates and stirs our souls. It is silence that rocks and awakens us to the truth of our dreams.

Tonight in the Cabeza Prieta, I feel the eyes of the desert bighorn. It is I who am being watched. It is I who am being counted.

KATHERINE MCNAMARA

Piety

One might say that Catholicism notices things, the particular.
Robert Lowell

Belief makes the mind more abundant.
William Butler Yeats

*H*ERE I SIT, looking out into a piney and deciduous wood as a squirrel frisks along the low unmortared fieldstone wall at the edge of the yard, as a mourning dove calls a cool, sensual lament, as young peepers whistle shrilly: *"Spring! Spring!"* This is a fat county in upstate New York, where I have come to stay a while; nothing like wilderness I've known, pointless to compare them. The house is not far from Hyde Park; its grounds are pleasing to the eye and easing of heart, as (says the playful mind) Hyde park is, in London. Each is a landscape of evocation, arranged to elicit a fine balance in the mind, between delight in nature and confidence arising from recognizing one's place in society, by birth or election. They are (disparate) examples of Man's ability to organize Nature for the benefit of Man. Each in its way is a *making* and a *seeming* of the balance between Man and Nature, where Man allows Nature to flourish, while shaping Her growth, so that Nature is never allowed out of hand, but yet always seems like Nature. I take my analogy, of course, from the English of the eighteenth century and their pleasure in landscape architecture, and the Germans' devotion to *Englische Gartens*, and from their philosophy of Nature. I am amused by the comparison, and feel at ease here: comfort and safety were long since established, and tolerance is the rule.

But what I am actually thinking about is piety: religious devotion to and reverence for God, devotion to and reverence for parents and family: from Middle English *piete*, meaning mercy, pity, from Old French, from Latin *pietas*, meaning dutiful conduct, from *pius*, dutiful. I did not come from such a county as this one, nor the social stability that governs it, but from a once beautiful Pennsylvania valley raked over by deep-mining coal barons, themselves long since gone with their riches, leaving the culm banks and hard need for making a living to us who remained; and even the miners were not the people I came from. I was born into the kind of family made up of doctor, priest, businessman, lawyer, and the dutiful wives (my mother still gardens, and loves English gardens) who stayed home with the children: the kind that anchor, or did anchor, the small-town middle class to property and propriety.

To those people, and that secular and Church hierarchy, I was no dutiful daughter of the home, but discovered a longing in myself to go traveling. I went to live in a place the people I came from certainly thought was wilderness, and was unimaginable to them: I went to Alaska, then moved farther out into the Interior, the great boreal forest that is the primeval home of people among whom I was a stranger and visitor, and of wondrous things that were revelations to me. I saw for myself its nature, in this respect: I saw it was nothing like what I had known, and came to believe it is alive with spirits: or animate, as a student of religions would say; and further, that spirits exist regardless of one such as myself, and are independent of whether or not I believe in them.

But this is too big a thing to assert from where I sit: I mean, rather, to offer it not as a tenet of belief, yet, but as an idea to be approached and contemplated from the ground of experience. I wish to recount an experience, and reflect on its meaning. If I sound certain, I am certain only of what happened; yet I would not be human, if I did not turn it over and over again in memory, to see if I can understand what it offers.

It begins in the Interior, where toward the end of the seventies and early in the eighties I made a small living as an itinerant poet. There I met a woman who became a friend to me: Malfa Ivanov, the name she gave me to use in writing. When we met I was living in the town of McGrath, where I worked for the local school district of which her village was part. We were introduced over school business, and formed a friendship; and, gradually, she let me know more about herself. She lived with her Athabaskan husband on the Yukon River, in the Athabaskan and Yup'ik village called In the Shelter of the Hill. They made a good living from the barge and hauling business they had built together, and in the winter he trapped. They had four children of their own, and had fostered others, who had grown and formed new families; and they had close friends and relatives along the rivers, the Yukon, the Koyukuk, the Kuskokwim, the Tanana. During the sixties, when the War on Poverty had encouraged many Native people to begin to speak out, a group of Yukon elders had trained her as a speaker, teaching her debate and argumentation.

But a young woman from Outside, as I was, living alone in that hard, masculine country was in a complicated position; and in time, I realized she was watching over me. When, later on, I asked her why, she explained, "We have to treat people according to their nature. I had to protect you and teach you as my daughter."

"You wanted to *know*," she said also. "I thought for a long time about that. What you needed to learn. What to tell you. Finally I realized: I told you, 'Pay attention to what's ordinary.' "

By 'ordinary' she meant the things I might overlook. For instance, one afternoon when I was at her house, she turned on the television. By then, bush households received television via satellite dish. We watched a performance by Yup'ik dancers and drummers from a village downriver. She was studying their language; it was akin to Aleut, her mother's tongue.

Yup'ik drums are bladder skins scraped thin as membrane, stretched over great hoops of light wood, usually birch, that have been steamed and curved into shape, and attached by sinew to a short handle. With one hand the drummer holds the drum; with the other he holds the stick, a slightly curved willow wand, and strikes the drum with it.

Those old men held drums made of green plastic garbage bags stretched over hoop-frames. The skin drums were difficult and expensive to make, explained one old man to the camera: for everyday use, plastic did just as well.

"Look at what it does," Malfa said, deeply stirred by their cadence. "That plastic—it's the drum; but not just the drum, it's the sound.

And it's the sound: but not just the sound, it's the effect. The lowly thing, the ordinary thing: the sound it produces, what it does to our hearts. It holds off the Mighty."

I PAUSE TO REMIND myself of all I did not know about the animals. During those years I scarcely saw wild animals, except for their beautiful skins, and the way women used them: but already I had glimpsed a small part of the enormous store of knowledge and belief by which people lived; and I had eaten animals; and I had heard old stories from the lips of respected tellers, and the more informal instruction adults give children.

As for myself, somehow I knew, and sensed, that the animals were there, beyond my sight, yet entwined in the lives of humans. I knew, or imagined, or sensed, that when the animals were offended, they withdrew from humans, who needed them to live. But, looking back, I cannot tell exactly how or when I knew it, or what I knew of animals and humans, hunting and trapping, at any given moment. The accumulation of my knowledge was slow and circular, formed from brief conversations, or in small observations, or some experience of the body, and by intuition, and in dreams.

But when I asked Malfa *why* and *how* and *what*: when I said, *I think that*, and *I saw this*: just when I thought I *knew*: she would nod, and look at me seriously, yet with kindness, and advise: "Pay attention to what things *do* in our country, not what they're *called* in yours."

A NEWCOMER DRIFTED INTO McGRATH, a white man, tall and good-looking, probably in his late twenties. Somewhere along the line he had learned to build elegant dog sleds, and he collected odd mementos—tin buttons, skulls of animals, old bottles unearthed in tumble-down cabins: relics of pioneer encounters with nature. One day he crossed my path in some out-of-the-way spot, and halted. Shyly, sweetly, he held out a small leather pouch and said, "I made this for you." He blushed, and walked away quickly. I opened the pouch and found a necklace and earrings, made of little bones.

The bones were perfectly shaped, creamy: miniatures of bones. He had strung them on dental floss, the new "sinew" in the bush, and glued them to gold-toned fixtures. Touched, but puzzled, I went to see him, and asked whose remnants these were.

They were wolverine toe-bones, he said. He had trapped their animal north of Anchorage, where he had built his best sleds.

Many Athabaskan women wore beads and quills beautifully worked as jewelry; doing this, they showed their respect for themselves and delight in the pleasure of adornment. I myself wore beads and quills; most often, I wore the long earrings that were the fine hand work of a young woman in Shelter. She and I had become friends, and I watched her when she worked skins or beaded. She had the ability the old people called *putting something special in it.* That *something* infused a quality that to an observant eye identified her work as Athabaskan. I could not seem to learn it: when I practiced beading with her, I make a bad imitation; we both knew it, though she was too polite to say so.

The bone necklace, the earrings made of tiny bones, were like that: imitations. He knew how to make handsome sleds, after his own design; but he had not mastered the use of the bones, and because of it his jewelry looked clumsy. Though I had been charmed, I was embarrassed for him, though I was sorry, too, to feel that way.

A feeling that was not esthetic, or romantic, also came to me: an uneasy sense that it was not correct for him or me to use this animal. I had never seen Athabaskan women wear wolverine and took that absence as a marker, for there was nothing accidental or arbitrary in the things women used, or did not use, in their hand work. Any part of the animal, even if used for decoration, invoked a quality particular to it. I did not know much about wolverine then: even so, when I tried on the pieces, I felt physically uncomfortable. I took them off and slid them back into the pouch, and, not knowing what to do with them, yet feeling they ought to be handled with care, tucked them into a box of odds and ends.

Around that time I went to Shelter on school business. I happened to talk with a teacher who was a friend of Malfa. It was trapping season. A wolverine had been taken. "It's their most powerful animal," the teacher told me, meaning *spiritually powerful,* "and they potlatch it when they catch one."

The word potlatch was used by Athabaskans for different kinds of celebrations. I asked what it meant in Shelter, where the Catholic church was strong. She described it as a ceremony to honor the animal. Before the hunter skinned it, his wife spread a blanket in the entry of the house, or more formally, in the place in the room where a guest of honor sat. There the husband arranged the animal's body, and there left it overnight with a small piece of moose fat or dried salmon in its mouth: so its body was honored, and so it was fed, to thank its spirit for having given itself to the hunter.

About a year later I found the small leather pouch again. What a poor thing the pieces in it looked; yet, the look on his face had been open and manly, and shy: sweet homage paid a woman amid the sexual carnage of that country.

But I couldn't bear to keep the ugly things, and (at some obscure prick of conscience) I couldn't bring myself to throw them away: until, tired of indecision, I threw away the fake gold. I cut the string and scraped off the glue; pushed the smooth, small bones into a pile, and rolled them into the pouch; and hid the pouch in the box of stuff. More time passed; I moved, then left Alaska. The pouch settled deeper into the box, where the bones remained safe, and with me; and I forgot about them.

For the sake of its beauty, or power, or, perhaps from spiritual pride, any pilgrim may long for a revelation that will rumble the earth; and instead, find that, if one is granted, it may only confuse her, being ambiguous, even banal. She might feel foolish, and not speak of it to anyone; she might decide to ignore it altogether. Or, if she is of a certain cast of mind, she will not; then she must accept what follows and study its nature.

The time must have been late January 1983, a mild winter; I had settled into a comfortable house on a hillside in Virginia. For days I had been sitting at the typewriter at work on a treatise far removed, I thought, from my former life in Alaska. The small black leather pouch had turned up in the box of odds and ends, and for some reason I had placed it formally on the desk; for—here was poetry, that this prose can scarcely evoke—I had begun to feel in my body the connection of the things of the world.

That sensation: I am not certain even now that I can describe it. It was like warm breath on the skin; it was a pricked-skin feeling, a tactile alertness, as if I could see behind things. The world appeared to me, and I saw it: I experienced the invisible become visible. The spaces between the trees in the woods at the edge of the yard were filled: I could see the very air between them: the ether; as something breathed.

For days I had been abstracted, vague, deep in concentration; but on that day, the weather was changing, turning gray and misty. A flock of crows circled—*yaw! yaw! yaw! yaw!*—above the treetops. I was staring idly out the window, thinking of nothing in particular. The insight I had been looking for came to me; it was complicated, but I was going to be able to give it form.

The leather pouch lay close at hand, and I felt safe. I was turning from window to typewriter: at the corner of my left eye a dark object, a blur of wing, sketched a movement, but at another window, not the one I had watched the crows from. I heard a raven's watercall— Alaskan sound! Old creaky voice: odd. For a moment I was surprised—not greatly surprised; aware that something seemed odd. Crows seldom flock with ravens.

—Something *was* odd: the sound I heard was very *odd*, and I *recognized* it. Trembling, I picked up the pouch. *Oh,* said the voice in the mind: *I know what I heard: but why did I hear that?* I laid the pouch gently on the desk. I was not afraid, and grew very calm; turned inward; and started to write.

When I finished writing, I knew I had to go back to Alaska. I needed help; I could not interpret the moment, I could not describe it, even to myself. Something had shifted—the psyche disturbed. I wanted to sit with an old woman who would explain it to me.

BUT MALFA APPEARED. Why were we both in Fairbanks? What were we doing at the university? An elevator door opened: there she stood, splendid in a handsome, fur-trimmed kuspuk, and her hair caught up in a beaded comb. We seized each other and went off to drink bad coffee; we sat and talked for many hours. I had been away for three years; they seemed like hours. Cautiously, then eagerly, we exchanged the news of our recent lives. Hour by hour, imperceptibly, as I opened myself to her, she became my mother again.

For, I trusted her more than myself. She came from people who had lived in a long spiritual relationship with their land, that in its nuances of power, had been kept veiled from the rude gaze of outsiders; and I did not wish to pull back that veil: but something had happened to me that I had small means of understanding, and I had to know what it was. Stammering—the words came hard; I had no natural language for this; this was not poetry—I told her how I had been given the bones, and had heard the raven's voice, and had felt protected by some quality that was—living about the bones.

Perhaps I hoped she would dismiss it all; could say, *Don't mix poetry with the unknown powers.*

Her face grew still; she did not laugh, or turn away; her tender eyes held steady. Gently, she explored my state of mind, asking careful questions: she must, I think, have been testing my mental balance and, I am sure, my sincerity. For some time she considered my answers.

"You cannot see if you are not supposed to see," she said, finally. "Things that are dangerous can be refused."

This was the delicate moment, the pivot, the tip into the future. I could not give my burden over to her: she gave it back, into my keeping, and my free will; but she stood with me. *Refused. Refuse it.* Over the years I heard this often from her; for a long time, I hardly knew what she meant. She had taken me seriously, and taken what I had said literally: and (though somewhat, still, to my own disbelief) so at last did I. I searched my memory of the experience. Something had touched me, and I had felt it: something beyond myself. It had felt like a nod, a sort of encouragement, I told her; then, confidant now: No, it had sounded like a grunt of approval from some old person I had not known was listening.

"That sounds like a good experience," she decided. "How do you feel?"

Stronger now, I said; happy and calm.

A question had been troubling me, a matter of moral etiquette. What should I do with the bones? They did not belong to me: should I keep them? In Alaska, my mind had cleared, I told her (I was almost light-headed with relief): one day when I was out in the woods, I would know where to step off the trail and bury them.

"Yes," she said. "Animals in the wild aren't buried, you know."

Maybe I would just lay them down, I amended.

"That animal is powerful, and sometimes there are spirit helpers. If you feel good and aren't afraid, I think it's all right."

I lived intensely in a state of unknowing. It was at first a gentle thing, never frightening; it was a heightening of attention, a deep focus on what I had no words for, an intent listening, a watching. I was responsible for the bones, but how to behave toward them, and where to lay them down, were not evident to me. It was not acceptable to ask Native people, those who did not know me, to speak of so intimate a matter. Occasionally, however, some non-Native friends offered insights. For instance, I was told that if an Athabaskan friend gave you meat, he never left the bones in it: the bones were put out in the woods for the animal's spirit to find, to return in a new body.

Remarks like that were rare, and were precious to me; for the remains of a Catholic conscience, which examines skeptically one's motive at every move, beset me. Often I became uneasy, believing, yet wishing not to believe. I wondered if I were trespassing on secluded ground, but could not make myself leave. In the long winter darkness, I wondered if I were losing my mind.

Surely this experience touches upon, and also is part of, an ancient, widespread human experience. Nearly a year after, that first intensity lifted. That was both relief and let-down: I was left in-between, neither in the air nor on the ground; I felt terribly serious, and slightly goofy.

The year that followed passed in a snap of fingers and was crowded with event. As I write I can see that passage clearly; all was confusion then. I traveled the bush, as a visiting poet; I moved without judgment, absorbed in the movement. I slept in airports, teachers' lounges, local hotels, or on couches in friends' small cabins. The daily business of life obscured the deeper progress of the story I lived in, and if, intuitively, I did not take its passage as random—I knew something ordered and coherent was happening, on a higher level of consciousness than my own—the days were hectic and banal. I had fun, and lost my head in love. Men were very attentive, and I was available to their appeal. Even so, I grew testy over ordinary things, and hardly knew where the feeling came from.

As often and for as long as I could, I cast myself upon friends, non-Native and Native, who recognized that in the bush existed something we did not understand. I talked, I wept, I complained about everything. They listened patiently, advised when they could; and politely concealed their exasperation. I tried to convince myself that I was being Literary, telling myself stories, that I had an overactive imagination and was given to self-drama; that I was making it up: but I would never accept that suggestion from anyone else. I tested everything. I *saw* and *saw* and *saw;* as if the land had pulled back its mask, and revealed its inner face. I dreamed of stern, demanding, but not unkind spirits, who required fortitude of me; that is, of everyone.

Nothing made sense. I wrote everything down, otherwise I could not remember it; then I ignored it, because it was confusing. I never doubted the fact of the visitation, only that I could be patient enough to see it through in its own terms.

IN THE EARLY SUMMER of 1984 I went to Shelter again, to Malfa. After the winter ice broke up she and her husband always traveled the rivers, hauling supplies and freight by barge to the Interior villages. They were going to make the first run of the season. She said decisively, "We'll take you with us."

For days we traveled up the slow, clear Koyukuk. Malfa watched me, though I hardly noticed it, and as we neared a certain village, announced: "We can visit Mrs. Reliance."

Mrs. Reliance was well known in the Interior. Her Koyukon family was an old one. Her grandfather had been a respected medicine man; she was known among white people for telling his traditional stories again, and for allowing them to be translated and published.

Tactfully, Malfa asked me about my time of the month. Off schedule, I had just come into my moon. She knew that I carried like a sacramental the pouch with the bones in it. With a sense of relief it crossed my mind that I could leave them beside this peaceful river, in the woods near Mrs. Reliance's village.

The village was calm and pretty, and looked like a park, with its log cabins built amid clumps of new-leaved birches, along well-tended paths laid with river gravel. Songbirds sang in the trees. The women who came down to greet the boat were Malfa's old friends: they welcomed her with pleasure, and handed her gifts of food. Among themselves they spoke their Athabaskan tongue; it sounded fluted and musical, like the birds.

Malfa took me with her on her round of formal visits, until at last we came to the big log house of Mrs. Reliance, who welcomed her old friend warmly and offered us tea. Formally, Malfa introduced me as her daughter, to signal I was in her care. Carefully, as writers of all sorts were deeply mistrusted, she explained that I was a poet, and spoke well of a biography of an elder, known to both of them, which I had recently finished. Mrs. Reliance accepted the information without comment. The two women exchanged news about their families and mutual friends, then talked of more private concerns. I sat beside Malfa, as gently and skillfully she moved the conversation toward her purpose; when the moment came, she gave me an opening and slipped away.

Mrs. Reliance looked at me pleasantly, a small query in the tilt of her head.

Who was I, before the old knowledge of this woman? I took a deep breath, and told her about the man's gift. I described the misty day, the movement at the window, the raven's watercall, the prickly flush, and the clarity that had come on me when I lifted the pouch; the inner certainty, the *yes*, that had followed.

I write and rewrite, until the words are clear and accurate, until they describe exactly, or as exactly as I can make them; but speaking was difficult, and I was aware that I spoke in a rush. At the end, I asked if I could leave the bones nearby, in the woods, because it seemed to me they might be safe there.

"What is 'poet'?" she asked.

"A shaper of words."

She thought for a while. How long had I had the bones? Where had they come from, and who had given them to me? She asked me to describe them exactly.

Again she was silent; then she told me two stories, that I remember imperfectly now. In each of them, a man found something—an old arrowhead in a fish's stomach; a rock shaped like a bear's paw—and had dreamed on them. It seemed that each man had used those objects to ask for power: instead, misfortune had followed. One man had developed a double personality; the other had lost children and grandchildren.

"We don't know if this is why," she said, "but it could be."

I was discouraged; the bones grew heavy in my pocket; and I was distracted by my predicament. Why had she told me her obscure stories? I wanted only words, not power; not medicine.

It was strange, she said: in the stories her people told, they called this animal *doyon*: chief. He never came to women; they could not even use his skin, except a little bit from the stomach, and on parkees, where it did not matter. When their daughter was still a baby, her husband had hung up the skin of a *doyon* inside the house. The baby would not stop crying, until her husband decided he had better remove it.

"He would not accept those," she said of the bones. "I know if I asked Grandma, she would not. We don't know who might find them, or what would happen with our people. This way it is orphan. It didn't come from here."

She explained that a word, even one spoken in ignorance, might insult the animal, who in revenge could hurt the person who had spoken. Her people spoke their own language among themselves: he could understand them.

She said again, firmly, that no one in the village would accept such a gift: the medicine people had known for a long time, since before the First World War, that their powers were failing. Not that the spirits were failing: but that no one could bear the burden of hearing and interpreting them.

"Maybe you should try to find out where it came from. If that man is not in McGrath, you could leave it there, since that is where you got the gift."

I had not known what was proper, I apologized; I had not grown up among people who knew how to behave this way toward animals.

"You could burn it, or bury it. Burn moose fat, and thank it for being kind to you, and say you never meant any harm. —But, as I think about it, I wonder. Maybe you should bury it in plastic. Don't destroy it. It might keep talking to you. If it wants to come back, you'll know where to find it."

For an awful instant I saw my free life gone, given over into an archaic service of this orphan animal's bones, that I carried from some unthought habit, the consequences of which had suddenly become too great to face. I felt rude and awkward, and wished I had never come to her. "I guess I was asking improperly," I murmured, downhearted. I thanked her, and left.

MALFA LIT A CIGARETTE, listened, then, full of thought, asked if I had told Mrs. Reliance the name of the animal's spirit. He had felt ancient, protective; I had called him Old Husband. My face grew warm again; but she was serious.

"A power has been trying to come back for a long time," she explained. "Even the young people who refuse it can suffer terribly."

I worried that by bringing the bones into the village, I may have placed these people in some danger. She shook her head.

"You are in your strongest time now, with your period, and the bones are in your care."

"What protected me?" I asked her. "What sent my period just then?"

"Women have a very strong power of their own, which is innate," she said. "It cannot be controlled, except through proper behavior. *Hʉtłaanee,* what they say for 'taboo,' isn't just negative: it's to keep the power from getting in the way of the men."

"If women have their own power," I said, "and animals have their spirits; and if medicine people can be either men or women: then what do men have that is their own?"

"They are the providers," she said, surprised I had to ask.

A disturbance of the psyche: an opening in the mind, into which pours something unknown, unexpected. What is its nature? It is a delicate matter to tell only part of the story; but the whole story, in its intricate detail, is very long. I've boiled it down to an essence, knowing every thought, every incident may also open out and unfold into a story of its own; and that all is connected to, is grounded in, the close-meshed network of old and new stories, personal histories and mythopoeae, that cover the cold North. Mine is the smallest of those stories, told briefly here, with the hope that others may find it of interest and benefit; for when we speak of such matters, are we not telling ourselves how we may be at home in this place?

MY STARTLED QUESTION about powers, especially the power of women, was a personal one. I understood that a spirit had made itself known to me, and that I had accepted an offer of relationship; but what sort of relationship? The two women seemed to think it a medicine call, of a kind their people were not prepared to answer. I listened to them, for they had given me much from their particular, scrupulous knowledge. I was only a struggling poet. The literature to which

I was devoted was rich with the writings of great religious and nature poets, and visionary fictions testifying to the immanence of the spirit in the world: but the practice of medicine, its exacting, indigenous rituals and enormous power *to make things happen* were outside my ken, and were not my desire. I was more Jesuit than anthropologist about this: I accepted the ontological reality of medicine, and believed—because I had heard the stories—that in former days, priests and medicine men had fought genuine battle for the care of souls. That the priests had triumphed was evident; equally, that an old power was trying to return, I had no reason to disbelieve.

But mine was another calling, and I saw that none of us—not Mrs. Reliance, not Malfa, not me—knew a precedent for it. What knowledge was mine, and what was appropriate to me? I did not know the proper behavior, the protocol of the sacred, which the wolverine-spirit might require of me. My intentions were kind. I was concerned that my ignorance might put others at risk: I did not even know what language my animal spoke, or what words might offend it.

I did not imagine myself to be at risk. I was filled with awe and surprise, the lilt of a highly developed curiosity, deepened to a sense of mystery, whose veil now covered my own face.

How grateful I was to Malfa. Her knowledge had been tested; she offered it judiciously; and I could trust it and use it for my own. *Women have a very strong power of their own, which is innate. It cannot be controlled, except through proper behavior.* I was a young woman, carrying a bag of bones whose home I had to find: in Malfa's teaching lay the clue to the strength I felt rising in myself. *What they say for* taboo *isn't just negative.*

The word she used, *hɵtłaanee,* was Koyukon, which was Mrs. Reliance's language, an Athabaskan tongue; I had often heard it used. Its root is *hɵtła,* the word for menses: similarly, *taboo,* the word we use for forbidden behavior, came from the Tongan word for menses. Captain Cook brought the word back to England in 1777. It passed into our tongue to mean *consecrated; set apart; forbidden for use,* especially forbidden to women. Within that application lies the Judeo-Christian connotation of womanhood as unclean, and morally inferior; or, as Catholic teaching has held since St. Paul and the Desert Fathers, and as I was taught in my youth, a near-occasion of sin; a vexed subject, theologically and socially.

But its native meaning was less narrow, I found: it spoke not of an absence, the absence of goodness and purity, but of an abundance, a metaphysical enlargement, from which I myself was not excluded. Native people of the Pacific and Alaska freely mention their feelings of kinship with each other. They know the world in similar ways; and the similarity between them may exist even in etymological form. Just as *taboo* and *hʉtłaanee* come from a similar root, so is the derivation similar in Iñupiaq, the language of the people of the North Slope. The word *agliganaq* refers to the laws of behavior toward the supernatural: the rules applied to personal relations between men and women; and to their treatment of fur-bearing animals. The same connection, of game-rules and taboo to menses, exists in Yup'ik, and, I suppose, in other Athabaskan tongues.

Thus it came to me that there in the center of my nature, in the innate, archaic power of the blood-taboo, lived the authority with which my imagination composed the rules of the game. From within 'my' own ancient, impersonal, feminine nature was formed the protocol by which I would act: the devotion and reverence, the mercy and pity, the sense of duty in which I carried the bones of a fur-bearing animal, though I was not wife nor mother nor was I allied to a hunter, as was expected in that country.

ACCORDING TO THE Catholic teaching in which my intellect was formed, animals have no souls. Soul, fateful word in the New World; its historical and theological echoes are very loud. Perhaps they have deafened us. For example I turn to the great and horrifying disputation of 1550, in Valladolid, between Bartolomé de las Casas, Dominican missionary and defender of the Indians of the Spanish colonies, and Juan Ginés de Supúlveda, chaplain to Charles V of Spain: who meant to prove, by rational argument, whether or not the Indians of the Spanish colonies possessed soul and intellect.

I still read Las Casas with admiration and sadness, for how often in the literature of travelers, those who find it in themselves to leave home and wander, to meet the various people of the earth: how often do we not find some subtle, or desperate, argument by which to prove that Others are as human as we are? For, we know how often it has been denied. Yet after all, in Las Casas's treatise I found a detail of Christian moral theology which drew my particular attention. There he argued, mightily and with love, in order to redeem the Indians from their enemies, that "the Creator of every being has not so despised these people of the New World that He willed them to lack reason and made them *like brute animals, so that they should be called barbarians, wild men and brutes. . . .*" (Emphasis added.) His analogy of savages to brute, soulless animals, incapable of redemption, was typical of the learning of his time and civilization; his great work was to portray the Indians of the New World as possessing souls: thus, being human. My point of exception is small; yet it marks a typical barrier between old and new beliefs.

A spirit came to me in the bones of an animal. In the North it is the old belief of Athabaskans that everything that lives has its own spirit, and that that spirit must be respected. It is the principle that underlies all life, reaching back to the dawn of human consciousness; it is revealed in the earliest stories, the explanatory myths of Creation. How did one like myself who had not been taught this belief, who had been taught that only humans are endowed with souls: how did she accept it, and imagine such a world, in its minute particulars? I was not from that country. In need, I turned to others for help.

I found then that I had to begin all over again. The emotional intelligence of people who had guided me, of Malfa who mothered me, had been of a reach beyond my own. I undertook a spiritual task: to register nuances of plain words; to trust myself to give form to feelings, when I would rather turn away from them; to find right words for images that had no words.

That work is very close to the work of poetry, and it is also part of the work of poetry; but it occurs in a realm of belief which is more finely articulated than I could have known. Catholocism had prepared me for it in this way, at least: through the Mystery at its center; its formation of the intellect as the handmaiden of intuition; its ceremonies; and its belief in the possibility of grace.

But the wolverine is a greedy, malicious, evil-natured animal, and Mrs. Reliance's warning, that he was dangerous for women and would retaliate if insulted, was not to be disregarded. The old Athabaskan stories tell this over and over; nothing good is said about him; he *is,* and must be recognized for his nature.

Fortunate for my peace of mind, a written source provided another kind of check against which to compare my own experience. In his admirable *Make Prayers to the Raven, A Koyukon View of the*

Northern Forest, the anthropologist Richard K. Nelson, who knew Mrs. Reliance and reported her teachings accurately, wrote of the retaliatory nature of certain powerful animals, including wolverine:

> Not all spirits are possessed of equal power. Some animal species have very potent spirits called *biyeega hoolaanh*, which are easily provoked and highly vindictive. These dangerous spirits can bring serious harm to anyone who offends them, taking away luck in hunting or trapping and sometimes causing illness, disability, or even death. Animals possessed of such spirits include the brown bear, black bear, wolverine, lynx, wolf, and otter. The beaver and marmot have similarly powerful spirits but are not so vengeful.

To the Dena'ina Athabaskans, among whom I lived before I met Malfa, wolverine was *yes hughn'u*. The word refers to the varied colors of his skin, and describes how he moves: he is a strong, powerful animal, shifting around inside his skin almost like a cat; he is "rough and tough," always on the move. But more familiarly, he was called *idashla*, "little friend," meaning (bad one) for a friend. Their stories about him are grim, particularly in his treatment of women: wolverine does no good to women.

But, looking back, I cannot tell exactly when I learned this. The accumulation of my knowledge was slow and circular, and inconclusive, because the story in which I lived was not over.

From curiosity, perhaps, or caution, I fell into the habit of carrying the small bag of bones in my pocket. On occasion, the bones seemed to move: not literally: metaphysically. At such times, perhaps two or three times, I found myself in the company of priests or expriests, Jesuits. Then, agitation amid the bones, restlessness, unease; power meeting power: mutual hostility in the air. For I noticed signs of agitation, also, in those priests and former priests, who also were highly placed men. I moved away from such encounters. They were fascinating, disturbing, whiffs of danger: small glimpses into a realm of power I had no wish to enter. I took them seriously; why not? It was I who carried the bones; and if I knew, in that country of stories, that I lived in a story, it was no fiction, not a novel, seldom poetry. For, *I* was the visible one. The agitation swirled around *me*.

I used to laugh then: my shoulders were broad, and could carry weight. On them I balanced everything: all possibility; all that I knew, and also did not know. I was going forward, and could not look back, until the story was over, and I was released by it.

Only then did I recognize that behind that strange experience had always breathed the sweet, secret circumstance of the gift: the man's intention, his boyish love, that had come to me with the bones. *Old Husband.* In Athabaskan stories, the wolverine's spirit was vindictive and evoked fear, subdued for survival into the grimmer form of respect; but the white man, who had so clumsily worked the bones, was innocent of fear.

Here was paradox, a literary jest, an irony of the sacred; a form, shall I say, of poetic justice? I had received a gift, and had taken it literally, object and word; and had accepted its consequences, though they perturbed me; but much remained hidden, until I came to learn how the word lived in my language. *Gift,* the word and deed, comes to us, in part, from the Old English *forgi(e)fan:* to give up, to leave off (anger), to forgive.

As the decade of the eighties took shape, oil prices dropped. The economy the old-timers called boom-and-bust was going bad. New people, the whites who had come north toward the end of the boom, once again moved away. As the money dwindled, the people who stayed grew fearful. The normal violence in the towns and bush, the abuse of women and children, the suicides, the unexplained deaths, increased rapidly. The economy of oil had bluntly imposed itself across the North and was beyond the reach of national governance. The Alaskan tribes felt the changes, and took them hard, and drew their boundaries in upon themselves. Even Malfa, feeling ambivalant, encouraged me to be silent about what I knew.

In those years many people, often unknown to each other, dreamed heavily. One summer in mid-decade, in my literature class at the university, young Native men and women spoke hesitantly, yet urgently to me of dreams. They described a state of leaden sleep, from which one cannot awaken; one dreams, yet the dream is as clear as daylight, as if the dreamer were awake. Disturbed, they compared their dreams, and asked me how to interpret them.

White women, friends, artists, poets, dreamed of animals. We described our dreams to one another: bear, wolverine, wolf: animals of power, looking at us, speaking, asking some act of us, in words we could not quite hear. There also were white men, I knew, who saw what they did not understand; many of them were frightened. To whom could they speak of such things?

The animals are crying, a woman told me, describing her dream.

Older Native women were cautious about speaking to me, unless they knew, as Malfa knew, why I cared to learn. Rather, often I heard, "We don't know."

A polite rebuff, or a fearful response: but also, a mark of empirical thinking, practiced by people who counted as knowledge only what they might verify from experience. Since the First Beginning, since the Distant Time, the animal protocols had been tested and considered. In the last century, newer powers had come on the land: the monotheism of the missionaries; the far reach of the law; the remarkable efficacy of American technology. To those watchful Native people these developments seemed to leave non-Natives, the people like me, immune to their old spiritual sanctions. It seemed, I was told, sadly, or in wonder, that we were not punished for violating the rules of the game.

But I began to think: We live now, in a new time. What do the animals make of us, who come North into their country so easily? What do we want? What can they tell us?

Troubled, wondering, I turned again to Mrs. Reliance, whom I saw now and then in town. I told her about these dreams that fascinated and disturbed me.

"But Katherine, you don't understand," she said, in pity and consolation. "The animals are trying to come to the women."

MY CIRCUMSTANCES CHANGED; I met the man of my life, and moved to New York, and married him; and I didn't go back to Alaska for more than a year, not till early April 1989.

The day I flew north was cloudless. From Seattle onward the great range of snow-covered mountains along the coast shone bright and hard in the April sun. Several hours into the flight the pilot announced that below us lay Prince William Sound, where a few weeks before a commercial oil tanker had struck a reef and poured eleven million gallons of crude oil into the living waters. We were at thirty-five thousand feet; passengers seated on the right could observe where the tanker had run aground. The pilot's voice was measured, even thoughtful. Trying to assimilate those separate facts, I looked down through the clear air and followed the line of the coast to Valdez Arm.

The lovely fjord that is the Arm was from that height a long narrow file of entry into the port. At its mouth six tankers faned out in a wide semicircle, ranked to go in. They were very long ships: next to them the great mountains, the St. Elias range, looked—docile. A distance away, but in sight from the plane, tugs were drawing the *Exxon Valdez* away from Bligh Reef. In the slant of the sun I couldn't make out the oil slick. The pilot reported its charted movement, and named the bays and ports along the coast toward which it was predicted to be heading.

Anchorage was a raw and rowdy place; but that city lay grieving and strangely still, as if shocked into silence by the disaster. In the previous year, friends told me, so many people, even white people, had taken their lives that the newspapers no longer reported them, for the public good. Exxon was spreading money along the coastline. In the villages around Prince William Sound, food was running low, as all available planes and fishing boats, which normally carried supplies, had been chartered for use in the clean-up. With the first wash of money came the first cover-up of despair, the new round of drinking and fighting and wife-beating and child abuse; as usual, but more severe than usual.

And the lost animals. After the spill, the media ran sympathetic pictures of dead and dying otters. It was said that the Aleuts call otters Half-Man, because their spirits pass into otters after death. I wondered: To whom could those human spirits go now?

TOWARD THE END of my visit I stayed alone in a house north of Anchorage. I had brought the bones in their small leather pouch. On the last day, for no reason, I remembered the man who once had sweetly courted me: he had trapped the wolverine near a town not far up the highway. On a hunch, I decided to drive there.

After about half an hour, I suppose, the road crested a hill, and descended the long slope into a small wooded valley. As I passed a certain spot, not at all remarkable, a muscle under my heart twitched slightly, as if I had had a small electric shock. *Pay attention.* I drove through the valley, felt nothing, turned around, and drove back to the same stretch of road; and drove it three or four times, testing, until my heart, I thought it was, was composed.

The place was a few miles from a small Athabaskan settlement, but not, I considered, within its boundaries. I pulled off the road and parked on the gravel shoulder. Across the way, houses appeared here and there among the trees. *White people,* I thought, and felt easy; surely no one would be at risk. I turned and went into the forest, which was calmly busy and took no special notice of me. The air was fresh, and spruce-sharp; but I was nearly weeping. The voice in the mind was bemused by that damp emotion. I walked among the trees; the ground was boggy and covered with dried needles. I was going on intuition, and, perhaps, desire. The stump of a fallen tree, and a hollow in the stump, stood out from its surrounds. *Here.* I shook the small, perfect, white bones into my hand and tipped them carefully into the hollow; set the black leather pouch in the stump-top; and turned away. And as I turned, there came a leap in the vitals, the small shock again: an impulse, as of a shadow-form, that had so long resided inside and outside of myself. In the same thrilling instant the shadow parted from me, and, released at last, bounded away into the forest: light, young, eager; at home.

I sit in this comfortable study and look out on a domesticated landscape, and find comfort in it, if never the awe and elation of the North where once I lived; but my mind is large and I can believe that here I may be blind: that another poet, some dreaming woman or man, may see what I cannot. I am content not to be in the North. The wheel has turned: I've finished what I was called to do there; it remains only to tell the story of what happened.

A squirrel runs from branch to high branch across the spruces, as if the air were a woodland creek, and the limbs of trees the stepping-stones across it: a small, usual movement, fleet and airy as a poem can be; and it pleases me to compare that dart of movement to the logic of a poem, which links things like and unlike by tracing the arcs of movement between them. Invisible trails above our heads.

In Alaska, during the dreaming years, when animals were coming to the women, I woke one morning into the wondering sense that a veil had been drawn back, and an important instruction given during the night.

In the dream, I was reading a paper before a group of Alaskan anthropologists—in fact I had given such a talk, a poet's reading of a fine Athabaskan story which described in mythopoeic figures the compace between humans and animals, by which each kind lived in mutual respect, need, trickery, and delight. In the dream, unlike in the actual meeting, I was seated among the audience rather than above them on a dais. In the dream, though only there, Native people, too, sat as participants. The topic of the meeting was Subsistence, as whites called it, referring to the intricate culture of hunting relations between humans and animals in that animate country, which Native people called "Our way of life." In the dream, the dreamer—I—knew all this in a moment.

I saw myself stand among the seated people, and read my paper. As I finished, feeling young and terribly ernest, a voice behind me called: *Kathy*. It was a man's voice, an Athabaskan's, calling me by a childhood name. From the corner of my eye I saw him: seated behind me and to the right, still dressed in his work-stained clothes, accompanied by his wife, who sat silent and composed beside him. "Kathy," he went on, "you've got it wrong. It's not that *your* spirit, *your* way of knowing, goes out toward what lives: but that the spirit of the animals and plants *rushes toward you*."

THE WORLD HAS CHANGED. Great powers are at play; every possible human behavior has come out of the dark and once more into the open. We are astonished and distressed. The world divides, as Alaska divided, into small and smaller groups of *us*. Fear grows; uncertainty feeds it, and smothers our courage. We stammer. We don't know what can happen next.

For all its confusion, I lived in a world where humans and animals do still speak to one another. Alaska is a great land, fragile and deeply sensitive to the terrible disturbances done to its body. The manifestation of its spirits compelled me to maintain a respectful watch, and reminded me to listen carefully to my dreams. I think the animals are terribly lonely. They miss their old relations with humans. They try to establish relations with us through dreams, but we can't hear them clearly enough. Perhaps we don't talk the same language, as we are not hunting people. They are trying to learn our language.

I observe that the experience of the sacred is open to anyone. It is a gift of grace, or luck, as it is called in the North; and having received this gift—a vision, a message from a bird, a sign from an animal, a dream—we must try to understand what we've been given, for it is not necessarily benign. But the North sits under a weight of imposed silence. "Let the old knowledge die with the old people," said many Alaska Natives: "It's too dangerous; they told us not to stir it up." Surely they are right, for themselves; and their desires should be honored.

But the stories of our dreams and visions might help us all to enlarge the relationships we seek with one another; for when this earthly gift comes to us, we are obliged to pass the news of it on to our neighbors, and ask for their help in understanding what has happened. The experience of the sacred is, intensely, a singular one: but its form, its expression, the art by which we share it, is an ancient social, and also a religious, one. We are given voices, we have marvelous languages: we are able to sing; we can praise. We can give warning. We can speak truth.

Notes

Malfa Ivanov: the name she asks me to use in writing. As well, I have given a fictional name to Mrs. Reliance. The town of McGrath and the rivers exist as written; "Shelter" is an alias, an English version of its original Athabaskan name.

Hʉtłaanee: The etymology of this Koyukon word is found in Kathleen Mautner, "The Role of Koyukon Athabaskan Women in Subsistence," in *Tracks in the Wildland*, Richard K. Nelson, Kathleen H. Mautner, G. Ray Bane. Fairbanks: Anthropology and Historic Preservation, Cooperative Park Studies Unit, University of Alaska, 1982. pp. 190–92.

Agliganaq: 'Eskimo rules,' comes from *aglinigaqtuni*, meaning 'to menstruate'; it also means 'to begin to grow full or big.' N. J. Gubser, *Comparative Study of the Intellectual Culture of the Nunamiut Eskimos at Anaktuvuk Pass, Alaska,* 1961 (unpublished monograph), p. 220.

Las Casas: Information about Las Casas and Supúlveda is from Anthony Pagden, "Introduction," to *A Short Account of the Destruction of the Indies,* Bartólomé de Las Casas, ed. and tr. by Nigel Griffin. London: Penguin Books, 1992. The quotation from Las Casas is from *The Tears of the Indians*, tr. by John Phillips (1656), new introduction by Colin Steele. New York: Oriole Chapbooks, 1972.

"Not all spirits are possessed of equal power. . . .": Richard K. Nelson. *Make*

Prayers to the Raven, A Koyukon View of the Northern Forest. Chicago: University of Chicago Press, 1983, p. 241.

Yes hughn'u: for his stories and commentaries about wolverine, and Dena'ina belief and language, I am grateful to the late Peter Kalifornsky; this material is adapted from *From the First Beginning, When the Animals Were Talking,* V. 2, an archival manuscript of my English versions of his writings, and our conversations about the old stories. (Unpublished, 1984–88)

W. SCOTT OLSEN

An Advent Nature

I. Summer Solstice: The Straight River

I cannot tell you how long the fox had been dead. And I cannot tell you how it died. My morning had been filled already with enough stories of the living to carry me home. Stories of brown trout that did, or more often did not, take to the small flies I was dropping in front of them as I stood in the middle of the Straight River, northern Minnesota. Stories of egrets, geese, red-wing blackbirds, pelicans, sparrows, and robins. Stories of bugs. Stories of the flatland prairie near my home, cultivated fields of grains and sugar beets, giving way to hills and clear lakes, forests of birch, pine, oak, and elm as I drove east. Stories of an early morning thunderstorm giving way to a crimson bright sunrise. A story about something very large moving through the river behind me, far enough around a bend in the river I could not see it, but not so far away I could not imagine its size from the sound it made. Imagined stories of moose, bear, timberwolf, deer.

It had been a daybreak with theater, with symphony, with thunderbolts, and fast river water, with fish leaping and birds diving. So much motion on what most people would call a quiet morning.

I am lucky to have seen the fox at all. I had stopped to fill a pipe, not unhappily offering some tobacco to the river in the process, and for some time just stood there feeling the water whirl its way around my waders. The thunderstorms were leaving, heading east, and the

331

wind was lessening. The trees, the grasses, the world was glimmering. I wasn't really thinking about anything, I suppose. Just looking. More than once I forgot the fishing, happy just to be a witness.

All I noticed at first were two ears sticking up from a reddish mat nestled in the crook of a fallen tree. I walked a little closer and still did not know what I was seeing. Only when I'd come around and could see it from head on did I make sense of the shape.

There is a part of me which would like to imagine this fox had a choice, that it somehow knew its time had come and that it picked this particular set of branches as the best place to discover whatever comes next for foxes. Its nose pointed west, toward where the sun sets at this time of the summer. And in northern Minnesota, mid-summer twilight lasts for hours. It could have been a leave-taking filled with happy retrospect and quiet anticipation. But even I know better than this.

I sat on a stump in the river and looked at this fox. Nothing in this morning suggested death, but here it was. Not eloquent or filled with metaphor, but elegant and sacred. There was no larger symbol here, no sadness or sense of loss. The death of a northwoods fox causes nothing. But for me, this fox completed the picture. The morning had been alive with sky and river and animals, easily taken in. This fox was evidence that the story of this river, this place, is larger than I will ever see.

"Amen," I said to the fox. Not as benediction. But as confirmation.

II. 308 ACADEMY HALL

I will never climb Everest. This much is already certain. In all probability, I will never hike the length of the Grand Canyon. I will not likely spend a season at the South Pole, although I'd like to, and I'll never get a chance to walk unhurriedly through the Amazon basin or the Chinese highlands.

Most days I walk the hundred yards or so from my home to my office, amble a bit from office to classroom and back, then walk the hundred yards back to my home. But those other places, those places I have not seen and will never see, those places I can only imagine, are not less real to me, nor less sacred. Maps and pictures of those places hang on my walls, journals and texts fill my bookshelves. The untravelled road has always been the one most anticipated, the one most imagined, the one whose promise we most desire.

I've had good fortune. I've travelled already more than most people ever will. And for me, the act of traveling, the act of encountering each new corner of the natural world, is bound to the idea of Advent. Advent is a season of preparation, of housecleaning, of getting ready for the miraculous. It's a season of joy filled anticipation. We know what's coming. At least we know the mundane elements, since we've done the routine before. But even with this knowing, the excitement builds. All through Advent, we make ourselves ready, get ourselves looking in a direction we too often ignore.

I think there is something essential in the idea of Advent, something we feel more deeply important than we've explained to ourselves. And the same is true for how we see nature. We live in our cities and towns, most of us, but we are constantly anticipating what exists outside the people-made places. I will never be most places on the planet, but I anticipate them every day.

My friends who are religion professors tell me that in Advent we are in fact getting ready for three Christmases. The first is the historical Christmas. The second is the metaphorical, present-day Christmas. And the third is the Christmas of the second coming. The kingdom of heaven will not replace this world, the one we're living in. This world will become that kingdom. Martin Luther made the point sometimes that we should stop saying God created the world, and instead speak in the present tense, that God is creating this world.

And this is troubling news. If I am going to claim we have an Advent relationship with the natural world, with both wildness and wilderness, then I am claiming a relationship with a historic Nature, which is troubling because we've romanticized it so much. And with a present-day Nature, which is troubling because no one disagrees about its metaphorical power—look at all the nature shows on television and the sheer weight of old National Geographics filling our basements—yet we can cut down forests so easily as well. And with a future Nature, which is troubling because simple population pressure seems to be the death knell of any open places. Still, despite the trouble, in an Advent relation with Nature, we are anticipating the very thing which can save us. All three relations are, in fact, calls to action.

Advent is a time to cleanse the imagination, to see the world sacramentally once again. Advent anticipates Christmas, divinity made real in the world, while in Nature there is simply the fragile promise of otherness. It could be that these two things are in fact the same.

III. Uluru

"Nganana Tatintja Wiya" means "We do not climb." It's all over the tourist brochures.

> What visitors call the climb is the traditional route taken by ancestral Mala men on their arrival at Uluru and the path is of spiritual significance. Although permission for climbing is given, the traditional owners, Anangu, prefer that you choose to respect the cultural significance of Uluru and do not climb.

Standing at the base of Uluru, what most people call Ayers Rock, in the central outback of Australia, I'm caught by the sight of people all over the rock. Tourists, by carload and busload, pull into the car-park and usually without hesitation race toward the climb. There's a line of people going up, and another line coming down. In a brochure I learn that Anangu call tourists Minga, which means ants.

"Did you climb?" I ask a young man sitting on a bench.

"Yes," he said.

"What do you think of the request not to climb?"

"Well, at first I thought about that. I mean, I suppose it's a bit like crawling all over a crucifix in a church."

"But you made the climb."

"Yes, I did. I finally decided to, since I'll probably never be here again."

Turning away, I begin what is called the Mala walk, a portion of the base of the rock, interpretive brochure in hand.

> Life and Land are One
> The Tjukurpa is not a dream; it is real. The landscape tells how the knowledge and wisdom of our ancestors came to be. The land was made at the beginning of the Tjukurpa, when ancestral beings created the landscape features and all living creatures including humans. The details of the activities and travels of the ancestral beings have been taught to us ever since, in story, song, dance, and ceremony. When Anangu

look at the land, and all the features and living things upon it, we see visible evidence that our ancestral beings still exist. Uluru, and its many different features, continue to tell us about the Tjukurpa. We have no need for special buildings to remind us of our religion or law. The Tjukurpa is all around us in the landscape itself.

I continue the Mala walk, reading about the Mala people coming to Uluru from the west and north, about how they would plant a Ngaltawata, a ceremonial pole, on top of the rock, which would signal that everything to follow would be ceremony. I read how other people came from the west and about the fatal disagreements that would follow. I pass the sites of this story, the story itself made manifest in the rock and caves and water holes.

At a cave called Mala Puta, I catch up with a park ranger giving a tour to about fifty people. In the brochure I read that

> Anangu believe that a site such as Mala Puta is too important to have its relationship with all the surrounding land ig-nored, removed and isolated in a photograph.

The ranger repeats the same request. Mala Puta, spiritually, is the pouch of the female hare wallaby.

The ranger and the group move on, but two men linger. When the group has gone beyond eyesight, they quickly shoot several pictures.

IV. 308 ACADEMY HALL

This much is certain. We have grown accustomed in stories to the sight of a wise man on a mountaintop. It seems perfectly reasonable for him to be there. Away from the noise of humanity, he can gain the ability to listen and the time to think. And we are no longer surprised by the location of monasteries in difficult and remote land-scapes, for the very same reason.

In the fourth century, the Desert Fathers took to the desert to discover more clearly what they meant by God. Only by shedding what they called their passions, their connections to the issues and politics of their daily lives, could they approach an appreciation of the physical world; and only from this appreciation could they approach theology.

The solitary spiritual quest in the wilderness is not limited to any cultural tradition. It is shared by Native Americans, Buddhists, Inuit, and Boy Scouts. If there is one thing we know as a species, it is that we must maintain our connections, and our participations, in a world that moves before politics and doctrine. We know this, and it scares us.

The Greeks defined themselves by membership in the city-state. If you were not a member, that is if you came from the wilderness, you were often the enemy. And nature itself was often the enemy. The city-state was order and rule and status quo while nature, both literally and metaphorically, was random, hard, lethal, by definition un-civil. From the time the first hut was erected to this very day, we have been working to divorce ourselves from the threat of nature.

Still, the stories work the other way. The desert did not kill Moses, or Jesus. It made them stronger. John the Baptist was the voice in the wilderness. For Christians, Advent readings begin with the kingdom of God becoming the highest peak on Earth, and from the mountain comes the news to turn sword into plowshare. Advent readings show John submerging Jesus in the river, and only then does a voice from heaven proclaim his readiness. If we have an Advent relation with the natural world, then we are aware, dimly, that the stories are not over, that the threat still exists, and that the threat itself is what may save us. "In Wildness," said Thoreau, "is the preservation of the world."

What do we seek in Nature? We seek what we fear, which is confirmation that we are incomplete.

V. Mount Cook

Nothing is more difficult to escape than our own stories. In Minnesota, when I speak the word "home," what I really mean is everything from Medora and the badlands of North Dakota to the St. Croix River at the Wisconsin border. This is the part of the world where I am most often. Between those two boundaries, I have stories, stories I've learned from other people and stories I've helped create myself. And, every story has its own setting, its own landscape and earth.

The closer I get to home, the more stories I have. Prairie land just east of home is not just prairie, it's the spot where I sat one morning in a blind with two others, watching and listening to the mating dance and song of prairie chickens. North of town is the spot I stopped to rest from too much driving and discovered a moose in some trees not twenty yards away. When I pass these places now, those stories insist themselves back into the present tense.

Usually, this insistence is a wonderful thing. Few things are more welcome among people than a good story, and good stories shared with others is what creates friendships, communities, security and love. But there are those other places where we have no personal history, no personal or community story to color the landscape for us in advance. And it's in those other places we can regain a sense of the wild.

This particular morning, I am sitting on a rock on a trail that leads to Kea Point, in the shadow of Mount Cook, in the Otago region of the south island of New Zealand. Mount Cook is the country's highest peak, permanently snowcapped, and this morning quite breathtaking set against a deep blue sky, set on fire by bright sunshine. The trail has led me through river washes, through dense brush, over small hills and up steep climbs. Not one step puts me anyplace I've been before, or anyplace the people I know have been before. For me, this morning, this is a landscape without human story, without interpretation, without metaphor or politics. Keas, a type of alpine parrot, fly overhead while glacier runoff wets my boots.

When I am at home, my sense of where I am holds years of history, years of community and people and politics and the thousand concerns of a social life. Here, looking up at a mountain I've never seen before this morning, my sense of where I am holds nothing more than rock, than water, than birds and trees and bush. Here, apart from the insistence of others, I am able to catch a breath of the Other. There is no past in this place today, and no future. Just a tremendous present-filling eternity. It's enough to fill the soul.

There are places on this planet that are sacred to me. Not because they have been sanctified by ritual, but because they have not.

VI. WRIGHT PASS

A sacred place can trouble as well as bring joy. In fact, trouble may be as necessary for the sacred as a fall is for salvation.

A fair distance north of the Arctic Circle, almost exactly upon a continental divide, at a place called the Wright Pass, I am marveling at the bright midsummer sun, despite the fact it's well past midnight.

This same sunshine, I realize, also falls on London, on Moscow, on Delhi and Johannesburg now, and the sentimental part of my nature want to cry out in this new connection with what I consider the other side of the planet. I am sharing something as simple and as physical and as joy-giving as sunshine on my face with places and people I'll never know. Right now, looking up from this mountain pass, with no other human within any reasonable distance, it's possible to imagine the size of the globe.

"Hello!" I yell northward.

Then, of course, I remember that my own home is in darkness now. Every step toward a new place takes us away from someplace we know. The wind at Wright Pass is strong, and I decide silence and reverence are the better ways of seeing this place. Brilliant red fireweed, the greens and browns of arctic tundra grasses and willows, the patches of snow still in the mountains have their own stories to tell.

I am at Wright Pass this night because of something called the Dempster Highway. More than four hundred miles of single lane gravel each way from Dawson City in the Yukon Territory to Inuvik in the Northwest Territory, it's the only public road in North America to cross the arctic circle. The fact that this road exists is what has brought me here, the strong call of a simple line on a map leading toward the imagined places. And the fact that this road exists is what troubles the picture for me.

Looking southward from the pass, I can see the landscape fall away toward a brown valley, then rise again into another range of mountains. And in the middle of the scene, the dark line of the road. It doesn't matter how long or where I look here, my eye is always drawn back to the roadway, to the very thing that connects me to a world I've been leaving. The Dempster Highway connects me, yes, with people I know and love. And it has brought me to ptarmigan and grizzly bear and views large enough to steal my breath. At the same time it connects me with other things, with my need for gasoline, with politics, with the million messy ways we've arranged ourselves, with money and greed and division.

To be at Wright Pass is to be in a privileged place. Here, and at other places like here, if we listen, we can begin to hear the sounds outside the insistence of humanity. Voices much older than our own. Voices we have a talent to forget. Voices we must not ever forget.

Yet, if I am able to hear or see anything here, if I am able to expand even for a moment my understanding of the natural world, the cost of my new understanding is several hundred miles of road interrupting what I've come to see. Anticipating the Other, I have come to Wright Pass. Anticipating me, other people have built roads, gas stations, hotels, restaurants, gift shops.

I resist turning nature into symbol or metaphor, to give it a meaning-made-human. The grizzly bear that lumbered away from me earlier today does not care how or why I was looking at it. But the road is a different matter. The road is a symbol of commerce, of ease, of accessibility. Yes, I am grateful for this road. And yes, I worry about how many others will come after me. I admit to this selfishness. But today I traveled several hundred miles of arctic landscape at more than fifty miles per hour.

At Wright Pass I catch a moment of illumination. And to get here, I committed a sin.

VII. Sixth Street

I live in an old house.

Built in 1929, it's filled with oak floors, heavy ceiling moldings and window frames, lath and plaster walls that crack anew every season, and the accumulated story-ghosts of every love and heart broken within its history. Like many old homes, nothing really fits anymore. The doors catch on their frames. The windows take some effort to convince. Every step on the staircase has claimed its particular note in the scales of squeaks and wheezes. If you sit very still in the living room, you can feel the footfalls of the others in the house come through the walls, the floor, up into the upholstery of the couch. I believe there's no other way to say it; old houses dance.

Still, old houses are not easy places. Entropy and the weight of Minnesota snowfalls have worked their way into the wood that supports a small deck off the second floor and into the spaces between the cinder blocks that make up the foundation. Each season the house shifts a little more and new cracks appear in some wall. I cannot imagine a time anywhere in the future when my house will not ask for some repair, for some help, for some participation on my part, for some small act of protection and love.

I love my house, not in spite of its creaks but in part because of them. My house will shelter me and my family from rain and snow, from heat and lethal cold, but only if we shelter the house from decay, from time and neglect and stupidity. It's a relationship in which we both must take an active and loving part. The rewards are substantial.

Last summer, one twilight found my neighbors and friends gathered in my backyard. Kids ran and played. Dogs barked and jumped. Long after the coals in the grill had gone to deep red and then ashen embers, the grownups fell quiet. From where we sat, we could see the many homes on this shaded street. We could see, in the failing light, visible proof of a very small planet's rotation through space. We could see the never ending game of tag turned into hide-and-seek turned back into tag. Past, present, future.

Somehow, for all of us at the same moment, there was a moment of clarity. A moment of connectedness. A moment when we could glimpse the promise that the universe and all its places will continue not despite or because of us, but with us. In the deepening blues of the evening sky, in the games of the children, in the comfortable silences of adults who have become friends, there were hints of the sacred. Yes, there is no other way to say it. We could see, we could almost touch and taste, the dance of time. Then one of the children ran up to her father.

"Daddy," she pleaded. "Can I have some more?"

The grownups, feeling suddenly very young, exploded into laughter.

There are stories here, like this one, I know. Stories which are, in one sense, chapters in my own history and the history of the people I love. And there are stories here I will never know beyond an imagined echo from people I will never meet. Other people have patched walls here, have braced a basement wall here, have planted gardens, have laughed and loved and cried here too. All of us have been writing the story of the future.

This, I believe, is what we mean by a sacred place. A place where the stories get large. A place where our own story meets, and joins, the stories of other people, other animals, other needs, others.

DAVID BAKER is author of four books of poetry, most recently *After the Reunion* (1994) and *Sweet Home, Saturday Night* (1991), both from the University of Arkansas Press. In 1996 his edited volume *Meter in English: A Critical Engagement* appeared from Arkansas. He teaches at Denison University, Ohio.

RICK BASS is the author of several books of fiction and nonfiction. His latest essay collection is entitled *The Book of Yaak*. He lives in Montana with his family and is working on a novel, *Where the Sea Used to Be*.

WENDY BATTIN is the author of *In the Solar Wind* and *Little Apocalypse*. She is currently Visiting Poet in Residence at MIT.

DAVID BENGTSON lives and teaches high school English in Long Prairie, Minnesota. He has received a Prize for Poetry from the Academy of American Poets and a Loft McKnight Award for Creative Prose. Most recently, his short prose has been published in *26 Minnesota Writers* (Nodin Press).

CAROL BLY is the author of five collections of essays and short stories, most recently *Changing the Bully Who Rules the World* (Milkweed, 1996). *The Tomcat's Wife and Other Stories* (HarperCollins, 1991) won a Friends of American Writers Award. Three stories from *Backbone* (Milkweed, 1985) were scripted into the award-winning American Playhouse film and video, *Rachel River*. She teaches ethics-in-literature at the University of Minnesota.

DAVID BOTTOMS won the Walt Whitman Award for his first poetry collection, *Shooting Rats at the Bibb County Dump* His most recent book is *Armored Hearts: New and Selected Poems* (Copper Canyon). He has been awarded the Levinson Prize, an Ingram-Merrill Award, and an award in literature from the American Academy and Institute of Arts and Letters.

DOUGLAS BURTON-CHRISTIE is an assistant professor of christian spirituality at Loyola Marymount University, Los Angeles. He is the author of *The Word in the Desert* (Oxford, 1993) and edits the *Journal of the Society for the Study of Christian Spirituality*. His next book, *The Quest for the Sacred Place*, is forthcoming from Univerity of California Press.

EDWARD BYRNE has written four collections of poetry, most recently *Words Spoken Words Unspoken* (Chimney Hill Press, 1995). He is a professor of American literature and creative writing at Valparaiso University, Indiana.

DOUGLAS CARLSON's essays have appeared recently in *The Georgia Review*, *Adirondac*, and *The American Literary Review*. He was guest contributing editor for *The Georgia Review*'s special issue devoted to nature writing.

KELLY CHERRY's recent books include *God's Loud Hand*, *Time Out of Mind*, and *Lovers and Agnostics*, poems; *Writing the World*, essays *The Exiled Heart*, a memoir; and *My Life and Dr. Joyce Brothers*, a novel in stories. A new collection of poetry is forthcoming from Louisiana State University Press in 1997. She teaches at the University of Wisconsin, Madison.

RICHARD CHESS is the author of a book of poems, *Tekiah* (U. of Georgia Press 1994). His poems have appeared in *Triquarterly*, *Poetry*, *Tikkun*, *The American Poetry Review*, *Prairie Schooner*, *New England Review*, and *Tampa Review*. He is an associate professor of literature and language at the University of North Carolina at Asheville. He also directs UNCA's Center for Jewish Studies.

KATHARINE COLES's first novel, *The Measurable World*, for which she won a New Forms Project Grant from the NEA, was published in 1995 by the University of Nevada Press; her collection of poems, *The One Right Touch*, was published in 1992. She received an Individual Writer Fellowship from the NEA in 1990.

PETER COOLEY was born in Detroit and has lived in New Orleans since 1975, where he is a professor of English at Tulane University. He has published five books of poetry, the most recent of which is *The Astonished Hours*. A new book, *Sacred Conversations*, will be published in 1997.

ANNIE DILLARD won the Pulitzer Prize for her *Pilgrim at Tinker Creek* in 1975. She is the author of nine other books, including *An American Childhood* and *The Living*. She has received fellowships from the John Simon Guggenheim Foundation and the National Endowment for the Arts. She was the first recipient of the annual Milton Center Prize.

HELEN FROST is the author of *Skin of a Fish, Bones of a Bird* (Ampersand, 1993) and the editor of *Season of Dead Water* (Breitenbush, 1990), and anthology of writing about the Valdez oil spill. She lives in Fort Wayne, Indiana and teaches poetry to children.

DIANE GLANCY teaches Native American literature and creative writing at Macalaster College in St. Paul, Minnesota. Her new collection of essays, *The West Pole*, is forthcoming from the University of Minnesota Press.

JORIE GRAHAM won the Pulitzer Prize in poetry in 1996 for *The Dream of the Unified Field* (Ecco Press). She has also received a John D. and Catherine T. MacArthur Fellowship and the Morton Dauwen Zabel Award from the American Academy and Institute of Arts and Letters. Other collections of her poetry include *Region of Unlikeness, The End of Beauty, Erosion*, and *Hybrids of Plants and Ghosts*.

ALVIN GREENBERG has other recent prose work, both fiction and memoir, appearing in *American Literary Review, Antioch*

Review, Kansas Quarterly, Mid-American Review, Nebraska Review, North American Review, and *Short Story.* His most recent collections of poetry are *Heavy Wings* and *Why We Live with Animals.* He teaches at Macalester College in St. Paul, Minnesota.

PAUL GRUCHOW's sixth collection of essays, *The Grace of the Wild,* will be published this spring by Milkweed Editions.

CATHRYN HANKLA is the author of four books, the most recent of which is *Afterimages,* a collection of poetry from LSU press. Her new collection, *Negative History,* is forthcoming from LSU Press. She is an associate professor and chair of the English Department at Hollins College, Virginia.

CHARLES O. HARTMAN is Poet in Residence at Connecticut College. His most recent books of poems are *Sentences* (Sun & Moon) and *Glass Enclosure* (Wesleyan). In summer 1996 Wesleyan will publish *Virtual Muse: Experiments in Computer Poetry,* and Northwestern will reprint in paperback *Free Verse: An Essay on Prosody.*

LINDA HASSELSTROM now owns the western South Dakota ranch where she lived and worked for thirty years, but lives in a Wyoming city. Her essays and poems have been widely published in small magazines and anthologies. Her nonfiction books include *Windbreak, Going Over East,* and *Land Circle.*

DAVID HOPES is Professor of Literature and Humanities at the University of North Carolina at Asheville, director of Pisgah Players Theater Company, and founder of Urthona Press.

WILLIAM KITTREDGE is in his final year of teaching English at the University of Montana before retirement. "The Bluest Water" is part of a manuscript in progress titled *Reimagining Desire.*

SYDNEY LEA is author of the novel, *A Place in Mind* (Scribner), a collection of naturalist essays, *Hunting the Whole Way Home* (U.P. of New England), and six verse collections, most recently

To the Bone: New and Selected Poems (U. of Illinois). He teaches in the MFA in Writing Program at Vermont College.

DENISE LEVERTOV's new book of poems, *Sands of the Well,* was published by New Directions. She has also published a book of memoirs, *Tesserae.* She has lived in the Northwest for the past six years.

BARRY LOPEZ is the author of *Arctic Dreams, Crow and Weasel, Field Notes, Of Wolves and Men, Crossing Open Ground,* and other works of fiction and nonfiction. He is the recipient of the National Book Award, the John Burroughs Medal, the Christopher Medal for Humanitarian Writing (twice), the Award in Literature from the American Academy of Arts and Letters, and other honors.

BRET LOTT grew up in Southern California and Phoenix, and now lives in Charleston, South Carolina. "War Story" is from his most recent book, a collection of stories titled *How to Get Home.* He is also the author of four novels, a second story collection, and a memoir.

KATHERINE McNAMARA lived in Alaska during the seventies and eighties; she now divides her time between the East Coast and Europe. "Piety" is from *Narrow Road to the Deep North,* a work of nonfiction.

JOHN McPHEE has written twenty-three nonfiction books on varied subjects. He lives in Princeton, New Jersey, and teaches a course in writing at Princeton University.

DAWN MARANO is a freelance writer and vice-president of Writers at Work, living in Salt Lake City, Utah. Her fiction, poetry, and nonfiction works have appeared in a number of local and national publications. She is currently at work on a collection of essays and a novel.

MICHAEL MOTT has published six collections of poetry, the latest of which, *Corday,* has just been reissued in paperback. *Woman and the Sea, Selected Poems* will appear soon. Mott is also the author of four novels and the award-winning biography, *The Seven Mountains of Thomas Merton.* He lives on a lake between Jamestown and Williamsburg, Virginia.

KATHLEEN NORRIS is the author of two nonfiction books, *Dakota: A Spiritual Geography* and *The Cloister Walk.* Her most recent book of poetry is *Little Girls in Church.* She has lived in western South Dakota since 1974.

SCOTT RUSSELL SANDERS is the winner of a Lannan Literary Award for his nonfiction and is the author of *Staying Put, The Paradise of Bombs,* and *Secrets of the Universe.* His latest work, *Writing from the Center,* won the Great Lakes Book Award. He teaches literature at Indiana University.

REG SANER is the author of several books, including *The Four-Cornered Falcon: Essays on the Interior West and the Natural Scene.* His essay in this volume is in a forthcoming book.

LYNDA SEXSON'S latest book is, *Hamlet's Planets: Parables* (Ohio State U.P.). She is the author of an acclaimed collection of stories, *Margaret of the Imperfections,* and *Ordinarily Sacred.* She is professor of humanities at Montata State University.

NAOMI SHIHAB NYE lives in San Antonio, Texas, where she walks along the once-sacred little river as often as she can. She writes poems, essays, and children's books, edits anthologies, and, along with her husband, photographer Michael Nye, is raising one lovely computer-literate son and eight muttering hens.

BETH SIMON is an assistant professor at Indiana University–Purdue University, Fort Wayne. "Widows and Dead Men" is from a manuscript based on the years she lived in India. Her prose has appeared in *Iowa Review, Massachusetts Review,* and *Triquarterly.* Her poetry collection, *Out of Nowhere, The Body's Shape* (Pecan Grove Press) was published in 1996.

JANET SYLVESTER's first book, *That Mulberry Wine*, was published by Wesleyan University Press. Her second, *Regardless*, will be published in 1997 by W. W. Norton. She is currently working on *A Visitor at the Gate*. Her poems have appeared in many journals and anthologies, including *Best American Poetry 1994, Boulevard, Triquarterly, Shenandoah, Michigan Quarterly Review*, and *Virginia Quarterly Review*.

ANN TOWNSEND's chapbook *Modern Love* appeared in 1995 from Bottom Dog Press. She is the recipient of a Pushcart Prize for Poetry (1995) and a "Discovery"/*The Nation* award for poetry. Her poems and stories appear in *The Nation, The Southern Review, Triquarterly, The Kenyon Review*, and many other magazines. She teaches creative writing and literature at Denison University in Granville, Ohio, where she directs the Jonathan Reynolds Young Writers Workshop.

INGRID WENDT's books of poems include *Moving the House* and *Singing the Mozart Requiem*, winner of the Oregon Book Award for Poetry. She has co-edited the anthologies *In Her Own Image: Women Working in the Arts*, and *From Here We Speak: An Anthology of Oregon Poetry* and is the author of *Starting With Little Things: A Guide to Writing Poetry in the Classroom*. Wendt has taught in the Arts-in-Education programs of several states and was a 1994–95 Fulbright Professor at the J.W. Goethe University, Frankfurt am Main, Germany.

RICHARD WILBUR received a second Pulitzer Prize for his *New and Collected Poems* (1988) and his latest translation from Molière's verse comedy is *Amphitryon* (1995). He divides his time between Key West and the Berkshires of Massachusetts.

TERRY TEMPEST WILLIAMS is Naturalist-in-Residence at the Utah Museum of Natural History. She is the author of *Pieces of White Shell: A Journey to Navajoland* (Scribners), *Coyote's Canyon* (Peregrine Smith), *Refuge: An Unnatural History of Family and Place* (Pantheon), *An Unspoken Hunger* (Pantheon), and *Desert Quartet* (Pantheon). She is a recipient of a Lannan Fellowship in creative nonfiction.

CHARLES WRIGHT published *Chickamauga,* a book of poems, in 1995 and *Quarter Notes,* a book of essays and improvisations on poetry. A new book of poems, *Black Zodiac,* is forthcoming. He lives in Charlottesville and teaches at the University of Virginia there.

ACKNOWLEDGMENTS

RICHARD WILBUR. "The Beautiful Changes" from *The Beautiful Changes and Other Poems*, copyright 1947 and 1975 by Richard Wilbur, reprinted by permission of Harcourt Brace and Company; "Clearness" from *Ceremony and Other Poems*, copyright 1950 and 1978 by Richard Wilbur, reprinted by permission of Harcourt Brace and Company.

CHARLES WRIGHT. "Looking Outside the Cabin Window, I Remember a Line by Li Po" from *Chickamauga*, copyright 1995 by Charles Wright, reprinted by permission of Farrar, Straus & Giroux, Inc.

KELLY CHERRY. "Natural Theology" from *Natural Theology—Poems by Kelly Cherry*, copyright 1988 by Kelly Cherry, reprinted by permission of Louisiana State University Press; "Lt. Col. Valentina Vladimirovna Tereshkova" from *Relativity* (Louisiana State University Press, 1977), reprinted by permission of the author.

ANNIE DILLARD. "Pastoral" first appeared in *Antaeus* (Autumn 1994); "Mornings Like This" first appeared in *Georgia Review* (Fall 1993); and "The Naturalist at Large on the Delaware River" first appeared in *Ontario Review* (Fall/Winter 1993–94). All poems reprinted by permission of the author.

DAVID BOTTOMS. "Under the Vulture Tree" and "Alatoona Evening" from *Armored Hearts: Selected and New Poems*, copyright 1995 by David Bottoms, reprinted by permission of Copper Canyon Press.

Peter Cooley. "A Vision" first appeared in *Borderlands, Texas Poetry Review* (Spring/Summer 1995), reprinted by permission of the author.

David Baker. "Yellow Lilies and Cypress Swamp" first appeared in *Antaeus* (1994), reprinted by permission of the author.

Ann Townsend. "In the Limbo of Lost Words" first appeared in *Southern Poetry Review* (Spring 1991), reprinted by permission of the author; "Evening Burning" from *Modern Love* (Bottom Dog Press, 1995), copyright 1995 by Ann Townsend, reprinted by permission of the author.

Paul Gruchow. "Visions" from *Grass Roots*, copyright 1995 by Paul Gruchow, reprinted by permission of Milkweed Editions.

Linda Hasselstrom. "Buffalo Winter" first appeared in *American Literary Review* (Fall 1994), reprinted by permission of the author.

Scott Russell Sanders. "Buckeye" first appeared in *Orion*, copyright 1995 by Scott Russell Sanders, reprinted by permission of the author. "Buckeye" also appears in the author's collection *Writing from the Center* (Indiana University Press, 1995).

John McPhee. Excerpt from "A Mountain" from *Encounters with the Archdruid*, copyright 1971 by John McPhee, reprinted by permission of Farrar, Straus & Giroux, Inc.

Douglas Carlson. "Tide Pools" adapted from portions of *At the Edge* by Douglas Carlson, copyright 1989 by White Pine Press, reprinted by permission of White Pine Press, Fredonia, NY 14063.

Kathleen Norris. "Getting to Hope" from *Dakota*, copyright 1993 by Kathleen Norris, reprinted by permission of Ticknor & Fields/Houghton Mifflin Company.

DOUGLAS BURTON-CHRISTIE, "Interlude: The Literature of Nature and the Quest for the Sacred" from *The Way Supplement*, Autumn 1994, Spirituality, Imagination and Contemporary Literature, reprinted by permission of the Editors, Heythrop College, Kensington Square, London W8 5HQ.

SYDNEY LEA. "Midway" from *No Sign*, copyright 1987 by Sydney Lea, reprinted by permission of the University of Georgia Press; "Over Brogno" from *Hunting the Whole Way Home*, copyright 1994 by University Press of New England, reprinted by permission of the publisher.

WENDY BATTIN. "Seven" first appeared in *Poetry* (February 1996), copyright 1996 by the Modern Poetry Association, reprinted by permission of the author.

DENISE LEVERTOV. "It Should Be Visible," "What One Receives from Living Close to a Lake," and "In the Woods" from *Sands of the Well*, copyright 1995 by Denise Levertov, reprinted by permission of New Directions Publishing Corporation.

DAVID BENGSTON. "Spiritual Fallout" first appeared in *The New England Review* (Fall 1992), reprinted by permission of the author.

DAVID HOPES. "The Soul May Be Compared to a Figure Walking" first appeared in *The Arts Journal*, reprinted by permission of the author.

BARRY LOPEZ. "Pearyland" from *Field Notes*, copyright 1994 by Barry Lopez, reprinted by permission of Alfred A. Knopf, Inc.

REG SANER. "The Real Surreal: Horseshoe Canyon" first appeared in *The Rocky Mountain News* (May 7, 1995), reprinted by permission of the author.

RICK BASS. "Out on the Wild Fringe" first appeared in *Audubon* (January/February 1994), reprinted by permission of *Audubon* and the author.

BRET LOTT. "War Story" first appeared in *The Southern Review* (Spring 1994), reprinted by permission of the author.

CAROL BLY. "In the Maternity Wing, Madison, Minnesota" from *Inheriting the Land*, edited by Mark Vinz and Thom Tammaro, copyright 1993 by University of Minnesota Press, reprinted by permission of the author.

KATHERINE MCNAMARA. "Piety" from *Narrow Road to the Deep North: A Work of Nonfiction*, reprinted by permission of the author.